GLASGOW

Town and City Histories

Town and City Histories
Series editor: Stephen Constantine

Glasgow

Irene Maver

Edinburgh University Press

Series Editor's Foreword

The books in this series are designed and written with a broad readership in mind: local people interested to know how the character of their town has been shaped by major historical forces and the energies of their predecessors; newcomers and visitors curious to acquire a historical introduction to their new surroundings; general readers wishing to see how the sweeps of national and international history have manifested themselves in particular communities; and the scholar seeking to understand urbanisation by comparing and contrasting local experiences.

We live, most of us, in intensely urban environments. These are the products largely of the last two centuries of historical development, although the roots of many towns, of course, go back deep into the past. In recent years there has been considerable historical research of a high standard into this urban history. Narrative and descriptive accounts of the history of towns and cities can now be replaced by studies such as the TOWN AND CITY HISTORIES which investigate, analyse and, above all, explain the economic, political, social and cultural processes and consequences of urbanisation.

Writers for this series consider the changing economic foundations of their town or city and the way change has affected its physical shape, built environment and interests of those who wielded power locally and the structure and functions of local government in different periods are also examined, since locally exercised authority could determine much about the fortunes and quality of urban life. Particular emphasis is placed on the changing life experiences of ordinary men, women and children – their homes, education, occupations, social relations, living standards and leisure activities. Towns and cities control and respond to the values, aspirations and actions of their residents. The books in this series therefore explore social behaviour as well as the economic and political history of those who live in and helped make the towns and cities of today.

Stephen Constantine
University of Lancaster

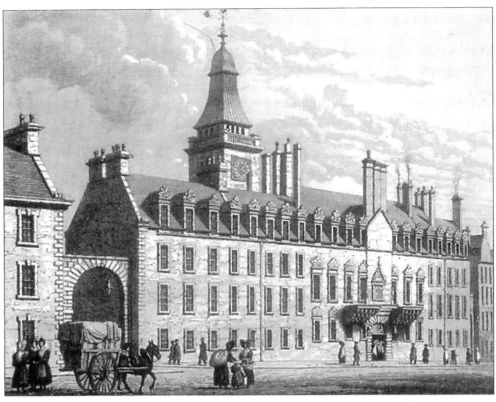

5. The old College (University) in the 1830s.
An engraving of the old College by John Scott. A sense of the university's dignified seventeenth-century style is captured here, even though the inflow of population was rapidly overwhelming the district and prompting the academic authorities to consider moving to a more salubrious location. (*By courtesy of the Mitchell Library, Glasgow City Libraries and Archives.*)

caused by the great fires.[21] However, trading and commercial opportunities continued to expand for the merchant community. A feature of the period was the trend towards company organisation, apparent when a pioneering woollen 'manufactory' was set up in 1681. According to McUre, a joint-stock partnership had been established in 1667 to process West India sugar, which along with tobacco became a vitally important new commodity for Glasgow.[22] So successful was the sugar-house that three others soon followed, and diversified into the distillation of rum. Such expressions of local confidence were in spite of obstacles to overseas trade arising from the English navigation laws of 1660, which specifically precluded Scots from dealing directly with English colonies. This was a source of frustration for Glasgow merchants, who were keen to consolidate transatlantic connections, and meant that smuggling became widespread as a means of getting round the restrictions. Nevertheless, navigational improvements helped to encourage the flow of trade. There were unsatisfactory attempts to build a quay within the burgh, but far more meaningfully in 1667 the Town Council acquired land some twenty-nine kilometres down-river for the construction of a substantial harbour. The community was subsequently known as Port Glasgow.

The expansion of trade in the burgh was all the more remarkable given continuing political tensions and the uneasy ascendancy of the restored episcopacy after 1661. As a particularly vigorous upholder of 'English' church practices, Archbishop Alexander Burnet polarised religious opinion in Glasgow, and unofficial Presbyterian gatherings, known as 'conventicles', were held repeatedly in defiance of his authority. The town was fined several times for allowing such laxity, and attempts to prevent conventicles could provoke disturbances, as in one riotous incident of 1678, when women were again among the ring-leaders. The next year an abortive insurrection was fought out at Bothwell Bridge, not far from Glasgow, and led to unprecedented government repression of Presbyterian dissidents. While there was initially a cautious welcome for the accession of the more tolerant Catholic King James VII in 1685, criticism of crown and clerical interference in civic government soon intensified. Despite a solid core of royalist support, especially among the wealthier burgesses, Glaswegians manifested little loyalty to James when the monarchy was challenged directly in 1688 by his nephew, William of Orange. One year later the constitutional revolution replaced James with his Protestant daughter Mary, who was married to William, and the couple reigned as joint monarchs. In 1689 episcopacy was abolished in the Church of Scotland, although direct action had already been taken by townspeople to 'rabble' or eject ministers associated with the old regime. The following year Presbyterianism was officially restored in the Established Church. While the short-term implications were political and religious, in the longer term the demise of the 'bishop's burgh' was important for redefining perceptions of Glasgow. For all the upheavals of the seventeenth century, the community was now firmly identified as the rising merchant city of Scotland, with aspirations to broaden economic horizons at home and overseas.

Notes

1. J. B. S. Gilfillan, 'The site and its development', in J. Cunnison and J. B. S. Gilfillan (eds), *Glasgow: the Third Statistical Account of Scotland* (Collins: Glasgow, 1958), p. 28.
2. Robert Renwick and Sir John Lindsay, *History of Glasgow, Volume I: Pre-Reformation Period* (Maclehose, Jackson: Glasgow, 1921), pp. 7–8.
3. Elspeth King, *The Hidden History of Glasgow's Women: The Thenew Factor* (Mainstream: Edinburgh, 1993), pp. 15–24.
4. John MacQueen, 'The dear green place: St Mungo and Glasgow, 600–1966', *Innes Review* 43 (1992), pp. 87–98.
5. James McGrath, 'The medieval and early modern burgh', in T. M. Devine and

Gordon Jackson (eds), *Glasgow, Volume I: Beginnings to 1830* (Manchester University Press: Manchester, 1995), p. 21.

6. Andor Gomme and David Walker, *Architecture of Glasgow* (Lund Humphries: London, 1987), pp. 24–5.

7. Quoted in Renwick and Lindsay, *History of Glasgow, Volume I*, p. 214.

8. Frank Arneil Walker, 'Origins and first growths', in Peter Reed (ed.), *Glasgow, the Forming of the City* (Edinburgh University Press: Edinburgh, 1993), p. 16.

9. McGrath, 'Medieval and early modern burgh', p. 27.

10. John Gibson, *The History of Glasgow, from the Earliest Accounts to the Present Time* (John Gibson: Glasgow, 1777), p. 80.

11. The legend of the crafts defending the cathedral features memorably in Walter Scott's novel, *Rob Roy*, first published in 1817. See Robert Alison, *The Anecdotage of Glasgow* (Thomas D. Morison: Glasgow, 1892), pp. 95–6.

12. Quoted in George Eyre-Todd, *History of Glasgow, Volume II: From the Reformation to the Revolution* (Jackson, Wylie: Glasgow, 1931), pp. 144–5. The commentator was John Lesley, Bishop of Ross.

13. Ibid. pp. 122–9.

14. M. Lynch, 'Continuity and change in urban society, 1500–1700', in R. A. Houston and I. D. Whyte (eds), *Scottish Society, 1500–1800* (Cambridge University Press: Cambridge, 1989), p. 106.

15. Eyre-Todd, *History of Glasgow, Volume II*, pp. 137–8.

16. Roger Mason, 'The aristocracy, episcopacy, and the revolution of 1638', in Terry Brotherstone (ed.), *Covenant, Charter and Party: Traditions of Revolt and Protest in Modern Scottish History* (Aberdeen University Press: Aberdeen, 1989), p. 7.

17. John McUre, *A View of the City of Glasgow* (D. McVean and J. Wylie: Glasgow, 1830 edition), p. 86. First published in 1736.

18. T. C. Smout, 'The Glasgow merchant community in the seventeenth century', *Scottish Historical Review* 47 (1968), pp. 55–6.

19. Quoted in McUre, *View of the City of Glasgow*, appendix, p. 307.

20. Gibson, *History of Glasgow*, pp. 314–17.

21. T. C. Smout, 'The development and enterprise of Glasgow, 1556–1707', *Scottish Journal of Political Economy* 7 (1960), pp. 194–6.

22. McUre, *View of the City of Glasgow*, p. 227.

CHAPTER TWO

The Rise of the Merchant City, 1690–1800

Despite the constitutional settlement of 1688–90, the decades up to the mid-eighteenth century were politically volatile in Scotland and there were recurring challenges to the established order. The 1707 parliamentary union with England tested Glaswegian loyalties, and subsequent Jacobite rebellions were a tangible expression of opposition to the new British state. However, from 1714 the city's rulers stood firmly behind the Hanoverian ascendancy, recognising it to be the best safeguard against social instability. As this chapter explains, the quest for security characterised the administration of Glasgow, to the extent that critics eventually branded the mercantile elite as oligarchic and inflexible.

Although the city acquired a politically conservative reputation, this sat uneasily with the developing enterprise culture that made Glasgow's merchants early advocates of freer trade. Commercial success had been encouraged, if not initiated, by the opportunities afforded by full Scottish entry into English colonial markets after 1707. The pivotal period for Glasgow's rapidly rising fortunes was between the 1740s and 1770s, when the transatlantic tobacco trade transformed the city into an international entrepôt. The golden age ended when colonial ties were severed during the American war of independence, but judicious investment in alternative growth areas ensured that the economy did not decline. As Glasgow diversified to become the centre of a major manufacturing region, the urban fabric altered indelibly to accommodate the expanding population. The city ultimately became one of the largest in the British Isles, with a population of over 77,000 by the 1800s.

Union, Trade and Tobacco

As the eighteenth century approached, colonial trade intensified its promise of profitable returns for Glasgow merchants. The consumer products of tobacco and sugar continued to head the list of transatlantic imports, often shipped to the southern ports of London, Bristol, Liverpool and Whitehaven, then re-exported to European markets via Glasgow. Much of the city's overseas activity was in spite of the continuing restraints imposed by English navigation laws. Glasgow's tobacco came overwhelmingly from

Virginia and Maryland, and for all the volume of legitimate trading, substantial quantities still entered the port as smuggled goods from the English colonies. At the same time, there were tentative moves in 1689 to promote commercial union between Scotland and England; a suggestion instigated by the provost of Edinburgh, and strongly supported by Glasgow Town Council.[1] Yet rather than relaxing trade barriers, attitudes hardened north and south of the Border as the Scots became ambitious to secure their place among the colonial elites of Europe. From 1695 the impressively-titled 'Company of Scotland Trading to Africa and the Indies' acquired huge amounts of Scottish capital to establish a colony at Darien, in the region of modern Panama.[2] The Glasgow share was some £56,000 sterling, more than a third of the total investment. Unfortunately, by 1700 English and Spanish pressure had forced the Scots to withdraw from their putative American empire, incurring heavy financial loss both for the city and the nation.

The Darien débâcle was a devastating blow to commercial confidence in Scotland, and English obstruction of the enterprise rankled deeply in the popular consciousness. Having exposed the raw reality of Scottish economic dependence, the spectre of Darien hovered over the negotiations which finally led to incorporating union with England in 1707. Whatever the desire to preserve political autonomy, the Scottish parliament was not in a position to undermine trading links by rejecting English proposals to create a United Kingdom, with centralised government in London. A common market would at least settle the vexed question of access to English colonies; a matter of no small significance to Glasgow's merchants. On the other hand, the prospect of union was violently opposed in a number of Scotland's urban centres, including Glasgow. Towards the end of 1706 the civic leadership authorised a series of measures to combat recent 'tumults and uproars', which at one point had involved an attack on the person and property of Provost John Aird.[3] Distrust of English intentions and suspicion of municipal complicity in the pro-union cause lay at the root of the riots, which were further fuelled (supposedly) by the call of one zealous minister to be 'up and valiant for the city of our God!'.[4] At the time there were widespread fears about the reimposition of the episcopacy under an English-dominated state church, which were allayed to some extent when the status of Presbyterianism in Scotland was guaranteed as an integral part of the union settlement.

Glasgow's subsequent commercial progress was not the inevitable outcome of 1707, despite the confident statement of historian John Gibson in 1777 that 'we may from this era date the prosperity of the city'.[5] In the first instance, definitions of 'prosperity' were open to interpretation, depending on the economic activity of particular traders, and it was generally the close-knit elite among overseas merchants who made substantial profits. There was also a counter-side to freer trade, notwithstanding the hopes arising from union. English ports remained ruthlessly competitive, certainly up to the 1750s, when trading specialism began to distinguish individual regions. Only in the longer term did Glasgow win out over its keenest rival, Whitehaven, as the southern seaport directed resources away from tobacco and into the coal export trade.[6] Continuity as well as change characterised the early eighteenth century, showing that 1707 was not wholly definitive in shaping Glasgow's fortunes. An international business network was already in the process of developing, with local merchants buoyed by access to London-based financial institutions as a means of providing credit. The success of the tobacco trade derived partly from economies of scale effected by the Glaswegians, who preferred to deal directly with colonial planters rather than rely on commission agents as an intermediary source of supply. This mode of operation was apparent in Virginia during the late seventeenth century, and such personal contact was to stand Glasgow interests in good stead as links were consolidated after 1707.

Nevertheless, if post-union opportunities did not immediately transform Glasgow, it was apparent that colonial trade was assuming greater importance for the local economy. The annual quantity of tobacco imports demonstrated the steady then spectacular scale of developments. Between 1715 and 1725 the volume doubled from two to four million lbs, then surged from eight million in 1741 to an unprecedented forty-seven million in 1771.[7] Moreover, official figures for the early period concealed the full extent of the trade. In their concern to evade customs duties, the smuggling proclivities of certain merchants continued until mid-century, when more rigorous preventative measures were enforced by the government. Fraud may have boosted competitive advantage, but there was ultimately a range of reasons for the concentration of tobacco imports in the city. One significant factor was Glasgow's strategic western location, which allowed for swifter sailing to the tobacco colonies. A combination of costs, convenience and shrewd commercial management allowed for Glasgow to become emphatically the premier tobacco port of the United Kingdom by the 1760s. The proportion of Scottish tobacco imports had reached 40 per cent of the national total, with city merchants virtually monopolising the trade. This regional focus is important, as it was the more favourably located outports of Greenock and Port Glasgow that handled the transatlantic cargoes. The vital connection forged between Glasgow and these fast-growing Clyde communities demonstrated that the fruits of colonial expansion were extending beyond the city boundaries.

To make profitable use of cargo space, the vessels bound for the tobacco colonies were freighted with assorted export goods. These were distributed among supply stores owned by Glasgow merchants and then purchased by planters or traded for tobacco. During the 1720s the English writer and journalist, Daniel Defoe, itemised the main commodities leaving from the city, making special reference to textiles and clothing.[8] By no means all the export merchandise was Scottish in origin, although Defoe was impressed

6. Tobacco fleet at Port Glasgow, 1760s.
The extent of shipping activity at Port Glasgow is conveyed by this view of the tobacco fleet during the 1760s. This was one of several illustrations produced by the Academy of Fine Arts, inaugurated by Andrew and Robert Foulis, and given generous patronage by the city's tobacco merchants. (*By courtesy of the Mitchell Library, Glasgow City Libraries and Archives.*)

by the quality of local linen. Of course, linen manufacture had a long-established base in the west of Scotland, and the districts of Calton and the Gorbals, contiguous to Glasgow, were developing as handloom weaving communities by the early eighteenth century. Linen, like tobacco, eventually benefited from the market opportunities arising after union, and between 1746 and 1771 the quantity stamped as of saleable standard in Glasgow rose from 861,000 yards to almost two million.[9] The example of the Stirling family illustrates how the profits accruing from colonial trade were being reinvested in the industry. From the 1720s the erstwhile 'sea adventurers' extended their sphere of operations into the textile processing sector, where technology was advancing in bleaching and printing.[10] By 1770 the firm of William Stirling & Sons had become so large that production shifted from Glasgow to the Vale of Leven, in rural Dunbartonshire, where more abundant water supplies allowed for increased levels of output to meet consumer demand.

Three substantial merchant partnerships, the Cunninghame, Spiers and Glassford groups, dominated the Glasgow tobacco trade by the 1770s. One of the giants, William Cunninghame & Company, has been described as 'an organisation of great stability and commercial influence', with an estimated capital of £100,000.[11] The wealthy Cunninghame partners could easily afford to invest in industrial enterprises, such as the Port Glasgow Sugar House, the Pollokshaws Printfield Company and the Dalnottar Iron Company. Not surprisingly, they were also at the centre of local financial institutions,

7. Glasgow from the south-west, 1760s.
A panoramic view from the south-west by Robert Paul. The shallowness of the River Clyde is apparent from the scene, as is the compact size of the city. Another illustration produced by the Foulis Academy of Fine Arts. (*By courtesy of the Mitchell Library, Glasgow City Libraries and Archives.*)

notably the Glasgow Arms Bank, founded in 1750. Given this scale of commitment, there seemed to be a lot for them to lose when the rebellious American colonists took their stand against British rule in 1775. The war of the revolution broke the tobacco monopoly and imports plummeted to around five million lbs in 1780. Yet for a variety of reasons the economy remained remarkably resilient. Vast reserves of tobacco enabled importers to make the most of wartime scarcity by raising prices. Contraband tobacco was channelled to Glasgow through neutral ports, notably in the Caribbean. The transatlantic focus was shifting, in any case, with a rapidly-expanding market for West India sugar, tobacco, spices, dyestuffs and raw cotton. The British territory of Canada offered new outlets, although the important timber trade was not fully established until the early nineteenth century. At the domestic level, investment in land and industry meant that tobacco fortunes were spread across several lucrative growth areas. Accordingly, diversification provided strength in depth for Glasgow's merchant elite, who by the 1800s continued to play an influential part in developing the economic infrastructure of the west of Scotland.

Politics and Government

Because of the burgess basis of authority in Scottish royal burghs, Glasgow's commercial interests were intricately bound up with the city's government.

Moreover, the power of the burgess institutions was strengthened in 1690, when William and Mary confirmed the right to free election of the magistrates. The civic leadership was determined to project a purposeful image from this time, and made every effort to distance itself from the discredited Restoration regime. Public finance was a particular preoccupation, given the unhealthy state of municipal finances inherited from the 'bishop's burgh'.[12] This was ironic, as overseas trading interests meant that councillors were by no means parochial in their outlook and nurtured grand ideas for promoting the city's prosperity. A sign of their ambition in 1696 was the investment of £3,000 sterling in the Darien scheme, which represented a substantial segment of the 'common good', as the patrimony of the burgh was known. As has been seen, there were dramatic political consequences arising from the failed imperial adventure, which was reflected in a split among the ranks of the Whig 'Revolutioner' majority on the Town Council. From 1700 the balance of power was remarkably fluid. For example, Glasgow's last member of the Scottish parliament, ex-Provost Hugh Montgomerie, did not represent the views of all his peers when he voted against union in 1707.[13] His antipathy to the proposed English connection derived from disillusion over Darien and commitment to radical Presbyterianism, sentiments that had considerable support among the wider community of Glasgow.

Each of the sixty-six royal burghs had returned their own MP to the Scottish parliament, but the quota was drastically reduced to fifteen when seats were reallocated for Westminster in 1707. Glasgow was combined with three other towns, Dumbarton, Renfrew and Rutherglen, and the grouping of the Clyde Burghs constituency prevailed until the onset of electoral reform in 1832. Up to this time there could be intense competition among the communities as to who should represent them, and Glasgow's superior size and status did not offer any significant advantage. As there was no proportionality in the nominating process, the city was strictly limited to a quarter-share in the MP. Nor had union allowed for an overhaul of the franchise qualifications, which were confined to serving town councillors in the burgh constituencies. Until 1832 Glasgow had a grand total of thirty-three parliamentary electors, which although sizeable for Scotland, still represented an extremely narrow power-base. The constraints of the closed electoral system came under critical scrutiny by the burgh reform movement during the 1780s, but even after this time Glasgow's rulers remained conspicuously aloof from complaints about lack of public accountability. They believed that the city was efficiently administered and that their personal business acumen stood them in good stead when it came to decision-making. Nor were they prepared to countenance constitutional change which might upset the political balance in Scotland and challenge their own entrenched position.

To an extent, they also were determined to reap advantages from the

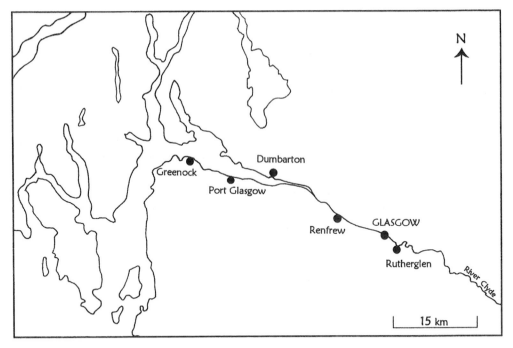

8. Clyde burghs and Clyde ports.
The geographical location of the Clyde burghs and Clyde ports, which were so important for furthering Glasgow's eighteenth-century political and economic status. (*The author.*)

intricate network of political patronage that prevailed in eighteenth-century Scotland. From 1750 a portrait of Archibald Campbell, the influential third Duke of Argyll, was prominently displayed in the town hall as evidence of the city's devotion to the Hanoverian ascendancy.[14] The formidable 'Argathelian' or Argyll interest had become apparent in Glasgow in the wake of the abortive Jacobite rebellion of 1715. This dramatic attempt to secure the British throne for the exiled Stuarts was the climax of years of uncertainty over the royal succession. As Jacobite power strengthened at Westminster towards the end of Queen Anne's reign, there was speculation that the monarchy would revert to Anne's Catholic half-brother, James, the 'Old Pretender'. In August 1714 the accession of the staunchly Protestant King George I of Hanover was greeted with considerable relief and rejoicing in Glasgow, where, as a symbol of loyalty, orange-coloured ribbons decorated the hats of the inhabitants. The following year, as Jacobite rebels mustered under the Earl of Mar, the magistrates raised a 500-strong citizens' militia to augment the Hanoverian army at Stirling Castle. John Campbell, second Duke of Argyll and commander-in-chief of the King's forces, returned 'most hearty thanks' for the zeal of the Glaswegians, and it was not long before his connection with the city became much more intimate.[15]

After 1715 Argyll was determined to ensure King George's peace in Scotland by extending his sphere of personal influence. Accordingly, in the localities he was served by individuals like Daniel Campbell of Shawfield, who became the Clyde Burghs MP in 1716. Campbell, unlike his patron, was no aristocrat, but a wealthy overseas merchant whose ambitions did not always accord with the greater good of his constituency.[16] His unpopularity intensified when he voted in parliament for measures believed to be contrary to the city's economic interests. Among these was the reimposition of the malt tax in 1724, which had the effect of increasing duties on Scottish ale by sixpence a barrel and provoking outrage in Glasgow. The quartering of troops in the city heightened tensions, their presence identified as government intimidation. Anger turned into tragedy in June 1725 when Campbell's substantial mansion at Shawfield was attacked by a mob. Renewed rioting erupted the following day, and at least eight people were killed outright as the military opened fire, and possibly twenty-eight more died later from their wounds.[17]

The civic leadership was made to pay dearly for the destruction of the Campbell residence, and a staggering compensation of £6,080 was awarded

9. The Shawfield mansion, eighteenth century.
The Shawfield mansion, looking solid and substantial, from a watercolour by Thomas Fairbairn. It was built for Daniel Campbell in 1711, with the frontage facing the Trongate and extensive gardens to the back. Fairbairn painted this scene long after the historic residence had been demolished in the 1790s. (*By courtesy of the Mitchell Library, Glasgow City Libraries and Archives.*)

to him from the common good. To rub salt in the wound, Campbell was returned again to parliament in 1727, under questionable circumstances, although he did not survive beyond the 1734 general election. Nevertheless, various scions of the Argyll family continued to dominate the city's politics well into the eighteenth century. While the Glaswegians initially had shown that they were not in awe of their Argyll patrons, from 1725 they were obliged to become more pragmatic about the relationship. There was considerable irony in this hegemony, as it cut across the autonomy secured in 1690 following the archbishop's departure. Instead, a Whig magnate had become the conduit of power, using the city as a base for his political placemen.

Despite the tensions arising from the malt-tax riots, loyalty to the House of Hanover retained particular resonance in Glasgow, because the regime was so firmly identified with the Protestant succession. In 1733 the city's first equestrian statue was erected at Glasgow Cross, depicting William of Orange, 'glorious and brave', as the great liberator from religious oppression.[18] Yet there was also some ambiguity behind the tribute, as it masked the uncomfortable existence of a small but solid core of Jacobite support in Glasgow. For instance, the Walkinshaw family of Barrowfield was one component of the mercantile elite who remained faithful to the old order, even though participation in the 1715 Rebellion drastically diminished their fortunes.[19] Moreover, the Jacobite threat continued long after this time. The worst fears of loyal Glaswegians were realised when Prince Charles Edward Stuart and his rebel army descended from the north in September 1745. The city could not offer military defence and Provost Andrew Cochrane was forced to hand over cash and goods to the value of £5,500. In December Charles returned in retreat from England, and lodged at the Shawfield mansion, by this time restored to a suitable state of splendour. Cochrane commented that the prince unsuccessfully tried to endear himself to the populace, appearing 'four times publicly in our streets, without acclamation or one huzza'.[20] As if to compensate for his frosty reception, Charles met a daughter of the Walkinshaw dynasty, Clementina, who subsequently earned Glasgow's place in royal history by bearing his only child, Charlotte.

After the '45 the Hanoverian ascendancy became more entrenched than ever, and political stability helped to create the context for further economic expansion. By 1755 the population had grown to over 23,500, indicating the attraction of the city as a regional centre. Understandably, Glasgow's administration became more complex, entailing an increasingly professional approach to civic responsibilities. These centred on law enforcement and the upkeep of assorted properties, including the cathedral and churches, the grammar school, the town's hospital (or poor house), and Glasgow Green (the burgh common lands). Municipal finances long had been a source of anxiety, although the losses arising from the Jacobite episode were eventually reimbursed from the Treasury. However, the appointment of a

City Chamberlain in 1755 to monitor expenditure represented a conscious effort to promote efficiency, especially in the collection of local taxes, market duties and rents.[21] The quest to bolster Glasgow's corporate viability contrasted starkly with the experience of Edinburgh, where the common good was eventually exhausted to help pay for the construction of the prestigious New Town. Whatever the subsequent claims of burgh reformers about civic profligacy in Scotland, Glasgow's canny councillors had gained too much experience (often the hard way) to involve themselves in risky entanglements. Faith in their achievements as custodians of the community came to be reflected in an assertive sense of civic confidence, as was shown by the elevation of the chief magistrate to the permanent status of 'Lord Provost' during the 1770s.

Notwithstanding the Town Council's input to the governance and parliamentary representation of the city, political expression was evident beyond the civic domain. For instance, Glasgow Chamber of Commerce sought to organise and inform business opinion on a range of issues, especially relating to the state of the economy. Founded in 1783, it was the first chamber of commerce to be established in the United Kingdom, and represented the views of individual merchants and also of manufacturers from the city and beyond. There was a radical edge to criticisms of measures like the government's Corn Laws, which regulated the price of grain to the frequent detriment of consumer interests. The Chamber's prevailing ethos has been summed up by one historian as 'a faith in freedom from restraint and a desire to seek independence rather than the protection of the state'.[22] Given the city's previous trading preoccupations there was nothing novel in this approach, although, significantly, it also looked forward to the mid-nineteenth century, when Glasgow had become a bastion of Victorian Liberalism.

On the other hand, such pioneering economic progressivism operated in a politically conservative environment. The American and French revolutions had redefined concepts of representative government, and the debate was opening out in Glasgow, albeit with acrimony. In 1792, at the same time as the Glasgow Society for Burgh Reform was urging its supporters to be 'asserting and constitutionally establishing the rights of man', the Town Council despatched a loyal address to King George III denouncing 'the cabals or seditious publications of a few discontented individuals'.[23] Chapter 4 explains the progress of the reformers in the uneasy context of the wars with France; suffice it to say that by the onset of the nineteenth century the 'constitution' had become central to very different notions of political legitimacy in Glasgow.

Culture and Society

During the course of the eighteenth century Glasgow acquired enviable fame for its attractive built environment; a reputation helped in no small measure by city publicists. In 1777 local historian and merchant, John Gibson, provided his impressions of structural progress:

> Every stranger is charmed with the appearance of Glasgow; the streets are clean and well-paved; ... the houses are all (excepting a very few) built of free stone, well hewed; a few of them exceed four floors in height, and many of them are in an exceeding good taste.[24]

Gibson made particular reference to the expenditure which had been

10. James Barrie's 1782 map of Glasgow. Barrie's map of the royalty was commissioned by the Town Council and published in 1782. The area around the Cross remains the most built-up part of the city, but the 'New Town' development centred on George Square is apparent in the gridded formation to the west of High Street. (*By courtesy of the Mitchell Library, Glasgow City Libraries and Archives.*)

11. Glassford family, 1760s.
Tobacco merchant James Glassford and his family at home in the Shawfield mansion during the 1760s. The artist was Archibald McLauchlin of the Foulis Academy. The scene exudes prosperity, with Glassford's power and potency reinforced by his brood of offspring. A missing proprietorial symbol is the black servant who originally stood behind Glassford, but whose figure was later deliberately obscured as anti-slavery sentiments heightened in Glasgow. (*Glasgow Museums: The People's Palace.*)

authorised by the Town Council on 'public works' and street development. There was often a commercial incentive behind such investment; for instance, the patriotically-titled King Street was built during the 1720s to accommodate Glasgow's growing assortment of food markets. The desire to display conspicuous consumption was a further reason for the embellishment of the city. Colonial wealth supplied the wherewithal for maintaining the mansions of the mercantile elite. The famous 1767 portrait of the Glassford family, in the prestigious setting of the Shawfield mansion, exudes a proprietary image of domestic comfort. Indeed, a black servant was originally featured as one of the more exotic possessions of John Glassford; a highly revealing connection with the transatlantic slave trade, which was later removed from the painting when the abolition movement established a significant base in the city.[25] Virginia Street, constructed in 1755, was another obvious tribute to tobacco prosperity and provided the route to the residence of George Buchanan, whose abundant gardens included vineries and peach-houses. The family name was perpetuated in Buchanan Street, where George's brother, Andrew, built his own mansion in 1760.[26] Although most of these imposing dwellings were later demolished, Buchanan Street went on to earn a different kind of prominence as one of Glasgow's most prestigious shopping thoroughfares.

Street and property development accelerated markedly from 1770 and there was an increasing tendency for the wealthy to move into peripheral districts, especially to the west of the city. Speculative building was securing lucrative profits for landowners, although, as will be seen, suburbanisation was identified more distinctly with the nineteenth century, when better roads and transportation made travelling more convenient. Accordingly, the most desirable residential address during the late eighteenth century was in the relatively small area of Glasgow's 'New Town', which included the public space of George Square, laid out in 1782. It formed part of a network of thoroughfares named after the royal family, including Duke Street, Frederick Street and Hanover Street.[27] Merchants, lawyers, clergy and even gentry had town-houses in this salubrious location, which was near enough to the commercial centre and the College campus. Public building was part of the same speculative impulse that directed the residential property boom, and became an area where the work of the Adam brothers, James and Robert, was particularly distinguished. Part of a formidable dynasty of Scottish architects, the pair had already left their distinctive mark on the Classical style of Edinburgh's New Town. Although their impact was not so pervasive in Glasgow, buildings like the Trades' Hall and the Assembly Rooms, constructed in the 1790s, conveyed much about burgeoning civic pride.[28] As a sign of changing times, the Adam-designed Royal Infirmary was erected on the site of the bishop's castle, the decaying remnants of episcopal authority having been cleared to make way for the hospital, which opened in 1794.

By 1791 the population of the city and suburbs was around 66,000, which represented one of the fastest urban growth rates in the United Kingdom. Glasgow was on the cusp of profound social change, with the surviving architecture of the old burgh combining with the splendid edifices of the merchant city to present an impressive townscape. Contemporary accounts, both from locals and visitors, were imbued with the rhetoric of energy and activity, memorably summed up by novelist Tobias Smollett when he described Glasgow as 'a perfect bee-hive in point of industry'.[29] On the other hand, industry and prosperity were not always mutually reinforcing. The smoke and effluent deriving from steam power had yet to arrive in the city, but pollution could be apparent in other ways. The Molendinar and

12. Glasgow cathedral and the Royal Infirmary, 1820s.
New Glasgow merges with the old in Joseph Swan's 1828 engraving of the cathedral and Adam-designed Royal Infirmary, opened in 1794. The view of the cathedral is particularly striking because the western towers remain a prominent and integral part of the building. They were demolished during the 1840s, in a misguided attempt to 'improve' the cathedral and its surroundings. (*By courtesy of the Mitchell Library, Glasgow City Libraries and Archives.*)

Gallowgate burns had fallen foul of industries developing along their banks, notably dye-works and tanneries. Pure water was becoming a scarce commodity in a community experiencing unprecedented demographic growth, with inevitable consequences for the quality of life. While several explorations of alternative sources were sanctioned by the Town Council from the 1770s, no action was taken, and the inhabitants had to make do with the inconsistent supplies from city wells. The cost of providing such a large-scale, municipally-organised water supply seems to have blocked progress prior to the 1800s, as there were fears that it would entail a prohibitive tax on property owners.

Conversely, policing proved to be an area where there eventually was willingness to pay. As the following chapter explains, the debate had emerged forcefully in the wake of violent disturbances by striking weavers in 1787, during a time of acute economic depression. Rioting was no new phenomenon in Glasgow, but this latest outburst highlighted a serious imbalance in policing arrangements for the increasingly populous community. The magistrates responded in 1788 by appointing an 'intendant of

13. The Assembly Rooms, Ingram Street, 1820s.
The Assembly Rooms, Ingram Street, designed by Robert and James Adam and erected in 1796. They served as a fashionable focus for concerts and dancing assemblies, and were so popular that the building was extended in 1807. Demolished in the 1890s, the central bay was rebuilt as a triumphal arch at Glasgow Green and named as a tribute to local councillor, James McLennan. (*By courtesy of the Mitchell Library, Glasgow City Libraries and Archives.*)

police', whose establishment consisted of a clerk and eight officers. To augment this meagre corps, it was found necessary to form a compulsory night patrol of able-bodied citizens; an arrangement that was scarcely conducive for efficiency, despite stiff financial penalties for defaulters.[30] Not surprisingly, the complaints continued, and were given added urgency by strident claims about the moral deterioration of the city. Thus, in 1793 Glasgow's contributor to the *Statistical Account of Scotland* pointed to the dark side of commercial success:

> Great crimes were formerly very uncommon; but now robberies, house-breakings, swindling, pick-pockets, pilferers, and consequently executions are become more common. These delinquents, as well as common prostitutes, are often little advanced above childhood.[31]

To counter the incidence of crime and public disorder, Glasgow's pioneering Police Act was sanctioned by parliament in 1800, and set up an elected authority with rating powers. The new constabulary employed a Master of Police, three sergeants, nine officers and sixty-eight watchmen. However, in accordance with the broad definition of 'policing' in Scotland, a range of environmental services was assumed by the Police Board, including lighting, street-paving, cleansing and refuse collection.

The social extremes represented by Glasgow's 'burgher aristocracy' and the shadowy criminal underclass were, of course, untypical of the population as a whole. The weavers' strike indicated the presence of a growing industrial workforce, which was quite prepared to take direct action to articulate grievances. Moreover, women were a major component of the industrial economy, because so much employment was still based in the domestic context. Linen, which was long a manufacturing mainstay, created particular opportunities for flax-spinning, and a revealing insight was made in 1726 by one visitor to Glasgow, who claimed that 'all the poor people in the west of Scotland spin'.[32] Towards the end of the century domestic service became another growth area, to provide household help for the residences of the rich. The extent of Glaswegian opulence should, however, be placed in perspective. Income tax returns for 1801, which were applicable only to the very wealthy, reveal that Glasgow's share of the Scottish burden was only 1.6 per cent, even though the city accommodated just under 5 per cent of the national population.[33] Those with substantial personal fortunes were thus unusual, while the vast majority of the 'middle-ranks' were of modest means. This was the community of shopkeepers, craftsmen, manufacturers and small traders who continued to cluster around the traditional heartland of Glasgow Cross, living in multi-occupancy tenements often directly adjacent to their businesses.

Most of the College professors fell into the exclusive ranks of the highly taxed, showing the prestige of the institution and the profitable returns for senior academics. Indeed, the university had been central to the efflorescence of Enlightenment thought in Glasgow during the mid-eighteenth century, which paralleled the much more celebrated intellectual developments at Edinburgh. There was a keen philosophical edge to the ideas emanating from Glasgow, which related to the quest for social harmony and concepts of civil and religious liberty. Francis Hutcheson, an Ulsterman of Scottish descent, was one of the trail-blazers when he became professor of moral philosophy in 1729. An ordained Presbyterian clergyman, Hutcheson nevertheless was a strong believer in religious moderation and the value of scientific enquiry. His views were regarded with profound suspicion by Presbyterian purists in Glasgow, although charges of heretical teaching could not be substantiated. However, his powerful impression on the younger generation was later acknowledged by one of his students, Adam Smith, when he paid tribute to 'the abilities and Virtues of the never to be forgotten Dr Hutcheson'.[34] Smith himself succeeded to the chair of moral philosophy in 1751, and spent thirteen years in the city. His writing was influenced by the optimistic outlook of his mentor, notably *The Wealth of Nations*, first published in 1776. That classic text of liberal economics also benefited from Smith's association with leading Glasgow merchants, although he could be damning about the cartel quality of some practices that seemed to contradict the city's much-vaunted support for freer trade.

One famous example of social interaction between town and gown was the political economy club founded by Provost Andrew Cochrane in 1743, which later included Smith among its luminaries. The second half of the century was characterised by the emergence of numerous clubs and less formal associations in the city, ranging from the serious to the convivial, and invariably catering for men. The Tontine Coffee Room, erected by public subscription and opened in 1784, was one of the more dignified enterprises, which prohibited the consumption of alcohol or tobacco. Its main function was to serve as a reading room for its subscribers, numbering over 800 by the 1790s.[35] Local, national and even French newspapers were made available, as well as periodical publications. This interest reflected the spectacular growth of the printing and bookselling trades from 1740, with unprecedented demand for religious and secular literature. The local press took off in 1741 when the *Glasgow Journal* appeared, and other newspapers soon followed. Between 1745 and 1760 the *Glasgow Courant* was produced by the Foulis brothers, Andrew and Robert, whose quality output revolutionised publishing in the city. Recognising Glasgow's ripe potential for newspaper publishing, Edinburgh printer John Mennons came west and founded the *Glasgow Advertiser* in 1783. The name was changed to the *Glasgow Herald* in 1802, then shortened to the *Herald* in 1992, and the newspaper still buoyantly survives as one of the oldest in the English-speaking world.[36]

Ironically, the discourse stimulated by the cultural milieu of the Enlightenment took place in a city that was carefully controlled by the institutions of church and civic government. The Town Council's patronage of Church of Scotland ministers reinforced the connection, although it should be stressed that not all Presbyterians accepted the law of 1712 that had restored such power to landowners. There came to be a significant dissenting base in Glasgow because of the patronage issue, predominantly in the Secession and Relief Churches. Within the Established Church allegiances eventually divided between moderates and evangelicals, the latter vocal advocates of the right of popular selection, vested in congregations. The university was a centre of moderate thought, but the evangelicals identified more directly with the cause of radical Presbyterianism, which for so long had struck a chord among the wider population. If the moderates articulated an optimistic outlook, the evangelicals were criticised for having an austere and 'gloomy' cast of mind, although their paradoxical blend of passion and piety was altogether more complex than this stark appraisal would suggest. Moreover, their vision of the godly, ordered society became increasingly relevant in the urban context, where the pace of change was seen as threatening the intricate social balance. As Glasgow's economy took off in new directions from the 1800s, there was the promise of yet more wealth, but with disturbing implications for the equilibrium of the relentlessly expanding community.

Notes

1. Robert Renwick (ed.), *Extracts from the Records of the Burgh of Glasgow, 1663–1690* (Scottish Burgh Records Society: Glasgow, 1895), p. 420.
2. Gordon Jackson, 'Glasgow in transition, c. 1660–c. 1740', in T. M. Devine and Gordon Jackson (eds), *Glasgow, Volume I: Beginnings to 1830* (Manchester University Press: Manchester, 1995), pp. 73–4.
3. Renwick (ed.), *Extracts from the Records of the Burgh of Glasgow, 1691–1717* (Glasgow, 1908), p. 399.
4. Quoted in George Eyre–Todd, *History of Glasgow, Volume III: From the Revolution to the Passing of the Reform Acts* (Jackson, Wylie: Glasgow, 1934), p. 67.
5. John Gibson, *The History of Glasgow, from the Earliest Accounts to the Present Time* (John Gibson: Glasgow, 1777), p. 105.
6. T. M. Devine, 'The golden age of tobacco', in Devine and Jackson (eds), *Glasgow, Volume I*, p. 146.
7. Ibid. pp. 140–1.
8. Daniel Defoe, *A Tour Through the Whole Island of Great Britain* (Penguin Books edition: Harmondsworth, 1971), pp. 608–9.
9. R. H. Campbell, 'The making of the industrial city', in Devine and Jackson (eds), *Glasgow, Volume I*, p. 195.
10. John Oswald Mitchell, *Old Glasgow Essays* (James Maclehose: Glasgow, 1905), pp. 1–13.
11. T. M. Devine, *The Tobacco Lords: A Study of the Tobacco Merchants of Glasgow and their Trading Activities, c. 1740–90* (Edinburgh University Press edition: Edinburgh, 1990), p. 82.
12. Eyre-Todd, *History of Glasgow, Volume III*, pp. 13–19.
13. Introduction to Renwick (ed.), *Extracts from the Records of the Burgh of Glasgow, 1691–1717*, pp. vii–ix.
14. Irene Maver, 'The guardianship of the community: civic authority prior to 1833', in Devine and Jackson (eds), *Glasgow, Volume I*, pp. 259–60.
15. Renwick (ed.), *Extracts from the Records of the Burgh of Glasgow, 1691–1717*, pp. 545–6.
16. Ronald W. Sunter, *Patronage and Politics in Scotland, 1707–1832* (John Donald: Edinburgh, 1986), p. 206.
17. Christopher A. Whatley, 'Labour in the industrialising city, c. 1660–1830', in Devine and Jackson (eds), *Glasgow, Volume I*, p. 379.
18. John McUre, *A View of the City of Glasgow* (D. McVean and J. Wylie: Glasgow, 1830 edition), pp. 255–6. First published in 1736.
19. 'Senex' (Robert Reid), *Glasgow Past and Present*, vol. II (David Robertson: Glasgow, 1884), pp. 510–18.
20. Quoted in Eyre-Todd, *History of Glasgow, Volume III*, p. 210.
21. Maver, 'Guardianship of the community', p. 244.
22. H. Hamilton, 'The founding of the Glasgow Chamber of Commerce, 1783', *Scottish Journal of Political Economy* 1 (1954), p. 48.

23. Quoted in Henry W. Meikle, *Scotland and the French Revolution* (James Maclehose: Glasgow, 1912), p. 76; Renwick (ed.), *Extracts from the Records of the Burgh of Glasgow, 1781–95* (Glasgow, 1913), p. 461.

24. Gibson, *History of Glasgow*, p. 302.

25. Mary Edward, *Who Belongs to Glasgow? 200 Years of Migration* (Glasgow City Libraries: Glasgow, 1993), p. 17.

26. Daniel Frazer, *The Story of the Making of Buchanan Street* (James Frazer: Glasgow, 1885), pp. 41–2.

27. Thomas Somerville, *George Square, Glasgow* (John N. Mackinlay: Glasgow, 1891), pp. 12–13.

28. Miles Glendinning, Ranald Macinnes and Aonghus Mackenzie, *A History of Scottish Architecture: From the Renaissance to the Present Day* (Edinburgh University Press: Edinburgh, 1996), p. 180.

29. Quoted in Richard B. Sher and Andrew Hook, 'Introduction: Glasgow and the Enlightenment', in Hook and Sher (eds), *The Glasgow Enlightenment* (Tuckwell Press: East Linton, 1995), p. 6.

30. Renwick (ed.), *Extracts from the Records of the Burgh of Glasgow, 1781–95*, p. 392.

31. Sir John Sinclair (ed.), *The Statistical Account of Scotland, 1791–1799: Volume VII, Lanarkshire and Renfrewshire* (EP Publishing edition: Wakefield, 1973), p. 329.

32. Quoted in Whatley, 'Labour in the industrialising city', p. 368.

33. Stana Nenadic, 'The middle ranks and modernisation', in Devine and Jackson (eds), *Glasgow, Volume I*, p. 280.

34. Quoted in R. H. Campbell and R. S. Skinner, *Adam Smith* (Croom Helm: London, 1982), p. 20.

35. James Denholm, *The History of the City of Glasgow and Suburbs* (A. Magoun: Glasgow, 1804), pp. 188–91.

36. Alastair Phillips, *Glasgow's Herald: Two Hundred Years of a Newspaper, 1783–1983* (Richard Drew: Glasgow, 1982), pp. 11–17.

Clyde, 679 in the Gorbals, and 3,552 within the burgh boundary.[3] Geographically, the Glasgow sphere of influence was even more extensive, stretching to towns like Paisley, Hamilton, Ayr and Dumfries, where local weavers directly supplied the city. In addition, there was a well-established connection with weaving communities in Ulster. Cleland also reported the existence of sixteen powerloom works connected with Glasgow, indicating a steadily developing branch of textile production.

Despite fluctuations in the economy, domestic weaving appealed to a significant section of the labour force, not least because of the ease of entry to the trade and the relative autonomy it afforded. However, mechanisation meant that the market became keenly competitive, with inevitable consequences for wages and living standards. By the 1830s hours of work could equal and exceed those of spinners in cotton factories, the weavers attempting to compensate for declining wages through increased output. Moreover, conditions in self-employed loom-shops were often claustrophobic and ill-ventilated, the atmosphere humid, malodorous and choked with fibre.[4] The progress of the powerloom impinged mostly in the production of plainer

15. Woodside mill, 1820s.
Woodside mill on the River Kelvin, from a painting by Andrew Donaldson. The scene is from the 1820s, although Glasgow's first substantial water-powered cotton mill was erected in 1784. (*Glasgow Museums: The People's Palace.*)

cloths like calico, affecting the less skilled, poorer and most numerous section of the labour force. This was the group displaced by the over-whelmingly female powerloom weavers, in a highly-mechanised sector that rapidly expanded from the 1820s. Yet long after this time handloom weaving could still be favoured for finer and fancier fabrics. Smaller textile firms also continued to employ this category of weaver for reasons of cost-effectiveness, and it was not until the end of the century that the sound of the handloom shuttle became a rarity in Glasgow. John McDowall, the last working handloom weaver in the Calton district, was reported in 1916 as still gain-fully employed, aged over eighty.[5]

The survival of handloom weaving indicated the uneven technical progress of the assorted textile processes during the early nineteenth century. If weaving remained predominantly domestic, mechanisation characterised cotton-spinning, and it was this branch of production that became a powerful metaphor for the spirit of Glasgow enterprise. James Johnson was a London tourist in the 1830s who was struck by the industrial vibrancy of the city, his views contrasting sharply with the anxious assessments of social reformers about the deteriorating urban fabric. Johnson was breathlessly effusive in his description of Glasgow: 'this vast emporium of operatives –

16. John McDowell and 'Wee Maggie', 1916.
McDowell, shown with his industrious niece 'Wee Maggie'. McDowell was distinguished at the time for being the last working handloom weaver in the Calton district. When he started work in 1846 as a ten-year-old apprentice, the East End of Glasgow was still a focus for the trade, despite the incursion of the powerloom. (*By courtesy of the Mitchell Library, Glasgow City Libraries and Archives.*)

this city of the shuttle – this community of cotton-spinners – this world of weavers and unwashed artisans, living in an atmosphere of smoke and steam'.[6] In 1800 there had been eight steam-powered cotton-spinning mills operating in Scotland; by 1834 (when Johnson was writing) the number was 134, overwhelmingly concentrated within a forty-kilometre radius of Glasgow.[7]

The inadequacy of water resources in and around the city had stimulated early interest in the steam-engine, although ironically James Watt's crucial invention was protected by his Glasgow friends, so that it was not extensively exploited until the patent expired in 1800. The loosening of constraints allowed scope for experimentation, although subsequent industrial expansion must be placed within the context of relatively high machinery costs and limited engineering expertise. Watt may have achieved heroic status in Glasgow, his statue proudly erected in George Square in 1832, but he had left the city for Birmingham during the 1770s to refine his technical skills. However, Watt retained close links with Glasgow, much of it derived from his early university connection. From the mid-eighteenth century Watt had helped to establish the College's reputation for promoting 'practical' science. Not only was this apparent in mechanics and instrument making, but in the application of chemistry for industry. For instance, the chemist Joseph Black took a keen interest in improvements to the bleaching process for fabrics; a concern also shared by Watt, with whom he collaborated.[8] These explorations were more deeply probed by Charles Macintosh, a student of Black's and subsequently world famous for his patent waterproofing process. Macintosh entered into partnership with Charles Tennant, who came from an Ayrshire weaving background, and their bleaching salt was patented in 1799.[9] The innovation meant that bleaching could be cost-effectively conducted indoors, instead of in the unpredictable environment of open-air bleachfields.

Such novel ideas could stimulate extraordinary entrepreneurial success. The application of bleaching to textiles was the foundation for the rise in fortune of Tennant's St Rollox chemical works to the north of Glasgow, in close proximity to the Monkland Canal. By the 1830s the business had become probably the largest of its kind in the world, employing over 1,000 people. The energetic proprietor had diversified his interests into an extensive range of products, including soda, sulphuric acid, fertilisers and soap. 'Tennant's Stalk' was the enormous chimney of St Rollox and represented striking testimony to his achievements. Over 150 metres tall, it loomed over the urban landscape for eighty years until its demolition in 1922. One of the very few chimneys to inspire a celebratory poem, 'St Rollox Lum's Address to Its Brethren' was written by John Mitchell in 1842.[10] The garrulous 'lum' was portrayed as a soaring monument to free trade and prosperity, although for many residents the dense pall of smoke that belched forth from St Rollox was ultimately a more telling symbol of the fruits of industrial capitalism.

17. The St Rollox lum, 1890s. An eerie depiction of the lum, as it looms through a haze of industrial smoke. The photographer was William Graham of Springburn, whose prolific output revealed much about the life and times of his community. However, mortality underpinned this particular view of the celebrated chimney, taken from Sighthill cemetery. (*By courtesy of the Mitchell Library, Glasgow City Libraries and Archives.*)

Like Tennant, the pioneers of Glasgow textile enterprise often came from a weaving background. David Dale was another Ayrshire man, whose shrewd assessment of growing yarn demand led to the construction of the famous New Lanark mill in 1786. James Monteith's roots were in Anderston, although, like Dale, his mills were located next to abundant water supplies outside the city. Most businesses during the early spinning boom took the form of partnerships, with landowners and farmers playing a leading role because they provided the sites necessary to set up production. Often the landowners were merchants who had made their fortune in trade and commerce, and were seeking a means of boosting their investments. West India capital was a particular source of funding for Glasgow's fledgling textile concerns. James Finlay & Company, which was the largest cotton firm in Scotland by 1801, forged extensive West India connections, not least because the Caribbean and Americas were such lucrative export markets.

Because of the dependency on imported raw materials, the city's long-established overseas trading network was being put to profitable use to develop the new industry.

However, not all Glasgow's cotton entrepreneurs initially had such close personal links with the city. Henry Houldsworth came from Nottinghamshire via Manchester, where he had set up a successful cotton-spinning business with his brothers.[11] Moving to Glasgow, he was the manager then owner of Gillespie's Woodside mill. In 1804, using Manchester capital, he constructed a substantial steam-powered mill in Anderston, which was depicted as one of the wonders of Glasgow textile innovation. The new premises were famous as the city's first substantial brick-built building, the architecture indicative of the lavish care Houldsworth took over fire prevention. Along with his sons, he established a virtual family fiefdom to the west of the city, serving repeatedly as provost of Anderston after the burgh was created in 1824 to administer and police the district. Houldsworth's strict controlling influence was apparent in the conditions of the mill-workers. According to his testimony to a parliamentary select committee on child labour in 1816, he required operatives to work a six day week, twelve hours and fifty minutes a day, which stretched over fourteen hours inclusive of mealtimes. In response to a question about the effect of reduced working hours, he claimed that the free time would be spent 'very probably in drinking and other immorality', as well as exciting a dangerous spirit of 'restlessness and insubordination' among the labour force.[12]

The growing corps of Glasgow manufacturers generally imposed a more onerous work regime than counterparts beyond the city, and health and safety were not foremost considerations when it came to productivity. In the spinning mills there was often a working temperature in the seventies or eighties Fahrenheit (the twenties Celsius), the finer the yarn the hotter the atmosphere necessary for quality production. Houldsworth's produced fine yarn for muslin, and employed a relatively large workforce of 429 in 1834, who were overwhelmingly Irish-born or of Irish descent. The management was therefore more likely to be concerned about factory discipline because of the scale of operations. Of course, there was a variety of textile factories in Glasgow by the 1830s, including numerous smaller firms concentrating on coarser fabrics to meet demand for exports to colonial markets.[13] Significantly, there was a comparatively high number of youngsters employed under age fourteen, comprising 36 per cent of Glasgow mill employees as opposed to Manchester's 23 per cent.[14] It was the fine-spinning mills that tended to employ children, usually as piecers to fasten together broken threads. The ratio of women employed was also proportionately high, reflecting the preponderance of female labour in Scottish textile mills. Their wages were roughly half those of men, which was doubly disadvantageous for the women, as Glasgow was characterised as a low-wage city for most of the nineteenth century.

While cotton was the primary product, the textile sector extended to much more in Glasgow. Wool and worsted manufacturers had established a significant niche by mid-century, notably in carpet production. James Templeton, a Paisley shawl manufacturer, patented his chenille Axminster carpets in 1839. Thereafter the family business flourished, producing a particularly luxurious product, noted for the quality of design. Lace and silk were also manufactured in the city, reflecting elaborate Victorian tastes in fashion. By 1851 the textile and clothing trades together employed over 41 per cent of Glasgow's industrial workforce, with the next most numerous group, engineering, tool and metalworkers, comprising almost 9 per cent.[15] The general occupational profile showed that 77 per cent of men and 71 per cent of women were employed in the industrial sector, although not predominantly in a factory environment. The prevalence of small-scale concerns revealed that the old workshop tradition was still very much alive. Even in the clothing trades, nearly two-thirds of businesses employed four workers or less. Small workshops also generated ancillary industry in the manufacture of combs, shuttles and other essential items for textile production.

Despite the concentration of the labour force in textiles and related industries, the heady days of cotton success were already eroding by the 1830s. Manufacturers came to realise the relative backwardness of production techniques in Glasgow, as the more efficient Lancashire industry overtook the Scots. Significantly, over a five-year period from 1838 a spate of fires destroyed a number of prestigious cotton mills in the city, and the proprietors did not rebuild.[16] While conflagration posed a threat to the larger enterprises, the smaller were vulnerable to market fluctuations, and several disappeared following the failure of Glasgow's Western Bank in 1857. Indeed, a few well-established businesses foundered spectacularly during the crisis, indicating the unstable position of cotton in the city's economy by mid-century. While the industry had recovered some ground by the late 1860s, overseas competition intensified in the production of coarser fabrics, and Glasgow shifted decisively towards specialism in finer muslins and zephyrs. However, decline became precipitant from the 1880s, as the products of Lancashire, Europe and America overwhelmed the ossifying industry. It was modern, custom-built firms like the Paterson brothers' Clyde Spinning Company (1875) and Thomas Reid's Glasgow Cotton Spinning Company (1883) that maintained steady profitability and survived into the twentieth century.

Significantly, the canny Houldsworth family had diversified their industrial interests early on. Henry Houldsworth's Manchester connections made him acutely aware of the importance of machine-making and repair for textiles, and in 1823 he established the Anderston Foundry, to manufacture equipment. The enterprise was an augury of grander ambitions to expand into the iron industry, which was displaying promising returns for investors by the 1830s. Houldsworth founded the Coltness Iron Company in 1836, his obliging brother Thomas providing the necessary capital of £80,000. This was symbolic generally of the direction that Glasgow's industry was taking, as the blackband ironstone in the rich mineral hinterland of Lanarkshire became a prime focus for investment. Technical developments helped to stimulate this flurry of interest. In 1828 James Beaumont Neilson, manager of the Glasgow Gasworks, applied his considerable expertise in chemistry to develop the 'hot blast' process; encouraged, it should be added, by the veteran Charles Macintosh. By boosting the temperature for smelting in furnaces, fuel costs were lowered and the quality of iron improved. As the 1830s progressed, home and overseas demand for Scottish pig-iron reached unprecedented levels, allowing others besides the Houldsworths to increase their fortune. Building on substantial coal-mining assets, the Baird brothers of Gartsherrie accrued profits of nearly £270,000 between 1833 and 1840, making them among the richest men in the United Kingdom.[17] The Scottish industry was concentrated overwhelmingly in Lanarkshire, where there were fifteen ironworks by 1848 which made use of ninety-two furnaces. Together with the number of blast furnaces and foundries established within the city, these added to the already sooty skyline as success in heavy industry began to take-off.

Transport, Commerce and Finance

Industrial growth during the early nineteenth century was stimulated by the advantages of geographical location, which placed Glasgow at the heart of an extensive region with exploitable resources, including a ready reservoir of Lowland, Highland and Irish labour. However, as has been explained, the city's commercial background also stood industrial entrepreneurs in good stead because they were able to build on established connections. Glasgow was a transatlantic port of long standing; or rather, throughout the eighteenth century Greenock and Port Glasgow continued to serve the city because of the Clyde's unnavigable channel. Tobacco and other colonial connections prior to the 1780s defined established routes for Glasgow shipping, which remained important even after the nature of the cargoes altered. Economies of scale, based on specialisation, created a corps of merchant-shipowners, often with business partners based overseas to act as company agents. Foodstuffs and raw materials became vital imports, to provide for the expanding population and the needs of industry. By 1841 the Clyde at Glasgow had been made sufficiently navigable to allow ocean-going shipping direct access to the city, and the Americas and Caribbean were still a substantial focus of trade. Just over half the total tonnage of ships entering the port of Glasgow was attributable to the transatlantic connection, with cotton for textile production a prime commodity, along with the old staples of Canadian timber, American tobacco and West Indian sugar.[18]

According to one municipal assessment of 1896, the massive engineering feat involved in deepening the Clyde had constituted an exercise in 'prudent assiduity'.[19] This was because the city coffers were kept solvent, despite the high cost of the ongoing improvements. From the early eighteenth century, civic leaders had been preoccupied with assorted plans for opening out their notoriously shallow, shoal-filled river, which at some stretches (depending on the tides) could be as little as forty centimetres deep. However, the quest for a more practical thoroughfare for vessels to and from the city did not begin meaningfully until 1770. That year the English civil engineering team of John and James Golborne was given sanction to implement an improvement scheme, and they duly set to work on blasting, excavating, dredging and dyking.[20] As a result, ships of up to seventy tons were able to reach Glasgow, and the number of smaller coastal vessels steadily multiplied. The Golbornes' success encouraged further efforts, and the next great phase of activity occurred during the 1800s. The scale of the improvements meant that from 1810 Glasgow was recognised by parliament as a seaport in its own right, although until mid-century ships of larger tonnage still used the more commodious ports down-river.

18.   Broomielaw, 1840s.
The notorious congestion of shipping at the Broomielaw is captured in this scene from the 1840s. Artist J. D. Nichol's work was characterised by his lively evocation of Glasgow's street life. (*By courtesy of the Mitchell Library, Glasgow City Libraries and Archives.*)

Of crucial importance for expanding horizons was the coming of steamers in 1812, when Henry Bell's paddle-driven *Comet* first plied the river. These new, swift vessels proved to be particularly suitable for conveying passengers, and services soon were inaugurated between Clyde coast towns, Ireland and north-west England. Initially fares were expensive, costing four shillings to travel to Greenock, and the voyage from Glasgow was often disrupted by lurking shoals and sand-banks. In the event of grounding, passengers could be called upon by the captain to move rapidly from one end of the vessel to the other to manoeuvre it back to mobility.[21] Despite the drawbacks, brisk business was generated as more steamers were brought into operation. George Burns, who ran the Belfast & Glasgow Steam-Boat Company, made a telling comment in 1834 about the effect on Irish immigration, which was 'progressively increasing since the introduction of steam navigation, and . . . has rapidly increased since the lowering of the fares during the last two years'.[22] He added that costs were from sixpence to a shilling for deck passengers from Belfast, the majority of whom were provision merchants, labourers and seasonal harvest workers. In the Glasgow area generally by the 1830s nearly two-thirds of all paying passengers were opting to use steamer and canal services, and water transport remained popular throughout the century.[23]

Canals were one of the archetypal images of early British industrialisation. Work on the Forth & Clyde Canal to the north of Glasgow commenced during the 1760s, and the waterway functioned for over 200 years. Its rationale had been to allow a direct route between Glasgow's port of Greenock and Edinburgh's port of Leith, and despite limitations on the size and type of shipping that could cut across central Scotland, over time the canal substantially increased the volume of city trade. The Port Dundas district and the area around Firhill (later Maryhill) became the focus for a range of industries which depended on the waterway, including chemical works, dye works, grain mills, grinding mills, distilleries, foundries and machine shops. The Monkland Canal was constructed at the same time, to serve primarily as a conduit for coal supplies to the city from Lanarkshire. It prospered from the 1820s, when the west of Scotland iron industry began its phenomenal rise in fortune. Nor did the coming of the railways seriously diminish the use of this route, which survived until Lanarkshire mineral resources became all but exhausted by the 1920s.

The waterways helped to secure the concentration of industry in Glasgow, and the deepening of the Clyde was a further crucial factor in this process. The result, as historian Gordon Jackson points out, was the emergence of the only British city in the nineteenth century which was both a major seaport and a major industrial complex.[24] Indeed, by the 1830s the river had become overburdened with the sheer volume of shipping, vessels docked at the quays sometimes nine or ten layers across. Throughout the century harbour expansion continued to be a priority of the Clyde Navigation

Trust, a joint agency representing civic and business interests. For contemporaries this was a tangible sign of flourishing trade and commerce, but also indicated that extraordinary pressures were being placed upon urban space. Land became an increasingly valuable commodity as harbour and industrial developers sought out the most strategic sites in a city already congested with people and properties. The development of railways made further territorial inroads. The Scottish roots of the new steam-powered locomotion lay very close to Glasgow, in the lines constructed during the 1820s for the mineral districts of Lanarkshire. It was not long before the first service reached the city, with the opening of the Garnkirk & Glasgow Railway in 1831. This was an industrial line, locally financed, and running thirteen kilometres from the Baird brothers' coal domain of Gartsherrie to Charles Tennant's St Rollox works.[25]

Tennant was an ardent railway champion, largely because his business consumed over 30,000 tons of coal a year and he was anxious to break the Monkland Canal's transport monopoly. The chemical magnate was also to the fore in promoting a direct line between Glasgow and Edinburgh, inspired by the success of the Manchester & Liverpool Railway, which had opened in 1830. The Scottish scheme had to battle its way through parliament against fierce objections from the directors of the Forth & Clyde Canal, among others. An integral part of the established passenger route to Edinburgh, the waterway was threatened by the swifter rail connection, which aimed to cut ninety minutes from the four hour journey. Eventually the railway was approved and the inter-city service inaugurated with an elaborate ceremony in February 1842. The *Glasgow Herald* devoted extensive column inches to the occasion, including the speech of company chairman John Leadbetter, who defended the massive £1.25 million expenditure. Leadbetter claimed patriotically that 'this national work will add greatly to the prosperity of Scotland', and added diplomatically that it reflected 'the great railways' system which the genius of Britain has raised as a monument of her science, her enterprise, and her wealth'.[26] The Edinburgh & Glasgow Railway was far more extensive than any previous operation in Scotland, and significantly 90 per cent of its capital came from south of the Border.[27]

The new line was launched during a period of intense interest in railway investment, as transport technology progressed and the potential of the new communications system was recognised. From the outset there was bitter rivalry among the major companies serving Glasgow, and over time competition coalesced between two powerful groups. On the one hand were the joint forces of the North British Railway and the Glasgow & South Western Railway, which were able to work together because they served different regions. Directly opposing them was the Caledonian Railway.[28] During the 1850s the companies' animosity extended to cut-throat price wars, which allowed passenger traffic to boom on all fronts. However, the prolonged inability to reconcile spheres of influence in Glasgow had the

19. Garnkirk & Glasgow Railway, 1830s.
The railway arrives, with the opening of the Glasgow & Garnkirk Railway in 1831. One of a series of illustrations showing the triumphal procession of this new mode of transport, the engine is approaching the St Rollox works. D. O. Hill, who was also a pioneering Scottish photographer, produced the engraving. (*By courtesy of the Mitchell Library, Glasgow City Libraries and Archives.*)

ironic effect of retarding plans for a collectively-owned, centrally-located terminus of sufficient size to meet the increased demand. After much parliamentary wrangling between the companies the requisite legislation was secured and St Enoch Station opened in 1876. The Caledonian refused to participate in the venture, and opened its own Central Station in 1879. As explained in Chapter 8, these construction projects were a catalyst for clearing the city of some of its most notorious slum housing; an aspiration that from the 1840s had been intimately connected with plans for railway development in Glasgow.

For many Glaswegians the railways symbolised the quickening pace of change in society, above all the economically-liberating impact of free trade and industrial expansion. To celebrate the opening of the Glasgow & Greenock Railway in 1841, radical poet Alexander Rodger wrote of 'Thou greatest of all Revolutionists – Steam', and the power it bestowed on manufacturers to penetrate even the remote regions of the world.[29] From a less lyrical perspective, there was optimism in Glasgow about the financial returns likely to accrue from investment at a time of particular entrepreneurial energy. Iron and railways represented the glittering El Dorado of the 1830s and 1840s, leading to unprecedented activity in the city's financial sector. Business was sufficiently buoyant for Scotland's first formal stock exchange to open in June 1844. The driving force behind the initiative was James Watson, a Paisley-born accountant and future Lord Provost, wryly described by one subsequent commentator as 'a living declaration to all his confrères that it is possible to be a dealer in stocks and shares and at the same time an honest and upright man'.[30] Dealing was stimulated not just by the expanding number of joint-stock companies, many created as a result of the railway boom, but because of falling interest rates after 1842. Share-holding could thus be highly lucrative for investors, although it also was a risky business, especially in the increasingly unpredictable railway sector. Nevertheless, Glasgow acquired a bullish reputation in the money market, and after the city's stock exchange was successfully established, Edinburgh and Aberdeen followed suit.

Banking also went through an aggressively expansionist phase in Glasgow during this time. Edinburgh was the banking centre for Scotland, and although there were a few indigenous Glasgow enterprises up to 1830, these did not share the status of their prestigious eastern counterparts. However, there was resentment within Glasgow business circles about Edinburgh domination, particularly the unadventurous lending policies of existing institutions. The speculative climate of the times encouraged the formation of locally-based joint-stock banks, beginning with the Glasgow Union Banking Company in 1830 and followed by the Western Bank of Scotland in 1832. The latter was intended to answer the need for 'Sufficient Bank Accommodation, on Liberal Principles', and from the outset the directors embarked on an ambitious policy of branch development.[31] The Clydesdale Bank, inaugurated in 1838, was another institution with a strong Liberal influence, and several of its founders were active in post-reform municipal government. It proved to be the most resilient of the banks created in the fever of financial activity up to the mid-1840s, when no fewer than six appeared, including the City of Glasgow Bank in 1839. Some had a transient existence, and were quickly absorbed by the longer-established institutions. 'Dynamic and dangerous' is one description of the prevailing ethos of these banks, a dualism indicating that while they were expansive, they were often high-risk ventures.[32] Lending strategy could be reckless, and over-stretched resources were one reason why the Western Bank foundered in 1857.

Workers, Textiles and Trade Unionism

As has been explained in relation to textiles, the boom in Glasgow manufacturing had a profound effect on work patterns, impinging even on traditional areas of technology like handloom weaving. Not surprisingly, this led workers to organise, to defend their status. Yet the response of assorted groups within the workforce was apparent even before steam power altered conditions so drastically. The abundant opportunities for weaving employment in and around Glasgow by the late eighteenth century demonstrated how much the traditionally tight craft restrictions were eroding, as apprenticeship regulations became more flexible. In 1751 parliament had intervened by removing constraints on the power of trade incorporations to control the employment of weavers in linen, a particular growth area in Glasgow. During times of economic buoyancy the freer market was not so disruptive of living standards, but the recurrence of recession towards the end of the century hit hard as demand for products dropped and price levels plummeted.

The severe economic downswing of the 1780s exposed mounting industrial tension in the city. Enforced wage cuts provoked a mass withdrawal of labour, which reached a violent climax in 1787 as strikers demonstrated their anger by raiding the looms of working weavers. On 3 September Glasgow's magistrates attempted to quell an unruly crowd, gathered in the Drygate district and throwing 'stones, brickbats and other missile weapons' at troops of the 39th Infantry Regiment.[33] After the Riot Act was read, the troops were ordered to fire their muskets, killing three weavers outright and (depending on different accounts) mortally wounding three or five. These traumatic events were eventually enshrined as a landmark in the development of the Scottish labour movement. So ingrained was the legacy that 200 years later one senior Labour councillor attempted to exorcise the ghost of his municipal predecessors by paying tribute to the weavers as 'the first Red Clydesiders'.[34] While an overtly political dimension to the 1787 dispute was not apparent, the spectre of public disorder created anxiety among Glasgow's elites and, as has been seen, fuelled debate about the need for a more professional policing structure to protect the city.

The strength of the weavers' response also demonstrated the growing economic importance of the textile sector, although collective action for redress of grievances was by no means a new phenomenon in Glasgow. From at least the 1730s assorted journeymen organisations had been combining to protect and promote their interests.[35] More like friendly societies than trade unions, they nevertheless participated directly in disputes involving wage rates and hours of work. An important dimension to their activities was recourse to the legal process in Scotland. Local justices of the peace, the burgh courts and Edinburgh's Court of Session were used widely as industrial relations arbiters. Indeed, in the unstable economic conditions of the late eighteenth century, bargaining procedures based on judicial intervention could defuse tensions between journeymen and masters, with decisions often going in favour of the former. Yet as was shown by the Glasgow magistrates in 1787, the paternalistic edge to the prevailing system was considered obstructive by the new generation of entrepreneurs, who preferred that market forces alone should set the conditions of production. The mounting scale of manufacturing operations helped to polarise attitudes. Although there was relative tranquillity on the industrial relations front after 1787, economic insecurity during the 1800s meant that weavers started to organise along identifiable trade union lines. The Glasgow-based General Association of Operative Weavers in Scotland was formed in 1809, with connections stretching to communities as far as Stirling, Perth and Edinburgh.[36]

The weavers were spurred into activism as the economy deteriorated. By 1811 the prices they could command had fallen to a third of 1792 levels, the cost of foodstuffs was rising, and war with France was seriously disrupting overseas trade. The association vigorously pursued the traditional method for fixing prices through the courts, and in 1812 secured a broadly favourable response from the Lanarkshire justices of the peace. However, the manufacturers doggedly stood ground, and refused to implement the decision. A strike ensued, with echoes of 1787, as the sinister-sounding 'Black Cat' hook was used like a claw to shred the webs of recalcitrant weavers. While violence officially was not part of the association's strategy, the government intervened by arresting its leaders. Both the Lord Advocate and Home Secretary acted out of fear that the dispute would become dangerously politicised during the emergency conditions of war. The trial which followed in 1813 had a devastating impact on the weavers' organisation. The General Association was dissolved, combinations north of the Border were legally circumscribed, and the long-standing statutes for price regulation were repealed. Employers were empowered to determine wages and conditions of employment without intervention by the judiciary. Manufacturing interests collectively had overridden the intricate controlling mechanism in Scottish industrial relations, depriving workers of an important outlet for articulating grievances.

To some extent political radicalism served as an alternative outlet for protest during the depressed years up to the 1820s, but as the next chapter explains, this could be a perilous course in Glasgow. Conversely, the intensification of the industrialisation process meant that while the old 'moral economy' had been eradicated, trade union organisation did not disappear. After 1813 progress was erratic, but during the early 1820s the economy showed a marked improvement, which in turn boosted the demand for labour and placed workers in a stronger bargaining position. By 1825 Glasgow had become a focus for organisation among certain groups of workers, the repeal of anti-combination laws in 1824 intensifying activism. Colliers and builders were involved in industrial disputes, weavers had formed a new association and cotton spinners were strengthening an existing one. While economic fortunes fluctuated again in the city after 1825, with periods of slump then boom, concern about safeguarding workers' status remained prominent on the trade union agenda.

20. Cotton spinners' tray, 1820s.
This tray from the 1820s commemorates the Glasgow Cotton Spinners' Friendly Association. As well as celebrating commercial success, it symbolically blends local and national patriotism, with the city's coat-of-arms accompanied by the thistle and the rose. Significantly, the authoritative masculine figure dominates the female. (*Glasgow Museums: The People's Palace.*)

Of the organisations that gathered support by the 1820s, the Glasgow and West of Scotland Cotton Spinners' Association was one of the most vigorous, building up an entrenched membership in larger mills like Houldsworth's. Its priority was fending off uncontrolled entry to the trade, including the influx of women workers, whose presence challenged the resolutely male-dominated hierarchy among spinners. The association's problems were compounded by the pace with which Lancashire spinning technology was moving ahead of its Scottish equivalent and the successful tactics of southern employers to reverse trade union expansion. In 1837 the leading Glasgow manufacturers resolved to take a united stance to reorientate their industry towards greater cost-effectiveness by reducing wages and introducing larger, Lancashire-style spinning mules. The changes inevitably would skew the employment profile of mills, cutting the number of experienced spinners but recruiting younger piecers to service the more intricate new machinery.

The threat of innovation and its impact on work patterns was the catalyst for the ill-fated strike of the Glasgow cotton spinners, which ran its bitter course during the spring and summer of 1837. Initially there was confidence within the association that the strike would be successful. The employers, for their part, were equally determined to hold out against the union. The use of strike-breakers heightened tensions, which reached a sensational climax in July when a Houldsworth operative was fatally shot late one night while out with his wife. The victim, John Smith, appeared to have paid a tragic price for continuing to work during the dispute. Four officers of the association and another (who had allegedly fired the shot) were charged with a litany of offences in relation to the crime, including conspiracy, the use of intimidation and murder.[37] Despite escaping conviction for murder, they were given the harsh sentence of seven years' transportation, although were never sent to Australia. There were lingering doubts about the case against them, and in 1841 they were pardoned after a public campaign. Nevertheless, the strike was deeply damaging to perceptions of trade unionism in Glasgow, which for years afterwards was tainted by the unsavoury atmosphere of violence and conspiracy hovering over the events of 1837. The movement in Scotland generally suffered a severe organisational setback, exacerbated by the depressed economic conditions that prevailed into the 1840s and generated widespread unemployment and distress.

More specifically, in 1837 a watershed was reached in relation to the question of control in the workplace. As in 1812 a group of workers had attempted to safeguard their position by resorting to industrial action, but the employers had outmanoeuvred them. However, the context of the 1830s was significantly different, as political attitudes had been redefined during the reform era. Cotton-masters like Henry Dunlop and Henry Houldsworth's sons, John and William, were professed Liberal progressives who passionately advocated unfettered market forces as the basis for prosperity. Accordingly, persuasive and powerful people had confronted the Cotton Spinners' Association, buoyed by their conviction that the union was all too conservative in its anxiety to hold on to the vestiges of semi-autonomous craft tradition. Dunlop's role in the dispute is worth stressing, as he represented the epitome of the successful Glasgow businessman and went on to secure assorted positions of public prominence. A founder of the City of Glasgow Bank, deputy-chairman of the Edinburgh & Glasgow Railway and a prominent Corn Law repealer, he was also a devoted evangelical Presbyterian, who joined the Free Church in 1843. An active councillor since 1833, he secured the Lord Provostship in 1837, only months after co-ordinating the employers' action during the strike.

Closely connected with Dunlop's dual industrial and civic interests was the issue of public order. This preoccupation was nothing new, but the growing scale of industrial unrest during the 1830s prompted serious questions to be asked about the adequacy of existing control mechanisms. A major part of the problem related to the unco-ordinated policing structure in the Glasgow area, where there were separate jurisdictions for the city and contiguous county districts. Archibald Alison, the Sheriff of Lanarkshire, was in no doubt that a centrally-controlled Glasgow constabulary should be extended to manufacturing districts like Anderston and Calton, where the 1837 strike had been particularly vigorous. He claimed personal experience of policing deficiencies during the dispute, although it must be cautioned that his recollections could be coloured with sensationalism.[38] In his testimony to a parliamentary select committee on workers' combinations in 1838, Alison indicated that he had been compelled to call on the military to be 'in readiness' to quell disturbances at Galbraith & Johnstone's Oakbank mill to the north of Glasgow.[39] The presence was apparently enough to restore order. An unswerving Tory, Alison had no sympathy for the Liberal ethos and its ambiguous definitions of freedom. None the less, there was sufficient common ground for Glasgow's predominantly Liberal councillors to endorse the case for an extended police authority and secure the requisite legislation in 1846. The textile districts, among others, were absorbed into the enlarged municipal entity of Glasgow, and criminal policing arrangements in the city were fixed for nearly fifty years.

After the trauma of 1837 an organised trade union movement did eventually re-emerge in Glasgow, as Chapter 6 elaborates. From the 1850s the focus was on smaller groups of workers, locally-based and predominantly craft-orientated. The decade was characterised by general improvements in working conditions, although the collapse of the Western Bank in 1857 had a temporarily destabilising impact on industrial employment. Yet as Sheriff Alison and the cotton-masters had hoped, labour relations in manufacturing became noticeably less volatile in the years following 1837. The changing climate was reflected by the sometimes ostentatious paternalism of Glasgow employers, who took a qualitatively different approach to the behaviour of their workforce than Henry Houldsworth earlier in the century. For instance, the Clark family of Mile-End (in the east of the city) were thread manufacturers of deeply-held evangelical convictions, who consciously encouraged social and recreational activities in their factories, often with a strong pro-temperance colouring. While drink obviously had a debilitating impact on efficiency, the Clark strategy was intended to instil a sense of workplace identity and harmonise employer-employee relations in an effort to counter incipient trade union truculence.

In this context, the growth of an effective passenger transport system in railways and steam-shipping allowed for the organised work excursion to become one of several morale-boosting devices for employers. Operatives still had little leisure opportunity to venture beyond the city and such benevolence generated invaluable publicity. Thus, the workers of the Oakbank spinning and weaving factory, who had caused so much anxiety in 1837, were reported in June 1853 as having sailed for the isle of Bute aboard the steamer *Mary Jane* on their second annual excursion.[40] The *Glasgow Herald* pointed out that this was part of a new welfare regime by their 'unassuming philanthropic employer', who also had erected reading and refreshment rooms near the factory. Two weeks later the *Herald* gave the following enthusiastic account of another summer 'day-away':

> ... on Monday the 20th, the workers in the printfield belonging to Messrs Todd and Higginbotham proceeded on a pleasure excursion to Ayr... They then walked in procession to Burns's Monument, accompanied by the fine band of the Pensioners from Glasgow. After viewing the monument, the statues of Tam O'Shanter and Souter Johnny, the twa brigs o' Doon, with its beautiful and romantic scenery, and other interesting spots, they returned to Glasgow... The expenses of the excursionists were defrayed by the generous liberality of Mr Higginbotham.[41]

Fresh air, education and a sense of inspiring Scottish identity were the benefits of this sober and ordered form of social activity for at least one component of the city's workforce.

By the mid-nineteenth century, Glasgow's industrial economy was maturing. Although there was still a high percentage of the workforce involved in the clothing and textile sector, the heavy industrial base was becoming increasingly important and contributed substantially to regional specialism in shipbuilding. Such progress had been helped by the engineering feats that had transformed river navigation and created extensive canal and railway routes. The growth of population from 77,000 in 1801 to over 395,000 in 1861 suggested much about employment opportunities, as more effective transport communications encouraged unprecedented numbers of immigrants and in-migrants to settle in the city. Yet although Glasgow consolidated a reputation for the flair and energy of its entrepreneurs, rapid economic expansion had introduced new work practices which, in certain sectors, generated industrial conflict. The expression of grievances could take a variety of forms, whether through trade union organisation or through direct political action. The following chapter considers Glasgow's politics in the context of economic and social change from 1800 and the ideological reorientation of the city in the wake of electoral reform during the 1830s.

Notes

1. Sir John Sinclair (ed.), *The Statistical Account of Scotland, 1791-1799: Volume VII, Lanarkshire and Renfrewshire* (EP Publishing edition: Wakefield, 1973), pp. 295-7.
2. R. H. Campbell, 'The making of the industrial city', in T. M. Devine and Gordon Jackson (eds), *Glasgow, Volume I: Beginnings to 1830* (Manchester University Press: Manchester, 1995), p. 185.

3. James Cleland, *The Rise and Progress of the City of Glasgow* (James Brash: Glasgow, 1820), p. 239.

4. Norman Murray, *The Scottish Hand Loom Weavers, 1790–1850: A Social History* (John Donald: Edinburgh, 1978), p. 152.

5. Peter Fyfe, 'A tour in the Calton', in *Old Glasgow Club Transactions* (1916–17), p. 279.

6. James Johnson, *The Recess, or, Autumnal Relaxation in the Highlands and Lowlands* (Longman, Rees: London, 1834), p. 186.

7. William Blackwood (publisher), *The New Statistical Account of Scotland: Volume VI, Lanarkshire* (Blackwood: Edinburgh, 1841), p. 148.

8. Richard B. Sher, 'Commerce, religion and enlightenment in eighteenth-century Glasgow', in Devine and Jackson (eds), *Glasgow, Volume I*, pp. 339–41.

9. Nancy Crathorne, *Tennant's Stalk: the Story of the Tennants of the Glen* (Macmillan: London, 1973), pp. 60–1.

10. John Mitchell, 'St Rollox lum's address to its brethren', in Hamish Whyte (ed.), *Mungo's Tongues: Glasgow Poems, 1630–1990* (Mainstream: Edinburgh, 1993), pp. 96–102.

11. J. L. Carvel, *The Coltness Iron Company: A Study in Private Enterprise* (Carvel: Edinburgh, 1948), pp. 6–11.

12. British Parliamentary Papers [hereafter BPP], *Select Committee on the State of the Children Employed in Manufactures in the United Kingdom*, 1816, III, p. 230.

13. John Butt, 'The industries of Glasgow', in W. Hamish Fraser and Irene Maver (eds), *Glasgow, Volume II: 1830–1912* (Manchester University Press: Manchester, 1996), pp. 102–3.

14. Christopher A. Whately, 'Labour in the industrialising city', in Devine and Jackson (eds), *Glasgow, Volume I*, p. 371.

15. Richard Rodger, 'The labour force', in Fraser and Maver (eds), *Glasgow, Volume II*, p. 168.

16. A. J. Robertson, 'The decline of the Scottish cotton industry, 1860–1914', *Business History* 12 (1970), p. 118.

17. Anthony Slaven, *The Development of the West of Scotland, 1750–1960* (Routledge and Kegan Paul: London, 1975), p. 120.

18. Gordon Jackson and Charles Munn, 'Trade, commerce and finance', in Fraser and Maver (eds), *Glasgow, Volume II*, pp. 62–4.

19. Sir James Bell and James Paton, *Glasgow, Its Municipal Organisation and Administration* (James Maclehose: Glasgow, 1896), p. 312.

20. John F. Riddell, *Clyde Navigation: A History of the Development and Deepening of the River Clyde* (John Donald: Edinburgh, 1979), pp. 32–44.

21. James Deas, *The River Clyde: An Historical Description of the Rise and Progress of the Harbour of Glasgow* (James Maclehose: Glasgow, 1876), pp. 29–30.

22. BPP, 'Appendix G: state of the Irish poor in Glasgow', *State of the Irish Poor in Great Britain*, 1836, XXXIV, p. 103.

23. J. R. Hume, 'Transport and towns in Victorian Scotland', in George Gordon and Brian Dicks (eds), *Scottish Urban History* (Aberdeen University Press: Aberdeen, 1983), p. 198.

24. Gordon Jackson, 'New horizons in trade', in Devine and Jackson (eds), *Glasgow, Volume I*, p. 235.

25. Crathorne, *Tennant's Stalk*, pp. 91–2.

26. *Glasgow Herald*, 21 February 1842.

27. Slaven, *Development of the West of Scotland*, p. 45.

28. John R. Kellett, *Railways and Victorian Cities* (Routledge and Kegan Paul: London, 1979), pp. 223–4.

29. Alexander Rodger, 'Opening of the Glasgow and Greenock Railway', in *Poems and Songs: Humorous, Serious and Satirical* (Alexander Gardner: Paisley, 1897), pp. 102–3.

30. 'Fairplay', *Clydeside Cameos: A Series of Sketches of Prominent Clydeside Men* (Fairplay: London, 1885), p. 131.

31. S. G. Checkland, *Scottish Banking: A History, 1695–1973* (Collins: Glasgow, 1975), p. 327.

32. Jackson and Munn., 'Trade, commerce and finance', p. 80.

33. James Denholm, *The History of the City of Glasgow and Suburbs* (A. McGoun: Glasgow, 1804), p. 93; Kenneth J. Logue, *Popular Disturbances in Scotland, 1780–1815* (John Donald: Edinburgh, 1979), pp. 155–60.

34. Councillor Philip O'Rourke in the introduction to Elspeth King, *The Strike of the Glasgow Weavers, 1787* (Glasgow Museums and Art Galleries: Glasgow, 1987), p. 5.

35. W. Hamish Fraser, *Conflict and Class: Scottish Workers, 1700–1838* (John Donald: Edinburgh, 1988), p. 43.

36. See ibid. pp. 81–99, where the background to the weavers' organisation is explained in depth.

37. Ibid. pp. 154–62.

38. Michael Michie, *An Enlightenment Tory in Victorian Scotland: the Career of Sir Archibald Alison* (Tuckwell Press: East Linton, 1997), p. 73.

39. BPP, *Reports of the Select Committee on Combinations of Workmen*, 1837–38, VIII, p. 97.

40. *Glasgow Herald*, 13 June 1853.

41. Ibid. 27 June 1853.

the government's controversial Corn Law of 1815. The legislation was introduced to regulate grain prices and protect British agriculture from foreign competition, but it was popularly believed that the government had pandered to privilege by keeping up the profits of landowners at a time of post-war economic strain. Emotions ran high, with serious disturbances occurring in urban centres throughout the United Kingdom. The Glaswegian response was especially vehement, with the complicity of the Clyde Burghs MP over the Corn Law providing added piquancy to the taunts of the crowd. Not long after the infamous parliamentary decision, the strength of local feeling was summed up by one young visitor to the city, who wrote back home: 'Yesterday about 3 o'clock poor Finlay was represented hanging upon a gibbet upon one of the pillars of the Tontine. This instantly collected a great multitude who testified their joy by means of huzzahs and laughter'.[8] Effigies and public ridicule, the traditional expressions of urban protest, were consciously directed against the most authoritative figure in Glasgow. Yet Finlay's ritual humiliation was part of a much wider manifestation of disgust, over a law which was identified as a euphemism for increased taxation. Condemnation was expressed in a flurry of petitions to parliament,

22. King William and horse at Glasgow Cross, 1841.
Lively scenes around Glasgow Cross, where the equestrian statue of William of Orange was a prominent feature of the landscape. This illustration by J. D. Nichol, dating from 1841, shows the spot (somewhere to the right) where Kirkman Finlay's effigy was dangled from a pillar during the Corn Law protests of 1815.
(*By courtesy of the Mitchell Library, Glasgow City Libraries and Archives.*)

including those from 'numerous and respectable' meetings of inhabitants as well as assorted commercial and trading interests.

The furore provoked by the events of 1815 was also a major catalyst in awakening slumbering radical assertiveness in the city. The rhetoric and style of the protests had been imbued with Foxite sentiments, not least the emphasis on petitioning as an effective means of raising the public consciousness. However, the deteriorating economic climate in the wake of the war meant that popular politics speedily took on a more outspoken tenor. The veteran English parliamentary reformer, Major John Cartwright, toured Scotland during the summer of 1815, and visited Glasgow three times. He found audiences receptive to his ideas, especially his own brand of petitioning, which was explicit in its call for fundamental change to the political system. In the autumn of 1816, amidst conditions of acute distress and unemployment, a monster public meeting took place at Thrushgrove, an estate owned by the tobacco dealer James Turner. The organisers claimed an attendance of 40,000, making it the largest political gathering to be held in Scotland at that time. The efforts of Cartwright and other prominent radicals were praised by successive speakers, who urged Glaswegians to 'Petition and Petition, and Petition in an orderly manner, and with perseverence'.[9] The authorities had been resolutely hostile to the prospect of such a show of strength, fearing a recurrence of the Corn Law disturbances which had so embarrassingly damaged the dignity of the local MP. Turner therefore took a calculated personal risk in allowing the proceedings to go ahead on his private property, but was amply rewarded by the exemplary behaviour of the crowd. As one enthusiastic report put it, 'even the boxwood borders of the avenue which led to the park were not in the least injured'.[10]

The same report recognised the predominance of 'work people' at Thrushgrove, showing how far the base of opposition to the government had opened out after 1815. Glasgow shared this politicisation process with other industrial centres in the United Kingdom, as the incidence of popular protest gathered momentum. Major Cartwright was busy forming local radical societies (the Hampden Clubs) south of the Border, and while the movement was not so strong in Scotland, links were undoubtedly forged between communities. The generally depressed state of trade created an even wider gulf between the government and opposition, and added a sense of urgency to radical demands. In Glasgow economic fortunes had been fluctuating from 1811, but the cessation of hostilities with France in 1815 introduced a further element of unpredictability, as industrial markets sharply reorientated and demobilisation forced thousands to compete for work. In this context, the iniquities of the Corn Law were perceived as particularly galling, with the people compelled to subsidise the rich while their own living standards were eroding. The radicals also questioned the values of a government which had repeatedly stressed the virtues of constitutionalism in its war-time rhetoric, yet was playing a key role in restoring manifestly undemocratic regimes across post-Napoleonic Europe. 'Retrenchment and reform' was the slogan encapsulating the radical crusade against apparent profligacy and corruption among the ruling classes, so glaringly exposed by the economic crisis in the immediate aftermath of the war.

The 1820 Radical Rising

The petitioning campaign made no positive impact on the government. Indeed, with protests and disturbances occurring throughout the realm during the winter of 1816–17, ministers were now unshakeable in their belief that subversion was insidiously spreading. Fearing that events might spiral out of control, concerted efforts were made to target likely areas of political flashpoint. Kirkman Finlay acted as a conduit for news about Glasgow, much of it supplied by Town Clerk James Reddie, who zealously took on the task of reconnoitring the radicals. Part of the Finlay-Reddie strategy involved the use of police and informers, who were urged to infiltrate radical groups and report back their suspicions.[11] Some of the returns indicated that the threat to public order was grossly overblown, but in the highly-charged political climate of early 1817 several arrests were made, on the express orders of the Home Secretary, Lord Sidmouth. By force of law, the government hoped to demonstrate its firm commitment to expose conspiracy and restore order, but the Glasgow sedition charges ultimately proved to be an embarrassment. While evidence did emerge of clandestine activity, especially in the textile communities, it remained unclear whether this had been encouraged by *agents provocateurs*. As Henry Cockburn wrote in his memoirs of 1856, a key witness claimed to have been 'tampered with' by the authorities in efforts to secure a successful prosecution.[12] The case slowly dissolved under pressure from a determined array of Whig defence lawyers, including Cockburn, and most of the accused were released without going to trial. Only weaver Andrew McKinlay appeared at Edinburgh's High Court, and was eventually found 'not proven'.

The events of 1817 were significant, despite the failure of the sedition charges. The intensity of the official reaction, both within and from outside the city, achieved the immediate objective of muting radicalism in Glasgow. However, the lull was short-lived, as the deteriorating economy and rising unemployment meant that the articulation of genuine grievances could not be constrained. A telling indication of the extent of social dislocation in the city was the first major outbreak of typhus fever in 1818, which one medical expert attributed to the conditions endured by a 'numerous, crowded, dirty, and poor population'.[13] By the summer of 1819, well-attended protest meetings were advocating political reform as well as relief of distress. In June, 20,000 'operative weavers' gathered peacefully on Glasgow Green to call for annual parliaments, universal suffrage and a diminution of taxation.[14]

Again Glasgow was by no means isolated in making such demands, and again there was mounting concern among the authorities about a nationwide conspiracy to subvert the constitution. In August 1819 Lord Provost Henry Monteith issued a proclamation describing municipal attempts to 'mitigate the pressure of the times' through relief works, but adding a cautionary warning about the need for order. His intention was unequivocal:

> The Magistrates, Sheriff and Justices, hereby declare their determined Resolution to maintain the Public Peace, and to Repress all Disorder, Riot, and Attempts at Depredation, and for these purposes to employ all the force, both Civil and Military, placed by the Law at their disposal.[15]

The Glasgow proclamation reflected the uncompromising attitude of those in power, not just within the city limits but throughout the United Kingdom. Later that month the notorious 'Peterloo Massacre' focused national attention on Manchester, where at least eleven people died and some 600 were injured at a public demonstration.[16] The local Yeomanry (who were not regular soldiers) lost control in an attempt to arrest prominent radicals on the platform, and panic had ensued. Nor surprisingly, this ugly turn of events heightened tensions in Glasgow. There were disturbances in the city and surrounding textile communities, and the language used at protest meetings became ominously angry. Throughout the autumn the city seemed to be in a state of siege, with 'well-disposed inhabitants' advised by the magistrates to keep their families and servants safe at home, especially after dark.[17] By December 1819 there were eight troops of Hussars and sixteen companies of infantry billeted in Glasgow, along with regiments of local Volunteers. Such a large military presence added to the already strained atmosphere of the city. Loyalties were tested as rumours of an incipient radical rising began to gain ground. Lord Provost Monteith kept up an anxious correspondence with the Borough Reeve of Manchester, hoping to pool information about disaffection in their respective communities.[18] The precise nature of the supposed conspiracy remained elusive, but the Glasgow authorities were convinced that it was part of a general plan to co-ordinate insurgency on a national scale.

The dénouement came with the distribution throughout the west of Scotland of an *Address to the Inhabitants of Great Britain and Ireland*, issued from Glasgow and dated 1 April 1820. The authors were radical activists from weaving communities to the east of the city, although the wide-ranging impact of the address showed that they were working as part of a much broader movement. The self-styled 'Committee of Organisation for forming a Provisional Government' bluntly stated that the time had come to take up arms for the redress of grievances. 'LIBERTY or DEATH' was the rousing motto of this fateful document, subsequently branded by the authorities as 'most *Wicked, Revolutionary* and *Treasonable*'.[19] Yet despite its melodramatic language, the address summed up the bitter mood of exasperation over government insensitivity to reform sentiments, especially the brusque dismissal of the petitioning campaign. To show their solidarity with the aims of the address, sympathisers were urged to go on strike, and it has been estimated that some 60,000 people in the Clyde region responded to the call.[20] In Glasgow most of the cotton mills temporarily ground to a halt, although there were accusations (notably from the Tory *Glasgow Herald*) that intimidation of workers had been involved.

Given the many imponderables still shrouding this traumatic event in the city's history, it is impossible to be accurate about genuine levels of support and how far the ubiquitous *agents provocateurs* influenced the course of events. All that can be certain is that the projected rising ultimately was unsuccessful, with the authorities taking speedy action against the insurgents. Lord Provost Monteith, Town Clerk Reddie and other designated protectors of the peace immediately imposed a curfew, and offered a generous reward of £300 for information about those who had issued the treasonable address. Approximately 2,000 regular troops were placed on alert in Glasgow and surrounding districts to ensure that any outbreak of armed rebellion would be nipped in the bud. There were consequently no major disturbances in the city, although serious incidents took place elsewhere, notably in Greenock, where eight people were killed and another ten wounded in an abortive attempt to break open the jail. Glasgow radicals also helped comrades from other communities. One ambitious venture involved a group of some twenty-five weavers, who joined forces with fellow insurgents from Lanarkshire in an attempt to seize armaments from the Carron Iron Works at Falkirk. However, before reaching their destination they were intercepted by a troop of cavalry, and after a desperate skirmish (the 'Battle of Bonnymuir') eighteen were taken prisoner. The conspicuous lack of planning suggests that there was no grand military strategy behind radical endeavours, although it is revealing that two of the leaders, John Baird and Andrew Hardie, were ex-soldiers.

The Bonnymuir fiasco had a demoralising effect on radical support in Glasgow, especially as the authorities began to round-up suspected sympathisers. Along with 100 others, James Turner (of Thrushgrove fame) was arrested and incarcerated in the city Bridewell, a prison which he later disdainfully described as 'a receptacle for the lowest outcasts of society'.[21] Turner was eventually released on bail, and the case was never brought to court. Of those who were tried and convicted, the Bonnymuir insurgents, led by Hardie and Baird, were found guilty of high treason and sentenced to be hanged, beheaded and quartered. Another veteran radical, James Wilson, was similarly condemned for his part in an abortive march on Glasgow. In the end, Hardie, Baird and Wilson were executed, and entered the pantheon of radical martyrs; the other sixteen were transported for life to Australia.

Whig contemporaries like Henry Cockburn subsequently claimed that the radical rising was deliberately exploited by the government to create a revolutionary scare. Determined to make an example after the post-war years of unrest, 'the folly and violence of our western weavers' was interpreted as civil war, and the most severe penalties imposed.[22] This view is partly correct, given the intensity of the official response. Yet it is also a back-handed compliment to the apparent strength of the radicals that they provoked genuine fear among Glasgow's ruling classes. Moreover, there can be no doubt that the events of April 1820 had a searing impact on the city's politics. The leadership of the radical reform movement was chastened in the traumatic wake of the executions. Thereafter adherents with 'physical force' sentiments were treated with extreme caution. The incidence of overtly radical political protest receded, and the initiative passed firmly to the respectable, middle-class opposition, who even by the 1820s were calling themselves 'Liberal'. On the other hand, as one historian has tellingly pointed out, Glasgow's population did not remain quiescent, especially when long-standing community rights were intruded upon.[23] For instance, the 'Harvie's Dyke' riot of 1823 became a *cause célèbre* in defence of popular right-of-way, and involved some 3,000 protesters. Throughout the nineteenth century a strand of pugnacious local activism remained prominent in Glasgow, which acted increasingly in tandem with electoral politics after the extension of the franchise in the 1830s.

The Reform Acts of 1832 and 1833

Glasgow's business elite conspicuously closed ranks during the turbulent period leading up to the radical rising, and many supported firm action against those subsequently arrested. When Kirkman Finlay spoke out against 'this treasonable confederacy', he represented a political cross-section of trading and manufacturing interests, collectively alarmed about the industrial impact of the general strike.[24] However, it would be misleading to interpret their ideological commitment as reactionary because of this stance. Indeed, Finlay's circle, which itself dominated the civic administration, was becoming increasingly forthright about the need for parliamentary and municipal reform. In 1819 town councillors took the bold step of endorsing a statement condemning self-election as detrimental to the public interest. They stressed the divisive nature of the prevailing system, which instead of nurturing 'the respect for those in power which is so necessary for the good government of the community', had created a dangerous spirit of discontent.[25] Underlying all this was also resentment against the lack of parliamentary recognition for Glasgow's dominant status among the communities of the west of Scotland. Even the redoubtable Finlay fell victim to the unpredictable support of the three smaller burghs, and was defeated in the general election of 1818. Although he almost immediately secured a more malleable seat south of the Border, Finlay by no means lost interest in the politics of his native city.

Reform sentiments therefore found favour among a range of political opinion in Glasgow during the 1820s, or as one prominent Finlayite put it, many from 'the thinking part of the community' were broadly in accord with the need for change.[26] On the other hand, there was a diversity of views about the precise definition of 'reform', and how best to achieve the proposed constitutional transformation. Over time, politics coalesced around competing 'Conservative' and 'Liberal' approaches. The former advised caution, while the latter was not so circumspect about attacking the prevailing system, largely because adherents still felt excluded from the power-base. A declaration of reforming intent from the Town Council was consequently not enough for critics to restrain their assault on self-election. They were helped by the activities of the Whig-led burgh reform movement, which had revived in 1817 and was conducting a high-profile campaign to make the Scottish municipalities more publicly accountable. Embarrassing exposures, especially about financial mismanagement in Aberdeen and Edinburgh, had seriously tarnished Glasgow's civic reputation, despite the Town Council's exemplary book-keeping record. The press became a vitally important vehicle for disseminating opposition opinion. In 1825 a Glasgow periodical, the *Scots Times*, was established to further the cause of reform. Humour and satire were used to undermine the credibility of the municipal regime, witheringly parodied as the 'Old Lady of Self-Election'.[27] As the *Scots Times* gleefully reiterated, the Old Lady's sense of style was grotesquely old-fashioned, and her demise was fast approaching.

John Strang, who was an early contributor to the newspaper, wrote retrospectively of the stirring climate of the times for Liberal partisans in Glasgow, when the 'mighty power of Toryism began to totter'.[28] He evoked the lively political discussions of 'the fraternity', who would gather regularly in city-centre taverns like the Shakespeare, the Crow and the Vine. Copious quantities of whisky-toddy and toasted cheese were consumed in the course of debate, 'and all for the good of the nation!'.[29] As the reform impulse gathered momentum after the return of the Whig Government in 1830, the press and politics in Glasgow became even more outspoken. The imminence of major constitutional change galvanised public opinion, and newspaper circulation soared. A feature of Glasgow was the appearance of multifarious 'unstamped' journals, which evaded the Government's tax on publication, and thus had a transient (if telling) existence.[30] For instance, the *Friend of the People* was edited by Strang to serve as a forum for the views of prospective Liberal parliamentary candidates during the 1832 general election. Its success in promoting the cause of the 'Clique', a group of wealthy businessmen, revealed how pivotal the press had become in the political process. A stamped newspaper, the *Glasgow Argus*, was founded on behalf of the 'Clique' the following year, and quickly became the dominant voice of free trade opinion in the west of Scotland.

The unstamped press also served the interests of radical opinion, notably the custodians of trade organisation in the city, whose cause found a far more favourable political climate during the early 1830s. Glasgow's United Trades' Committee launched the *Herald to the Trades' Advocate* in the autumn of 1830, hoping that it would stimulate enough popular support to launch a fully-fledged working-class newspaper. The mission statement was to 'instruct the operatives in their pursuit of physical and mental attainments', showing how deeply-ingrained the notion of self-improvement had become.[31] The proposed newspaper did not get off the ground, and the unstamped prototype was eventually forced to close under threat of prosecution; however, its appearance up to May 1831 was a clear indication of the diversity of reform sentiment in the city. In addition to the Trades' Committee, other organisations had also emerged to represent distinct interest groups. The solidly middle-class Reform Association and the artisan-orientated Political Union were among the most vocal, and they often worked together, with the focus determinedly on 'peace, economy and reform' as the summation of shared Liberal values.[32] Such collective action was conducive to an impressive show of strength, with over 100,000 reported as participating in Glasgow's two great reform demonstrations in October 1831 and May 1832.

During the course of 1831 there were indications that electoral reform was becoming a tangible reality, despite persistent obstacles to the progress of the legislation in parliament. In March considerable excitement was generated in Glasgow when the Reform Bill for England and Wales passed its second reading in the House of Commons by one vote. To celebrate, the magistrates authorised a general illumination of the city and, as John Strang put it, 'all cheerfully obeyed the summons save the most bigoted of Tories'.[33] The buoyant mood of expectancy was maintained up to the time when the Scottish Parliamentary Reform Bill eventually became law in July 1832. The resulting electoral provisions represented a considerable advance on the previous exclusive arrangements in Glasgow, whereby the franchise had been confined to the thirty-three serving town councillors. The vote was extended to all males who occupied property to the value of £10. The legislation also recognised the city's identity as the commercial and industrial centre of the west of Scotland. The uneven and acrimonious Clyde Burghs' connection was dissolved, and the self-contained Glasgow constituency was allowed to send two MPs to Westminster. Yet for all that the legislation was generally received with enthusiasm, the achievement of reform was double-edged. In Glasgow's first parliamentary election under the new regime, held in December 1832, only 7,204 men were enfranchised out of a population of over 200,000. The £10 property qualification proved to be a

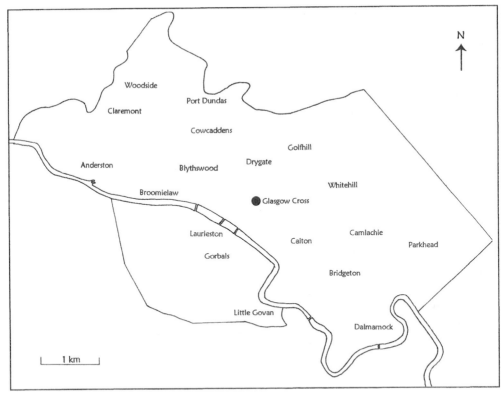

23. Parliamentary constituency, 1832.
The new parliamentary boundaries of 1832. Two MPs were returned for the unitary Glasgow constituency. The map shows the location of better-known districts within the constituency, with Glasgow Cross at the centre. (*The author.*)

relatively high threshold for voting in Scotland, and proportionately more were excluded from the electoral process than in cities south of the Border.

It also seemed paradoxical that in Glasgow a Conservative, James Ewing, should have topped the poll in the 1832 general election, even though a Liberal, James Oswald of the 'Clique', was returned as the city's second MP.[34] Ewing, from a West India trading background, was the serving Lord Provost and a long-standing political ally of Kirkman Finlay. His victory indicated that despite the plethora of propaganda outlets for the Liberals, support for the Conservatives remained strong. Their self-promoted image of cautious progressivism was attractive to many voters, and they were able to articulate their arguments through friendly newspapers such as the *Glasgow Courier*. Moreover, despite accusations of decrepitude in the Liberal press, many of the most ardent Conservative adherents came from the younger generation of businessmen in the city. Not only were they aware of the inadequacies of the self-elected system, but they realised that constitutional constraints were retarding meaningful administrative reform of civic government. The events surrounding the radical rising had helped to shape their

24. James Ewing and dog, 1831.
A silhouette of James Ewing and his dog by the celebrated French-born artist Augustin Edouart. Ewing's mansion was in Queen's Street Park, famous for its rookery, but today the site of Queen Street railway station. Edouart lived in Glasgow during 1831 and 1832, when he took Ewing's striking portrait. (*In a private Scottish collection.*)

consciousness by suggesting that stricter urban control was one appropriate mechanism for preventing community fragmentation. The policing strategies of Sir Robert Peel consequently appealed to the Glaswegians, and his 'liberal-Tory' economic ideas struck a similarly enthusiastic chord. Another Conservative hero was the Revd Dr Thomas Chalmers, the Church of Scotland evangelical, who preached a paternalistic vision of class harmony. His mission was to 'reclaim' the urban poor through the intervention of more prosperous citizens, who were urged to use moral exhortation to foster responsible attitudes and thus mute troublesome tendencies towards anti-social behaviour.

With the right to elect burgh MPs bestowed on the £10 householders, parliamentary reform in Scotland led inevitably to municipal reform. However, the 1833 Burgh Reform Act did not alter the role or function of town councils. While the £10 property qualification now prevailed, the quota of thirty-two Glasgow councillors was fixed to conform as closely as possible to the number (thirty-three) who had served under the old system. A further connection with the past was the continuing influence of the Dean of Guild and Deacon Convener, who were automatically returned as non-elected councillors. Their presence represented an important concession to Glasgow's burgess institutions, which ended only with local government reorganisation in 1975. For voting purposes in 1833, the relevant districts of the city were divided into five wards, which returned six councillors each. Reflecting the limitations of the £10 franchise, 4,821 Glasgow men were able to vote in the first open municipal poll, held in November of that year. The municipality covered less than half the territory of the parliamentary constituency, creating considerable confusion as to the exact definition of the geographic entity of Glasgow. However, in 1846 the municipal and parliamentary boundaries became conterminous and forty-eight elected councillors were returned for sixteen wards.

As with the general election of 1832, a lively campaign was conducted in 1833 by the candidates standing for the reformed Town Council. The *Glasgow Argus* adopted a crusading stance, urging Liberals to 'boldly and nobly' come forward to defeat 'Tory corruption'.[35] This call was generally supported and the return of twenty-seven declared Liberal councillors sharply reversed previous Conservative control of civic affairs. In recognition of this famous Liberal victory Robert Grahame was elected Lord Provost. He represented a direct link with the reform movement in the 1790s, when as a young lawyer he had helped to defend Thomas Muir against sedition charges. Grahame had also been involved with Charles Tennant in the establishment of the St Rollox chemical works, and was consequently a wealthy man by 1833.[36] Like the veteran Lord Provost, Glasgow's new councillors came overwhelmingly from the city's business elites. Approximately a third of those elected in 1833 were directly connected with the textile trade, while others represented the coal, iron, financial and retail sectors, as well as the law. This occupational profile was not significantly different from that of the unreformed Town Council. Indeed, the business basis of representation remained constant up to boundary extension in 1846, although significantly the Liberals lost ground to the Conservatives as the 1830s progressed.

In 1882, some fifty years after the passing of the reform legislation, historian Andrew Wallace wrote evocatively about the symbolic importance of the period for Glasgow:

What may be termed the romantic age, characterised by a pure atmosphere, pellucid streams, intra-mural gardens, orchards, cocked hats and silken hose, one o'clock dinners, and 'what you please' clubs, gave place to the practical age of coal, gas, iron, machinery, manufactures, smoke, sewage, steamboats, and all the other ungainly accessories of modern civilised life.[37]

Nostalgia for pre-industrial Scotland was lucrative literary business in the nineteenth century, and Wallace was reflecting contemporary preoccupations in depicting the past as much more Eden-like than the present. In reality, the chronology of industrialisation was not so clear-cut, with problems such as slum housing and smoke pollution identified in the city long before the 1830s. On the other hand, the decade did constitute a political dividing line. The achievement of reform, which had involved such a broad range of opinion in Glasgow, starkly exposed the previous inflexibility of the old order. The need for constitutional change had been acknowledged by the government and implemented. This conceded an important point of principle, which over-rode concerns about the exceptionally narrow base of democracy in the immediate wake of the two Reform Acts. Moreover, the mood of euphoria also meant that conscious efforts were made to undermine the culture associated with the old regime. It was identified as elitist and anachronistic, and so 'retrenchment and reform' was revived as an appropriate slogan for the future conduct of affairs. For many reformers, particularly of radical leanings, this meant an onslaught against ostentation and excess, which to them seemed grossly out of place in a more politically mature society.

Glasgow Chartism

The 1830s and 1840s were decades of considerable ideological flux in Glasgow, as constitutional issues remained to the forefront of political concerns. All shades of opinion, from radical to Conservative, struggled to come to terms with their post-reform identity. The extended franchise had seemed an easy goal to aim for, compared with the range of causes that intruded into the political agenda after 1832. Municipal reform, patronage within the Church of Scotland, Corn Law repeal and Chartism were among the most prominent. However, the intensity of debate should not be surprising, given the role that reform had played in heightening the collective political consciousness of the city. Perceptions were far more acute, which meant that the limitations of electoral change quickly began to be recognised.

Within the Liberal ranks there was growing resentment against the dominance of Oswald's 'Clique' group, which had publicly harnessed the issue of Corn Law repeal yet seemed reluctant to broaden out the organisation to include radical activists.[38] Moreover, while Glaswegians had enthusiastically responded to the repeal cause, with a petition of over 60,000 signatures presented to Parliament in 1834, the negative response of the Whig government prompted probing questions to be asked about its reform commitment. The deteriorating economic climate of the late 1830s also tested Liberal credibility. As has already been explained, the cotton spinners' strike of 1837 was quelled not just by the intervention of the outspoken Tory, Archibald Alison, but by the combined forces of predominantly

Liberal cotton masters. Depression dented reform buoyancy, with many Glaswegians compelled to seek poor relief. Visible manifestations of distress, notably the recurring incidence of typhus, sharpened demands for redress of grievances.

However, Liberalism was not easily fractured in a city where so much concerted effort had been put into the reform campaign. The shared values still mattered, notably the stress on individual self-improvement, moral elevation, rational argument and peaceful protest. While this approach was certainly not unique to Glasgow, it was underscored in the city by the bitter memory of 1820. The fate of the Glaswegians Baird and Hardie had not been forgotten by radical activists, and (in a highly symbolic gesture) a monument to them was erected at Thrushgrove in 1832. The previous confrontationist strategy and its consequences had taught a cautionary lesson about tactics, and the need to work subtly through the system in order to change it. Co-operation was thus recognised as an instrument of power, given the constitutional concession of 1832, and did not equate with deference to the ruling order for those who sought further extension of political rights.

This approach was to characterise Chartism in Glasgow, which first established a local base in 1838. The famous six-point 'Charter' originated in London during 1837, with universal male suffrage foremost among the list of objectives. It reflected radical demands that had been articulated since the late eighteenth century, and so there was nothing novel about the ideological focus. The Chartist emphasis on the efficacy of petitioning for parliamentary reform also had deep historic roots. However, organisationally the movement had learned much from the reform agitation. It was concerned to pool experience among communities and maintain the propaganda momentum. Glasgow's first Chartist rally took place in May 1838, and easily matched the earlier reform demonstrations in terms of its impressive turn-out.[39] The veteran James Turner repeated his role at Thrushgrove in 1816 by chairing the proceedings, showing concern to maintain continuity with past struggles. Up to 1842 Chartism attracted considerable local support, with Glaswegians dominant among the leadership of the co-ordinating Central Committee for Scotland. There were also some electoral successes, although understandably not in the parliamentary domain, despite the pro-Chartist George Mills standing for the Glasgow constituency in 1841. However, James Turner had been able to exorcise old grievances with his return to the reformed Town Council in 1833 and sat continuously for an East End ward until 1846.

While Chartist municipal representatives were rare at this time, Glasgow Police Board had a more significant presence. Chapter 2 explained the origins of the Board in 1800, at a time when concern about public order and the protection of property had compelled civic leaders to reappraise policing strategy. The administration of a professional constabulary was one of several functions of the elected Board, whose representatives were returned by the £10 householders long before this criterion prevailed for parliamentary and municipal elections. Environmental services, such as street-cleansing, were directed by the police commissioners. Indeed, Glasgow's night watchmen initially had the dual responsibility of guarding the streets and keeping them clean. As the urban population grew, the police establishment became more extensive and spheres of working activity became clearly defined. A corps of full-time 'scavengers' was employed for street-cleansing, a fire department was established in 1807, and the maintenance of the city's thoroughfares became a Police Board function in 1837. As for law and order, Glasgow's revised Police Act of 1821, passed in the wake of the radical rising, allowed for more vigorous surveillance of the community. A criminal investigation department was created and by the 1830s employed six specialist officers, to augment a constabulary that approached 200.

Although police commissioners were elected independently of the Town Council, Glasgow's civic magistrates – as designated protectors of the peace – remained intimately involved in Board affairs. Over time this led to differences of opinion about policing strategy, which became especially contentious following the cotton spinners' strike of 1837. Above all, there was municipal concern about the political orientation of certain Board representatives. The Board's constitution required aspiring police commissioners to stand for election in the wards of their domicile, which meant that the working-class communities (predominantly in the East End) were inclined to return locally-based radicals. Chartists James Moir, William C. Pattison and George Ross were elected during the early 1840s and demonstrated characteristic conscientiousness in Board deliberations.[40] The fact that Chartists and a few Irish-born Catholics were making their presence felt at this level undoubtedly contributed towards successful efforts to abolish the Board and absorb its functions into the Town Council in 1846. While the immediate anxiety was about direct radical involvement in such a sensitive area as policing, there was also fear that the commissioners might become a focus of political opposition, upstaging the more patrician Liberals who by this time controlled municipal affairs.

It was ironic that the whiff of subversion should have hovered around men like Moir, Pattison and Ross, because they were eminently respectable citizens, who consciously tried to project such upstanding qualities as hard work and moral probity. Like many among Glasgow's Chartist leaders, they were financially self-sufficient. Moir, for example, was a successful tea dealer in the city's Gallowgate district. All three outspokenly eschewed the violence that was tarnishing the movement's reputation in industrial centres south of the Border, culminating in the disastrous attempts to launch a general strike in 1842. They doggedly continued the campaigning reform strategy that they believed had yielded positive returns during the 1830s, especially in terms of consciousness-raising. Their opinion was not necessarily representative of the Scottish movement beyond the city, where the ideology was more varied and where there was greater scope for militancy, especially in some of the smaller manufacturing communities.[41] Indeed, Chartism's general loss of direction after 1842 was partly because of the failure to reconcile the ideological differences and co-ordinate a cohesive national movement, notwithstanding a brief resurgence during the acutely depressed conditions of 1848.

This was the year that James Moir sensationally defeated the sitting Lord Provost, Alexander Hastie, in a keen municipal contest for an East End ward. In particular, the magistrates' recent mishandling of the notorious 'Bread Riots' had provoked much bitterness, because of the deaths of three

25. James Moir, 1872. Moir in the autumn of his long political career, as portrayed by the newly-launched satirical magazine, *The Bailie*. The cartoon conveys a sense of Moir's continuing reputation as an iconoclast, with the exotic representations of 'the leaf of China' indicating his successful occupation as a tea-dealer. (*By courtesy of the Mitchell Library, Glasgow City Libraries and Archives.*)

men during the disturbances. A demonstration against unemployment and rising food prices had deteriorated into a violent confrontation between police and protesters. While a few retrospective accounts luridly evoked the spectre of anarchy, at the time it was generally recognised that the loss of life could have been avoided had the authorities exercised firmer control. Lord Provost Hastie became the focus of particular resentment, which Moir, as an erstwhile police commissioner, successfully exploited. Thereafter his municipal progress exemplified that of the upwardly-mobile element in Chartism, which eventually embraced the cause of Liberalism. Moir became an influential figure for future generations of activists, who looked admiringly to his pioneering experience in the reform movement and Chartism. In particular, he was a prominent figure in the Scottish National Reform League during the 1860s, which agitated for a further extension of the franchise. There was even talk of Moir standing as a Liberal parliamentary candidate for Glasgow. Yet intriguingly, his status as a symbol of radical continuity in the city stretched back to 1820. Although he was only an adolescent at the time, his elder brother Benjamin's arrest, trial and transportation as one of the Bonnymuir insurgents must have made an indelible impression on his political development.

The Mid-Victorian Liberal Ascendancy

During the 1850s, Glasgow Liberalism altered to accommodate radicals like Moir. As a successful local politician, Moir's constituency mattered, even if electoral numbers remained extremely small. According to Glasgow's 1862 register of voters, 16,568 were enfranchised out of a population of over 395,000, showing that parliamentary and municipal affairs were still con-fined to a relatively exclusive social class.[42] By this time Liberalism had long shed the ambiguous 'Clique' image. The resolution of the Corn Law crisis in 1846 by Peel's Conservative government had deprived James Oswald and his allies of their main campaigning platform, and the *Glasgow Argus* ceased publication the following year. For this and other reasons, shortly to be elaborated, there was no longer the need to fend-off an assertive Conserva-tive challenge. The pressure to hold together the Liberal electorate gradually eroded and a new generation of activists emerged, whose ideology was shaped by the post-reform experience. The identification of mid-Victorian Liberalism with the ethos of self-improvement was crucially important in Glasgow, because it offered an incentive to men with sufficient energy and motivation to penetrate the political power-base. The quest for individual freedom also meant that there was an enthusiastic reception in the city for international causes. The issue of slavery, which sparked the American Civil War in 1861, had long provoked strong pro-emancipation sentiments in Glasgow, while the nationalist movements of Italy and Hungary were ardently championed by Moir and others.

Locally, issues like city improvements became a focus of heated debate, especially after the boundary extension of 1846. By this time the leading civic players were almost invariably professed Liberals who were anxious to show how much they were taking the city's deteriorating fabric to heart. The next chapter provides more detail about policies undertaken to enhance the quality of urban life, notably in the crucial area of public health. However, it is important to stress that the predominantly business background of councillors made them acutely aware of the need to project a positive image, in order to instil a sense of civic pride and demonstrate that Glasgow could compete successfully with other cities. As Lord Provost Andrew Orr stated at the forum of a public dinner in 1856, their aim was to make Glasgow a 'model municipality'.[43] Orr's personal contribution to this ambitious project was his role that year in the acquisition of a civic art collection, complete with custom-designed galleries. There was considerable public unease at the time about the expenditure of £44,500 from the common good on the art works and properties, which comprised the estate of Orr's deceased civic colleague, Archibald McLellan. However, the Lord Provost responded briskly to his critics. He suggested that such a prestigious asset placed Glasgow on a par with 'almost any other city of importance on the Continent' and showed that the community was prepared to do something meaningful to promote the 'instruction and gratification' of the people.[44]

Ironically, a key factor in bolstering Liberal hegemony was the dramatic disintegration of Glasgow Conservatism during the early 1840s. The circumstances related overwhelmingly to the bitter conflict within the Church of Scotland over the patronage issue, that complex and sometimes arcane debate, which had been to the forefront of religious concerns since the early eighteenth century. From 1834 the evangelicals had been in the ascendancy after gaining a majority in the General Assembly. They immediately invoked the hostility of moderates within the Church because of moves towards vesting greater autonomy in congregations over the right of selecting ministers. The argument raged throughout the 1830s, with the two sides vying for control of the General Assembly. The Conservatives nationally had been sympathetic to the evangelicals, but the intensity of the struggle between the competing interest groups eventually alienated Peel, especially after he became Prime Minister in 1841. Two years later the evangelicals finally seceded from the Established Church, in exasperation over the refusal of the government to endorse their claims over patronage. Over half the worshippers in Glasgow left to form the Free Church of Scotland, under the charismatic leadership of Thomas Chalmers. Among this number was James Ewing, the former MP for Glasgow, whose previous belief in the fundamental Conservative principles of crown, church and constitution was shattered in the breach.

The Disruption, as it was called, has been described as 'the most important event in the whole of Scotland's nineteenth-century history, overshadowing even the Reform Act in its repercussions'.[45] This is a contentious opinion, which historians could argue over interminably, but there can be no doubt that the event was an ideological watershed, which profoundly and irrevocably reshaped Scottish politics. In Glasgow, the Disruption almost immediately obliterated what had been a promising base for Conservatism, and consigned its organisational structure to oblivion. There was no longer a designated Conservative group on the Town Council, and so Liberalism became the prevailing political orthodoxy as if by default. Although the Conservative cause did begin to revive after the Second Reform Act of 1868, it could never hope to match the formidable machine that the Liberals had been busily constructing in the intervening period.

Yet erstwhile evangelical Conservatives did not withdraw from public life in the aftermath of 1843. On the contrary, they pugnaciously crafted a new identity, which retained the sharp missionary edge of the pre-Disruption days. They positively repudiated the Establishment, and with wealth and influence behind them used politics as a vehicle to promote their idealised vision of society. Issues like temperance reform, education, slum clearance and public health were enthusiastically promoted, in accordance with the Chalmersian commitment to social activism. Common cause was made with like-minded Liberals; indeed, the evangelical craving for organisation was sufficient to redirect many talented activists into key positions within the Liberal party. For instance, William Collins was the founder of an internationally famous Glasgow publishing firm, a close personal associate of Chalmers and a declared Conservative. His transfer of spiritual allegiance to the Free Church in 1843 realigned the family politics, and his son (also William) became a prominent civic figure and one of the city's leading Liberals. However, the Conservative roots remained important, with Collins junior sharing the particularly warm regard of many Glaswegians for the brand of Liberalism articulated by William Ewart Gladstone, himself a refugee from the old party.

Conservative reorientation reflected the blend of continuity and change that characterised Glasgow's political power-base between 1800 and 1860. It was a time of ideological flux, but elements from the past still lingered. Thus, the old mercantile wealth of the city was apparent in the influence of men like James Ewing, even though individuals who had made their fortunes in relatively new growth areas, such as textiles, coal and iron, became increasingly prominent. The achievement of reform was also contradictory. Despite electoral limitations, it broadened aspirations and raised hopes that there could be further constitutional change. In the longer-term this had wide-reaching consequences for Glasgow, as the city became recognised as a bastion of Liberalism. Moreover, the strength of support was evident across a broad class spectrum. The next chapter places the political as well as economic changes in the social context of the period and considers the different ways they affected the city's fast-growing population.

Notes

1. James Denholm, *The History of the City of Glasgow and Suburbs* (A. McGoun: Glasgow, 1804), pp. 99–100.
2. Quoted in Henry W. Meikle, *Scotland and the French Revolution* (James Maclehose: Glasgow, 1912), p. 17.
3. Michael Fry, *The Dundas Despotism* (Edinburgh University Press: Edinburgh, 1992), pp. 167–8.
4. Quoted in John Brims, 'From reformers to "Jacobins": the Scottish Association of the Friends of the People', in T. M. Devine (ed.), *Conflict and Stability in Scottish Society, 1700–1850* (John Donald: Edinburgh, 1990), p. 43.
5. Quoted in Meikle, *Scotland and the French Revolution*, p. 131.
6. *Glasgow Herald*, 26 January 1810.
7. James Cleland, *The Rise and Progress of the City of Glasgow* (James Brash: Glasgow, 1820), p. 71.
8. Quoted in Jackson and Son (publisher), *James Finlay & Company Limited: Manufacturers and East India Merchants, 1750–1950* (Glasgow, 1951), pp. 27–8. The correspondent was Matthew Allison.
9. W. Lang (publisher), *Account of the Proceedings of the Public Meeting of the Burgesses and Inhabitants of the City of Glasgow* (Glasgow, 1816), p. 29.
10. Ibid. p. 13.
11. W. M. Roach, 'Alexander Richmond and the radical reform movements in Glasgow in 1816–17', *Scottish Historical Review* 51 (1972), pp. 6–7.
12. Henry Cockburn, *Memorials of His Time, 1779–1830* (T. N. Foulis: Edinburgh, 1910 edition), p. 319. First published in 1856.
13. Robert Graham, *Practical Observations on Continued Fever* (John Smith: Glasgow, 1818), p. 66.
14. *Glasgow Herald*, 15 June 1819.
15. Ibid. 2 August 1819.
16. Alan Kidd, *Manchester* (Keele University Press: Keele, 1996), pp. 92–7.
17. *Glasgow Herald*, 17 September 1819.
18. W. Hamish Fraser, *Conflict and Class: Scottish Workers, 1700–1838* (John Donald: Edinburgh, 1988), p. 110.
19. The *Address* is reproduced in W. Hamish Fraser, 'Patterns of protest', in T. M. Devine and R. Mitchison (eds), *People and Society in Scotland: Volume I, 1760–1830* (John Donald: Edinburgh, 1988), p. 288.
20. F. K. Donnelly, 'The Scottish rising of 1820: a re-interpretation', *Scottish Tradition* 6 (1976), p. 29.
21. J. Smith, *Recollection of James Turner, Esq., of Thrushgrove* (Glasgow Examiner: Glasgow, 1854), p. 73.
22. Cockburn, *Memorials of His Time*, p. 343.
23. Christopher A. Whatley, 'Labour and the industrialising city, c. 1660–1830', in T. M. Devine and Gordon Jackson (eds), *Glasgow, Volume I: Beginnings to 1830* (Manchester University Press: Manchester, 1995), p. 389.
24. *Glasgow Herald*, 14 April 1820.

25. Robert Renwick (ed.), *Extracts from the Records of the Burgh of Glasgow, 1809–1822* (Glasgow Corporation: Glasgow, 1915), p. 488.
26. Cleland, *Rise and Progress*, p. 67.
27. Irene Maver, 'The guardianship of the community: civic authority prior to 1833', in Devine and Jackson (eds), *Glasgow, Volume I*, p. 264.
28. John Strang, *Glasgow and Its Clubs* (Richard Griffin: Glasgow, 1856), pp. 525–6.
29. Ibid. p. 552.
30. Fiona A. Montgomery, 'The unstamped press; the contribution of Glasgow, 1831–1836', *Scottish Historical Review* 59 (1980), pp. 154–70.
31. Quoted in ibid. p. 163.
32. I. G. C. Hutchison, 'Glasgow working-class politics', in R. A. Cage (ed.), *The Working-Class in Glasgow, 1750–1914* (Croom Helm: Beckenham, 1987), p. 104.
33. Strang, *Glasgow and Its Clubs*, p. 543.
34. John F. McCaffrey, 'Political issues and developments', in W. Hamish Fraser and Irene Maver (eds), *Glasgow, Volume II: 1830–1912* (Manchester University Press: Manchester, 1996), pp. 189–92.
35. *Glasgow Argus*, 31 October 1833.
36. Maver, 'The guardianship of the community', p. 267.
37. Andrew Wallace, *A Popular Sketch of the History of Glasgow* (Thomas D. Morison: Glasgow, 1882), p. 93.
38. Fiona A. Montgomery, 'Glasgow and the movement for Corn Law repeal', *History*, 64 (1979), pp. 365–6.
39. W. Hamish Fraser, 'The working class', in Maver and Fraser (eds), *Glasgow, Volume II*, p. 315.
40. Irene Maver, 'Glasgow's civic government', in ibid. pp. 452–3.
41. Tony Clarke, 'Early Chartism in Scotland: a "moral force" movement?', in T. M. Devine (ed.), *Conflict and Stability in Scottish Society, 1700–1850* (John Donald: Edinburgh, 1990), pp. 106–21.
42. William West Watson, *Report Upon the Vital, Social and Economic Statistics of Glasgow, for 1863 and 1864* (James Maclehose: Glasgow, 1865), pp. 32–3.
43. *Glasgow Herald*, 10 October 1856.
44. Maver, 'Glasgow's civic government', pp. 458–9.
45. Michael Fry, *Patronage and Principle: A Political History of Modern Scotland* (Aberdeen University Press: Aberdeen, 1987), p. 52.

CHAPTER FIVE

Remaking Society

At the beginning of the nineteenth century Glasgow was a territorially compact and self-contained entity, still set within the bounds of the medieval burgh. However, the sharp economic downswing in the aftermath of the Napoleonic Wars finally put paid to pre-industrial perceptions of the city. The immediate post-war years were characterised by chronic unemployment, social distress and the incidence of fever and disease. From this time there were recurring references to the deteriorating urban heartland. The image of corrosion was compounded by the flight of wealthy Glaswegians to developing suburbs on the periphery of the city. By mid-century a strong sense of residential polarisation had emerged, especially between the predominantly proletarian eastern districts and the middle-class west.

Yet while the demographic pressures could cause severe social strain in some sections of the city, there were conscious efforts towards environmental improvement. Civic and community leaders were determined to counter the reputation of Glasgow as one of Europe's most industrially blighted communities. The evangelical impulse, derived from the Scottish Presbyterian tradition, played an important part in shaping ideas. It aimed to project distinctive moral values on behaviour, especially by instilling such socially desirable qualities as self-control and moderation. This attitude was not necessarily imposed from above, as political radicals often forthrightly repudiated extravagance and indulgence in their quest for self-improvement. As this chapter shows, the growth of alternative cultural outlets added to the eclectic range of activities on offer to Glaswegians, with traditional forms of recreation and entertainment co-existing (albeit uncomfortably) with the new.

The Deteriorating Urban Fabric

Glasgow had become Scotland's main population centre by 1821, when the number of residents (147,043) at last exceeded Edinburgh (138,235). The extensive Barony and Gorbals parishes were included in the census evaluation, thus adding to the traditional territory of the burgh, but this did not have the effect of exaggerating the western city's newly-acquired status. The scale of growth was evident between 1801 and 1861, when the demographic base increased more than five-fold from 77,385 to 395,503 inhabitants. A principal contributory factor to these unprecedented levels of expansion was the number of immigrants and in-migrants, largely from Ireland and other parts of Scotland, who came in search of work and improved prospects.

By 1851, the Irish-born presence in Glasgow constituted over 18 per cent of the population, with obvious ramifications for the social and cultural direction of the city. Many who came over after 1846 were escaping from intolerable living conditions in their homeland. The potato famine revealed the traumatic impact of demographic pressure at a time when the staple food resource had failed. Some contemporary accounts estimated that Glasgow was the recipient of around 1,000 persons a week at the height of the crisis in 1848, although by no means all of those arriving intended to remain. Glasgow long had served as a temporary stepping-off point for seasonal labourers, seeking agricultural employment beyond the city limits. Nor did Irish immigrants inevitably derive from rural origins, as links with urban centres could be strong. For instance, prior to the famine displaced handloom weavers from Derry and Belfast came to Glasgow in the hope of stable employment, their mobility rendered easier by the availability of cheap and regular steamship transport from the 1820s.[1] As for the Scots, the bulk of Glasgow's migrants came from the counties in close proximity to the city, notably Lanarkshire, Renfrewshire and Ayrshire, which had an abundance of small-town communities.

Incomers to Glasgow were sometimes concentrated in particular areas of the city. Thus, large number of Highlanders resided in the western textile community of Anderston. There was also a relatively high proportion in the Broomielaw, on the northern banks of the River Clyde, where the men were employed as transport workers.[2] The Irish were prominent in East End and northern districts, such as Calton and the Garngad (where Thrushgrove was located). However, the relative density of Glasgow's overall population did not allow distinctive ethnic enclaves to develop. There was no equivalent of Manchester's notorious 'Little Ireland', despite the Scottish city having one of the highest proportions of Irish settlers in mainland Britain. Instead, the Irish came to be associated generally with the poorer districts. Being more visible, the connection between poverty and ethnic identity seemed more readily apparent, at least to contemporary observers. As early as 1818, Dr Robert Graham provided a graphic description of conditions in a city-centre lodging house, where 'twenty-three of the lowest class of Irish' were reported as inhabiting two rooms, with only three beds.[3] The incumbents, not surprisingly, had succumbed to typhus fever, and thereafter the periodic epidemics of disease were frequently attributed to the Irish, especially during the famine years. Whatever the reality, the intrusion of contagion could be rationalised as a product of the perceived alien presence in the community. In 1849 John Strang, erstwhile campaigning journalist and now City Chamberlain of Glasgow, explained at the height of the cholera epidemic that stringent measures were necessary to check the 'growing evil' of uncontrolled Irish immigration, 'otherwise Glasgow will become a city of paupers and of the plague'.[4]

The examples of typhus and cholera illustrated the pressures arising from population growth and how this contributed to the city's rising mortality levels. A peak was reached between the fever years of 1845 to 1849, when crude death rates averaged almost forty per 1,000 living inhabitants, one of the highest figures in the United Kingdom.[5] In addition to the recurring epidemics, measles, scarlet fever, smallpox and respiratory diseases (notably pulmonary tuberculosis) had become deeply entrenched in Glasgow, the last a pervasive symbol of the pollution and dampness penetrating the city. The incidence of infant mortality was a telling indicator of the state of community well-being, with the deaths of those under five years of age constituting over 50 per cent of all Glasgow deaths by the 1850s. In his capacity as the city's official statistician, Strang was acutely aware of the city's notorious record. He speculated in 1858 about reasons for the high levels of child mortality, even suggesting that this might be attributable to working mothers, who exposed their offspring 'to greater danger from the mortal influences which ever surround such helpless beings'.[6] Yet the death rates were not quite so surprising given Glasgow's unusually high birth rate and young population profile, with half of its residents under the age of twenty by mid-century. Strang also pointed out that the city's health was seen to improve when mortality statistics were compared for those in the fifteen to sixty age group. What he called 'the *productive* class' was proportionately more likely to survive than counterparts in some major English cities, notably Liverpool and Manchester.

Strang was one of many contemporaries who argued that Glaswegians were dissipating their human assets by inattention to drastically deteriorating living standards, especially in the slum districts. From the time of the first typhus epidemic in 1818 pressure had been exerted for the creation of formal mechanisms to implement change. As part of this process, successive medical experts and social reformers contributed disturbing images relating to conditions in the warren of wynds and closes located in the city's heartland. An oft-quoted account of life in the 'low districts of Glasgow' was given in 1838 by Jelinger Symons, the English social investigator. His description of the area around the Trongate, Bridgegate and Saltmarket was uncompromising:

> I have seen human degradation in some of its worst phases, both in England and abroad, but I can advisedly say, that I did not believe, until I visited the wynds of Glasgow, that so large an amount of filth, crime, misery, and disease existed on one spot in any civilised country. The wynds consist of long lanes, so narrow that a cart could with difficulty pass along them; out of these open the 'closes', which are courts about

fifteen or twenty feet square, round which the houses, mostly of three storeys high, are built; the centre of the court is the dunghill, which probably is the most lucrative part of the estate to the laird in most instances, and which it would consequently be esteemed an invasion of rights of property to remove.[7]

The dunghill's pivotal importance to the internal economy of the slums was a powerful metaphor for the skewed priorities of landlords, who seemed more concerned about the quantity of sellable manure produced by their tenants than the quality of life. Indeed, queasy references to putrefaction began to pervade commentaries about the city's mounting

26. High Street Close, 1860s. Overbuilding has given a warren-like appearance to this High Street close, depicted during the 1860s. This was one Thomas Annan's celebrated series of photographs, commissioned by civic representatives to as serve a record of conditions prior to slum clearance and city improvement. (*T. and R. Annan & Sons Ltd.*)

health and housing problems, which appeared regularly in the press from the 1840s and considerably shocked the predominantly middle-class readership. In the autumn of 1848, George Troup, editor of the *North British Daily Mail*, wrote about a visit to the netherworld of the notorious Old Wynd, and consciously echoed Symons's earlier report by stating that he had 'never seen anywhere a district so pestiferously bad'.[8] The labyrinthine nature of the wynds, the lack of basic amenities such as water, the exclusion of sunlight and ventilation, the malodorous atmosphere, all represented a gross inversion of normality, which evangelicals like Troup equated directly with moral corrosion. Accordingly, child neglect, domestic violence, prostitution, alcohol abuse and other manifestations of anti-social behaviour, classed generically as 'vice', were indelibly associated with the unsavoury environment prevailing in the Old Wynd and similarly 'wretched' communities.

It should be stressed that Glasgow was much more diverse in terms of living standards than the rhetoric of Troup or Symons suggested. Yet the intensity of the inner-city housing problem was compounded by factors which related to local traditions of residential building. Multi-occupancy tenements had emphatically shaped Glasgow's landscape. Some examples could be impressive, such as architect Alexander Kirkland's monumental sandstone terrace in St Vincent Crescent, built in the 1850s to the west of the city. On the other hand, tenements were often far from commodious, and during the nineteenth century the city came to acquire an unenviable reputation for the number of one-roomed dwellings, or 'single-ends'. All this, understandably, created the conditions that fostered congestion. As the older, inner-city attracted increasing numbers of incomers, there was a rush by speculators to provide accommodation. Often this was located in the space behind existing properties, and the phenomenon of Glasgow's 'backlands' emerged. Rows of poor-quality tenements were built in what once had been the gardens of elegant, eighteenth-century residences, the original inhabitants having long departed to more salubrious homes elsewhere. Tenement owners were anxious to maximise their profits by renting out as many individual units as possible, which further encouraged the cramming process in the central districts. The profit motive even applied to the former houses of the mercantile elite, which were divided into multi-occupancy dwellings, serving numerous families and thus helping to meet insatiable demand.

Despite the efforts of speculators, by the 1840s a serious housing shortfall had become apparent in the inner city. The 1841 census revealed a population increase of some 33,000 people in ten years, but only 3,500 additional dwellings.[9] Over a broader time-scale, the average number of occupants per dwelling rose from 4.6 in 1821 to 5.2 in 1841. By mid-century acute overcrowding was recognised as a threat to the general well-being of the city and a blot on the much-vaunted image of progressivism. As one

crusading newspaper bluntly stated in 1845, 'The existence of such houses is
a reproach to Glasgow'.[10] The *Glasgow Examiner* went on to recommend an
extensive programme of slum clearance and rebuilding; a prospect that was
not immediately feasible because of the costs involved, but which nevertheless made a profound impression on a group of wealthy businessmen,
including the future Lord Provosts John Blackie junior and James Watson.
They passionately believed that moral corrosion could be reversed and
more wholesome values restored by using practical, if elaborate, measures
to open out the decrepit districts. However, there were other reasons behind
the impulse towards Glasgow's regeneration. The economic factor was
crucial, as it made sound business sense to clear the inner city for the freer
flow of traffic, especially the rapidly developing railway network, which
operated most efficiently with centrally-located terminals. Over time, the

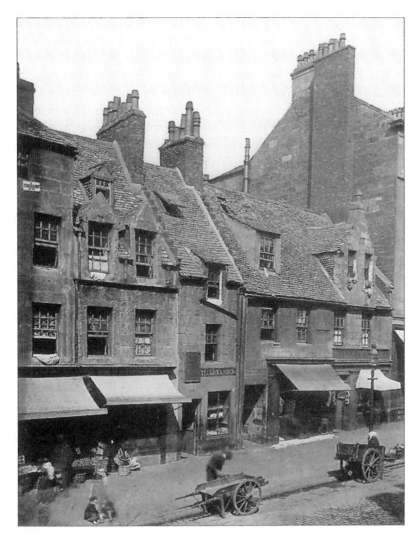

27. Gallowgate in
the 1860s.
Gallowgate,
showing the
co-existence of
dilapidated older
dwellings with
more solid-looking
tenements. This
Annan photograph
is also a fascinating
evocation of East
End street life prior
to city improve-
ment restructuring.
(*T. and R. Annan &
Sons Ltd.*)

idea acquired solid substance, taking formal shape as the municipally-controlled City Improvement Trust, inaugurated in 1866. In the interim, the traumatic impact of cholera did much to reinforce the need for reform.

Cholera and Urban Regeneration

In November 1848, not long after George Troup had published his shocking exposé of conditions in the Old Wynd, cholera made its second, searing appearance in Glasgow. The first epidemic had struck in February 1832, despite elaborate preventative measures having been taken by the authorities. The prospect of a second visitation prompted zealous efforts to scrub and scour the potential plague-spots, but over 3,700 people still died during the winter of 1848–9. Spread by the cholera bacillus, carried in water, the disease flourished in congested and insanitary conditions, and thus found a ready reception in the slum districts of Glasgow. Yet ironically, cholera seemed to be random in the choice of victims. Habits of scrupulous personal cleanliness manifestly did not secure a safeguard against attack, especially in the 1848–9 epidemic, when many better-off Glaswegians died. The bacillus was firmly identified as the carrier only in the late 1850s, which meant that prior to this time there was considerable fear and uncertainty surrounding cholera's unpredictable progress. In 1853 cholera erupted again in Glasgow, and the Revd Dr Robert Buchanan, influential minister of Glasgow's Free Tron Church, made a dramatic statement about his perception of the disease. It was, he claimed, 'the voice of God' to the people:

> When, like the vulture guided by an unerring instinct to its prey, the cholera alights among the undrained marshes and moral cesspools of such a city as this . . . when this mysterious visitant, issuing forth from these dark and foul recesses where his victims abound, soars up to a higher level, and flaps his deadly wing over our most princely terraces and squares, and fills ever and anon some abode of wealth and splendour with lamentation and woe – what does all this mean? Does it not imply that there is a voice in the cholera both to the rich and poor – both to the enlightened and the ignorant – both to the pious and the profligate?[11]

The vivid Gothic imagery used by Buchanan shows how much cholera had come to represent the grim harbinger of social disintegration to many Glaswegians. That the disease served as a divine warning gave emphasis to evangelical calls to further the dual mission of improving the spiritual and material welfare of the community. For Buchanan, a purer environment meant a more godly city, although he consistently stressed that activity confined solely to the sanitary sphere would not bring about a meaningful regeneration of Glasgow. 'Moral government' was the answer, because it aimed to transform the habits of the people, from all classes, and direct them into behaviour which eschewed extremes and excess.

As a protégé of Thomas Chalmers, who had made such a profound impact on Glasgow during his residence as a city minister between 1815 and 1823, Buchanan was saying nothing substantially new. Chalmersian evangelicalism was based on the endeavours of 'righteous men', whose moral leadership would ensure harmonious co-existence between the classes, and thus mute 'malignant antipathies'.[12] Implicit was a fear of the unrest which had characterised Glasgow immediately after 1815. As one historian said about Chalmers, 'In post-war Glasgow he saw radicalism, demoralisation and destitution as a descending series of logical consequences; they all flowed from a deep inner dereliction of personal duty'.[13] The message was as potent as ever in the cholera-stricken years of the late 1840s and early 1850s. Whatever the undercurrent of social control, 'moral government' indicated a way forward, offering an identity for Glasgow that combined the much-needed qualities of efficiency and order in public affairs.

Significantly, Glasgow's municipal public relations machine began to build up momentum in the wake of the 1848–9 cholera crisis. The surge of activity was not wholly tied in with the intrusion of the disease, but was also the product of the boundary extension of 1846. The burgh more than doubled in size from 960 to 2,295 hectares, thus resolving the confusion about what precisely constituted the territory of the city after the creation of the parliamentary constituency in 1832. Districts like Anderston, Calton and the Gorbals, all with sizeable working-class populations, became subject to the jurisdiction of the Town Council; a practical arrangement, that made for more effective administration and law enforcement. Of course, there had been official concern from the end of the eighteenth century about the corroding environment, and after 1800 Glasgow Police Board had made strenuous efforts to maintain the integrity of the urban fabric by providing such essential services as cleansing and policing. Yet its remit was restricted, and it was only after councillors took over the Board's functions in 1846 that the enlarged municipality could more readily co-ordinate substantial initiatives, especially in the sphere of public health.

Energies quickly became concentrated on the quest for an improved water supply. The matter long had been a public preoccupation, and in 1819 it was even suggested by a *Glasgow Herald* correspondent that the civic authority should operate its own water enterprise in order to reduce costs to the consumer.[14] The debate was given added urgency after the second cholera epidemic, amidst calls for meaningful intervention to cleanse the urban heartland and regenerate Glasgow. Direct municipal provision seemed to offer several advantages to the city. The existing private water company had origins in enterprises founded during the 1800s, and its outdated infrastructure consequently was unable to cope with the demands of the rapidly growing population. The old system had become notorious for its erratic output, both in standards of purity and regularity of supply. Moreover, the company was not in a position to raise the necessary capital for improvement, unlike the Town Council, whose extensive community assets made it eminently creditworthy. Public accountability meant that unpredictable market forces could be over-ridden, and a stable service provided. On the other hand, the profit motive was still an influencing factor, given the importance of steam power to the city. With a predominantly business and manufacturing orientation, councillors came from the kind of background most likely to benefit economically from a plentiful water supply.

Notwithstanding the strong element of vested interest, public control of water eloquently exemplified the beneficence of 'moral government' in Glasgow. Indeed, the civic leadership astutely played on the connection once the firm decision was made to municipalise in 1852, amidst the threat of another cholera visitation. While there was concern about the prohibitive cost of such a venture, criticism was temporarily muted following passionate appeals from the Council Chambers for practical preventative measures, rather than a hazy dependence on Providence to protect the city. The choice for the source of the proposed water supply also made a direct appeal to the Glaswegian consciousness. Loch Katrine was located in the Perthshire Highlands, some fifty-five kilometres from Glasgow, and thus well away from the polluted and disease-ridden city. Celebrated for its spectacular mountainous setting and apparent crystalline purity, the loch conveyed a Romantic image of unspoiled nature, which was compounded by its literary associations with Sir Walter Scott's best-selling epic poem *The Lady of the Lake*, first published in 1810.

The Scott connection undoubtedly helped to convey the visionary qualities of the bold feat of gravitational engineering, which ultimately cost the city some £1 million. The new municipal waterworks took time to construct, once the initial surveys and complex parliamentary negotiations had taken place. However, the official opening by Queen Victoria on an appropriately wet autumn day in 1859 was an event of enormous significance for Glasgow. A major step forward had been taken to improve the quality of life. Loch Katrine was tangible evidence that dirt, disease and their blighting impact could be challenged. Thereafter, the success of the water enterprise became inextricably bound up with civic progress in Glasgow. Loch Katrine was unquestionably the prime municipal showpiece for the city, combining the wonders of Victorian technology with the nurturing quality of pure Highland water. It was a reputation that endured into the twentieth century, with Glaswegian schoolchildren proudly informed by one official publication in the 1950s that their water was the cheapest, purest and softest in the United Kingdom.[15]

Back in the 1850s the loch's regenerative spirit gave added impetus to other

28. Queen Victoria at Loch Katrine, 1859.
A historic moment, as Queen Victoria (with Prince Albert) inaugurates the Loch Katrine water supply in
October 1859. The ceremonial handle for opening the sluice-gates is clearly shown. This was one of
Glasgow's most elaborate civic occasions to date, and Thomas Annan, recently established as a photographic
artist, was called upon to record it. (*T. and R. Annan & Sons Ltd.*)

civic endeavours to improve the environment. Several of the initiatives
consolidated work commenced by the pre-1846 Police Boards for Glasgow
and surrounding districts, particularly in relation to tightening up procedures for cleansing and refuse removal. The Dean of Guild Court, which
traditionally approved building plans for the city, was used far more
frequently as a mechanism for demolishing properties constituting a hazard
to health. In 1856 parliament passed the Nuisance Removal Act for Scotland,
which gave greater powers for tackling a range of environmental problems.
The civic authority immediately inaugurated a public health infrastructure
for the city, under the energetic direction of councillor John Ure. With
characteristic thoroughness, Ure (a successful flour merchant and devoted
evangelical) embarked on an extensive tour of Scottish, English and Irish
cities, to see what could be learned from experience elsewhere.[16]
Accompanying him was James Moir, and both men identified the claustrophobic conditions encouraged by Glasgow's speculative building practices
as a particular obstacle to progress. 'Breathing space', the quest for the
vital element of air as well as water, began to feature prominently in the
municipal agenda.

Suburbanisation and the Middle Classes

While the uncontrolled nature of building in Glasgow contributed substantially to the rapid deterioration of the inner city during the first half of the century, there was a qualitatively different dimension to speculative developments taking place in the outlying districts. As Chapter 2 explained, the first boom in middle-class property construction dated from the 1780s, when a 'New Town' began to take shape in the streets surrounding George Square. 'The buildings here are very elegant', reported James Denholm in 1804, 'which from the beauty of the design and taste displayed in the execution, surpass by far any other in this city or in Scotland'.[17] Whatever the veracity of such a claim, the land to the west of the Square attracted wealthy Glaswegians, concerned to distance themselves from the older and increasingly unsavoury district around Glasgow Cross. Two properties, the Cunninghame Mansion and Queen Street Park (the latter subsequently occupied by James Ewing), were notable examples of Georgian town-houses, set in their own spacious grounds. There were benefits for landed proprietors in encouraging such developments because of the lucrative returns from feuing, the uniquely Scottish system of land law.

29. The Cunninghame Mansion, 1820s.
Virginia merchant William Cunninghame's mansion was erected in 1778, and this engraving by Joseph Swan shows the original structure early in the 1820s. Towards the end of the decade the residence was transformed into the Royal Exchange, complete with imposing Corinthian columns. The building on the right of the illustration is the Theatre Royal in Queen Street. (*By courtesy of the Mitchell Library, Glasgow City Libraries and Archives.*)

Speculative building could substantially increase revenue, especially if the territory was not otherwise profitably utilised. The financial factor did not simply relate to private landlords. The Town Council was feudal superior over the lands of the medieval burgh, and civic officials diligently investigated assorted plans to increase income from this patrimony. One notable municipal money-making venture was the terrace of Monteith Row, named after Lord Provost Henry Monteith and commenced in 1818 immediately adjacent to Glasgow Green.

Just beyond the traditional burgh boundaries, further prestigious developments had emerged earlier in the century. The brothers David and James Laurie devised ambitious plans for the lands immediately to the south of the River Clyde, including the importation of Italian craftsmen to embellish the dwellings of the new suburb of Laurieston. The terrace of Carlton Place dated from 1802, and was stylish testimony to their optimism. Unfortunately, the relentless approach of industry towards the river deflated their initial mood of buoyancy, and the area soon slid down-market. On the other hand, more fruitful territory for residential building remained to the west of the burgh, in the 194-hectare estate of Blythswood. Plans had been first promoted in the 1790s, when Archibald Campbell, the feudal superior, realised that the time was right to make something of his inheritance. The resulting development adhered to a gridded street formation, based on Edinburgh's New Town, which set high standards for urban emulation throughout the United Kingdom. Regrettably, Blythswood did not have the impressive rugged landscape of central Edinburgh and so the effect of the Glasgow scheme was more consistently regular, or as one architectural historian has diplomatically put it, 'unexceptional but practical'.[18] By 1830 Blythswood's grid network had been largely built upon, and that year the district was formally absorbed into the city. Although the prospect of increased taxation held little appeal for the inhabitants, they were well aware that only the Glasgow authorities could provide adequate police protection for their expensive new properties.

Ironically, it was during the 1830s that Blythswood lost its reputation as Glasgow's most desirable residential district. As the demands of business for office accommodation began to encroach westwards, the middle classes fled even further to the fringes of the city; a movement that was made much easier by improved transport communications. The major thoroughfare of the Yoker Turnpike (subsequently Argyle Street and the road to Partick) helped to open up a cluster of pastoral estates beyond Blythswood, beginning with the development of South Woodside in 1830. Prospective purchasers were wooed with assurances that the lands were 'effectively secured against any kind of nuisance', showing the continuing determination of wealthy Glaswegians to detach themselves from the tainted urban heartland.[19] A second thoroughfare of vital importance to the city's spatial development was Great Western Road, which opened in 1841. Although at first slow to

30. Woodside from Blythswood Square, 1840s.
A bucolic vista of the developing middle-class residential area of Woodside, from Blythswood Square, taken in 1841. J. N. Nichol was the artist. The Grecian edifice to the right was originally St Jude's Episcopal Church, a striking building which by the end of the twentieth century had come to serve a less spiritual purpose as a restaurant. (*By courtesy of the Mitchell Library, Glasgow City Libraries and Archives.*)

make an impact in terms of residential building, this broad, straight, two-kilometre route was ultimately the key to the success of Kelvinside, an exclusive community of imposing villas and terraces. Its proprietors were lawyers Matthew Montgomerie and John Park Fleming, whose strict estate management ensured consistently high standards, both structurally and aesthetically. One particularly innovative example of Kelvinside design was the 1855 Italian-style Grosvenor Terrace, the product of architect J. T. Rochead and considered a *tour de force* of intricate yet monumental construction.[20]

The development of Glasgow's West End continued throughout the nineteenth century, although other middle-class suburbs emerged as transport facilities improved, especially to the south of the city. For instance, Pollokshields constituted part of the extensive estate belonging to Sir John Maxwell, whose ambitious feuing plans were implemented from the 1850s. The early South Side suburbs were notable for Alexander Thomson's contribution to villa design. He was a visionary architect, whose style reflected Greek revivalism, but whose inspiration derived from the evangelical ideal of the godly city, or Zion. Thomson claimed that religion

31. Caledonia Road church, mid-nineteenth century. Architect Alexander 'Greek' Thomson's first church, round about the time it was built in 1857 in the Gorbals. It served his own faith of United Presbyterianism, and reflects his distinctive Classical influences. The church was seriously damaged by fire in the 1960s and languished unused for decades until plans were implemented in the 1990s to restore it. (*By courtesy of the Mitchell Library, Glasgow City Libraries and Archives.*)

represented 'the soul of art from the beginning', and went on to substantiate his beliefs in such elaborate buildings as Caledonia Road Church and St Vincent Street Church, both constructed in the 1850s and serving his own faith of United Presbyterianism.[21] However, the strong spiritual dimension to Thomson's work did not deter him from making the most financially from Glasgow's mid-Victorian property boom, and like many civic activists he dexterously blended moral and material considerations in his commitment to urban improvement.

Another architect who reflected this dual motivation was Charles Wilson. Along with a group of city builders and financiers he suggested in 1850 that a public park should be constructed in the West End.[22] It was initially intended that the venture would be run on a commercial basis, but the

failure of the promoters to raise the necessary capital prompted civic
leaders to intervene. In 1852 they paid £77,945 on behalf of the Town
Council for the estates of Kelvingrove and Woodlands, extending over
twenty-seven hectares. Joseph Paxton, Britain's leading landscape designer,
was commissioned to lay out the grounds. The new West End Park (subsequently renamed Kelvingrove Park) proved to be an expensive item for the
municipal coffers, and the purchase prompted much criticism, especially
from the radical press. Correspondents repeatedly stressed the park's
remoteness from the main centre of population, eliciting the response from
one councillor that a brisk walk to the West End was 'part of the advantages
arising to all classes from exercise in the open air'.[23] While the health-giving
virtues of the new park continued to be lauded in civic circles, the original
purpose behind the project – to stimulate speculative building – resulted in
Wilson's inspired design for the exclusive Park district, whose elevated
prospect overlooked Kelvingrove. Nor did the initial controversy prevent
the Town Council from purchasing farmland to the south of the city in 1857

32. Kelvingrove Park, 1860s.
Kelvingrove, Glasgow's first custom-designed municipal park, was acquired in 1852. This view shows the park
in the 1860s. An integral part of the development was the construction of prestigious middle-class residences,
designed by architect Charles Wilson. For all its lustrous landscape, Kelvingrove proved controversial, given
civic commitment to embellish the well-heeled West End, but over time other parks were acquired throughout
the city. (*By courtesy of the Mitchell Library, Glasgow City Libraries and Archives.*)

for the proposed Queen's Park. Property development again featured as a prime rationale, and middle-class districts such as Crosshill and Langside grew up in close proximity.

Up to the 1860s, the proliferation of new middle-class suburbs was evidence of the city's fragmentation into separate residential spheres, thus reversing the traditional class cohesion of Scottish burgh centres. Ironically, the boundary extension of 1846 had been intended to make Glasgow more self-contained, but the addition of outlying communities only served to heighten the contrasts between the predominantly proletarian eastern districts and the middle-class west. The gulf was cultural as well as geographic. East End residents were often disdainful of what they saw as the *nouveaux riches* aspirations of West Enders, and political tensions could surface over issues like the allocation of amenity resources. The two public spaces, Glasgow Green and Kelvingrove Park, came to represent radically different perceptions of the way the city was developing. The Green was seen as declining in status because of its proximity to industry and the congeries of inner-city slums. Kelvingrove, on the other hand, was depicted as a repository of purer air, located well away from corrupting influences. The latter became yet another showpiece for the extended city, the park's meticulously landscaped setting serving as a positive affirmation of attempts to improve the environment and give citizens an attractive place for recreation.

Such display was far from convincing for the veteran campaigner, James Moir, who in a shrewd move to publicise the claims of the eastern districts led a public demonstration across the city in 1860, and made an ostentatious show of walking on the grass of Kelvingrove, in defiance of the by-laws. As a direct challenge to apparent middle-class pretensions, the incident revealed much about the strength of East End feeling. Indeed, residential polarisation during the mid-nineteenth century was often used as a polemical device, in order to highlight the differences between the old city and the new. However, Glasgow was not so sharply divided as the rhetoric of the radicals liked to imply. Western districts like Anderston retained substantial working-class communities, and the suburb of Dennistoun was first promoted in the 1850s as an attempt to entice the middle classes eastwards. There were also sizeable communities of a more mixed residential profile, just beyond the city limits. The Clydeside villages of Govan and Partick began to alter their rural character from the 1840s, as the growth of the fledgling shipbuilding industry attracted an influx of workers, anxious to settle near their place of employment. Round about the same time, in the northern district of Maryhill, substantial numbers of incomers appeared seeking work in connection with the railways and latterly the construction of the Loch Katrine pipelines.

The sharp population increase worried the longer-established, usually better-off inhabitants of these outlying districts, both in relation to the

33. Govan and the Clyde, 1820s.
The village of Govan, from a Joseph Swan engraving. The sailing boats are ferrying passengers across the River Clyde. Despite the idyllic landscape, the silk-mill in the distance was evidence of encroaching industry. Built in 1824, the mill employed 250 at the height of its operations. (*By courtesy of the Mitchell Library, Glasgow City Libraries and Archives.*)

arrangements for effective law enforcement and the provision of environmental services. Accordingly, a mechanism to ease the problems of populous places outside the scope of traditional burgh government was contained in the General Police (Scotland) Act of 1850. This allowed for the creation of elected local authorities, known as Police Burghs. At first they related to communities of 1,200 inhabitants or more, but amending legislation in 1862 substantially lowered the threshold to 700. Petitioners did not require to go through complex parliamentary procedures to achieve Police Burgh status, and thus saved considerable time, effort and expense. In 1852 Partick was the first area to take advantage of the new Act, with Maryhill and Govan following suit in 1856 and 1864. Thereafter, an array of predominantly middle-class districts to the south and west of Glasgow opted for similar self-government. Hillhead (1869) was followed by Crosshill and Kinning Park (both 1871), Pollokshields West (1876), Govanhill (1877) and Pollokshields East (1880). Scotland's Police Burghs were generally considered to be an important concession to local autonomy, encouraging the active participation of communities in public affairs. However, Glasgow's

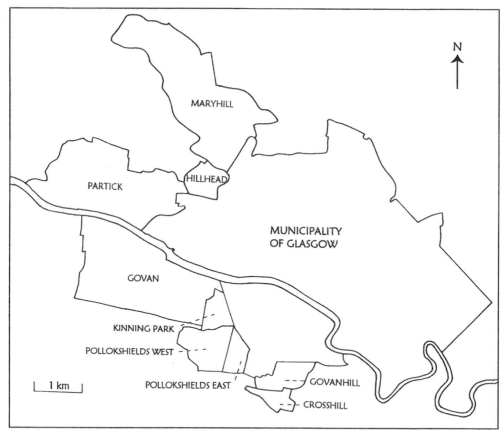

34. Glasgow Police Burghs by 1880.
A map showing the Police Burghs created to the south and west of Glasgow between the 1850s and 1880s.
All were eventually annexed to the city by 1912. (*The author.*)

civic leaders remained much more cynical. For them, the new administrative entities constituted a serious obstacle to the city's outward expansion, which by the 1850s was being articulated as an integral part of the municipally-inspired regeneration process.

Entertainment and Popular Culture

The anxiety expressed by representatives from the Town Council, churches and assorted philanthropic agencies over the deteriorating urban fabric helped to highlight the gloomier aspects of city life. Glasgow's blighted image, as presented by investigators like Symons and subsequently elaborated by journalists, left little room for projecting the rich variety of cultural experience in the city. Nevertheless, rising press readership from the 1820s was an important indicator of the expanding range of social activities that Glaswegians could enjoy, with newspapers a crucial vehicle for publicity, especially through advertising. While access to the press remained largely the preserve of the middle classes, given the prohibitive price of newspapers due to the continuation of government taxation until 1855, the buoyant circulation of unstamped periodicals revealed that a market for news and information existed beyond elite circles. Glasgow's rapidly increasing population generated demand for entertainment and leisure outlets. This phenomenon was identified as early as 1805 by the civic authority, alarmed about the moral impact of mushrooming 'tippling houses, and retail spirit shops' within the burgh.[24] However, it would be misleading to interpret such concern as a new phenomenon, a product of the social dislocation associated with urbanisation from the 1800s. Throughout the eighteenth century, the more zealous Presbyterian clergy had been outspoken guardians of public morality, their mission to prevent Glaswegians from sinking too deeply into the mire of self-indulgence.[25]

The struggle to establish a Glasgow theatre was indicative of the tensions that long had been simmering over appropriate forms of recreation. There was initially bitter religious opposition to the prospect of such an enterprise, and it was not until 1782 that a playhouse eventually opened in the city. This was Glasgow's first Theatre Royal, operating under the sanction of the Lord Chamberlain, who up to 1843 had legal powers to limit venues for the performance of drama. However, from the 1800s other theatres did emerge, notably the spacious and sumptiously-decorated Queen Street playhouse, built in 1804 and quickly taking over the coveted Theatre Royal title. The huge construction cost of £18,500 was indicative of changing times, especially the social aspirations of wealthy Glaswegians. In an effort to emulate metropolitan grandeur, the Queen Street theatre became a fashionable resort, and not just for drama. An advertisement for a fancy-dress ball in 1815 gave an idea of what patrons expected, with the interior fitted-up to resemble London's famous pleasure gardens at Vauxhall and the costumes imported from a specialist English masquerade warehouse.[26] As for performance, much inspiration derived from Edinburgh and the prolific output of that city's flourishing Theatre Royal. The dramatised fiction of Sir Walter Scott was crucially important for attracting audiences, with *Rob Roy* (partially set in Glasgow) achieving legendary status as the mainstay of the Scottish theatre throughout the nineteenth century and beyond.

However, performance was by no means confined to the theatre. In the 1860s journalist Robert Reid recalled the eclectic range of entertainments he saw as a child during the late eighteenth century, usually in hired halls or taverns. He recalled the popularity of animal and freak shows, and the thrill for youngsters of the perennial 'Punch's Opera'.[27] This last was staged in a penny booth, with the puppets performing to the music of a barrel organ. Such entertainment was not classed as drama, and therefore did not come under the strictures of the Lord Chamberlain. The unusual and bizarre featured frequently in popular preferences, as did displays of dexterity and daring. The young Reid was impressed with the talent of Herman Boaz, the 'celebrated sleight-of-hand performer', who was a recurring visitor to Glasgow. Boaz was resident over the 1809–10 festive season, where his 'Magical Illusions' and 'amazing deceptions with Gold Boxes, Machineries, &c', attracted considerable interest, notwithstanding the steep admission price of two shillings.[28] The appeal of showmanship reflected the growing commercialisation of popular entertainment, which was especially apparent in the rise of the circus from the 1800s. The Olympic Circus, which visited Glasgow in 1815, was one successful English company which saw potential in the lucrative Scottish market. Featuring a fast-moving show of horses and acrobats, the company made the most of its stay in the city by teaching those who could afford it the 'Polite Art of Riding' at seven shillings a lesson.

From the 1820s entertainment became cheaper and more accessible to Glaswegians. In the theatrical domain, competition for audiences intensified. Indeed, the well-publicised and highly personal conflict between two consummate showmen, John Henry Alexander ('Alexander the Great') and John Henry Anderson ('The Wizard of the North'), did much to arouse public curiosity and ensure that their respective theatres were well-patronised.[29] The introduction of 'free trade' in drama after the removal of performing restrictions in 1843 gave further momentum to theatre construction. Anderson's City Theatre could accommodate up to 5,000 people. Designed deliberately as the biggest playhouse in Scotland, this 'Temple of Magic' opened in time for the 1845 Fair holiday. The first performance featured acrobatic dancers, the Ethiopian Minstrels and a troupe of musical bell-ringers, plus the star attraction of Anderson, with his mesmerising conjuring act.[30] For five months the new theatre generated brisk business until it was sensationally destroyed by fire. The Aberdeenshire-born Wizard subsequently left Glasgow to travel the world as an illusionist and inspire a future generation of stage magicians (notably Harry Houdini) with his flamboyant style.

Originally Anderson had established his reputation in the forum of Glasgow Fair. As Chapter 1 explained, the burgh had been granted the privilege of holding an annual trade fair during the twelfth century. However, by the 1820s the event had become transformed into a carnival extravaganza, held in mid-July when most of the working population was on holiday. Around this time, weaver-poet John Breckenridge wrote a lively vernacular account of 'funning and sporting' at the Fair, where eating, drinking and impromptu dancing featured as much as the professional entertainers.[31] Show-folk were permitted to erect temporary booths in the Saltmarket, next to Glasgow Green, and popular performers like Anderson did extremely well financially from the arrangement. In 1844 the *Glasgow Herald* provided a detailed description of the summer's offerings, which

35. City Theatre playbill, 1845. A rare playbill from the City Theatre, which opened in July 1845 and was destroyed by fire only five months later. The proprietor was the flamboyant 'Wizard of the North', John Henry Anderson, who spared no expense in setting up his mammoth, ill-starred enterprise. The city's coat-of-arms appears as part of the patriotic tableau at the top of the playbill. (*By courtesy of the Mitchell Library, Glasgow City Libraries and Archives.*)

included Cooke's Circus, two wild- beast shows (Wombwell's and Hilton's), and a plethora of penny theatricals. The correspondent went on to describe the kind of drama most favoured by the predominantly working-class audience:

> Pieces which have a touch of the horrible in them generally do best for the Fair, and accordingly mimic scenes of blood, and treachery, and rapine are served up pretty extensively. The performers, however, always treat the public to a dance outside, and a procession, with banners, to the tune of *God Save the Queen*, before enacting the diabolical work within . . .[32]

Town councillors initially encouraged the commercialisation of the Fair, largely on the initiative of James Cleland, one of the formidable offi-cials who kept a tight rein on civic administration during the nineteenth century. Inspired by the example of London's Bartholomew Fair, Cleland arranged in 1815 that show-folk should be charged for each steading of ground they used on municipal property. As well as providing a source of civic income, control could be exerted as to who was permitted to perform. Yet despite Cleland's efforts to instil some order into the proceedings, the temporary release of social inhibitions associated with Fair-time jarred increasingly with the mood of temperance and restraint in the city. Alternative outlets for the energies of the population were encouraged by those concerned about moral welfare. The availability of cheap holiday excursions, due to the expanding railway and steamship network, was espe-cially welcomed as more wholesome recreation. In marked contrast, the freaks and performing animals that had appealed to previous generations were now considered gross and unnatural, a disturbing reflection of the inner-city's tainted environment. The 1844 *Glasgow Herald* correspondent was firm in his conviction that the Fair's status was swiftly declining, and that for all the 'noise, glitter, and outward show', the popularity of pleasure trips would 'altogether supersede the interest attaching to the penny drama, or the fat woman and fat hogs on the Green'.

Combatting the Fair's apparently corrosive influence was only one of several strands to the campaign for moral regeneration in Glasgow, which had been steadily gathering momentum after 1815. Efforts covered a broad range of activities, from encouraging educational and literary pursuits to the crusade for temperance. Evangelicals were to the forefront of promoting access to education. Free Churchman David Stow became famous well beyond the bounds of Glasgow for his programme of 'moral training'.[33] Given that no co-ordinated schooling system existed in Scotland until 1872, Stow faced an uphill struggle. Moreover, literacy standards had been identified as falling drastically in Scotland's cities, with inadequate school accommodation for the younger population. To counter the decline, Stow

36. Glasgow Green, 1840s.
A view of Glasgow Green, depicting aspects of work and leisure in the city. To the fore, women from the public washing house have laid out their laundry to dry. Glasgow industry is evident from the smoking chimneys and ships' masts on the horizon. However, the promenaders seem to be heading straight for the Fair-time carnival. (*By courtesy of the Mitchell Library, Glasgow City Libraries and Archives.*)

established influential model institutions during the 1820s, under the auspices of the Glasgow Infant School Society. His schools were notable for encouraging play as a constructive outlet for youthful energies and prohibiting corporal punishment. The focus on cleanliness and healthy outdoor activity indicated the growing awareness of the detrimental impact of the urban environment, especially on children, and the fear that the population was deteriorating physically as well as spiritually. 'Moral training' was thus another aspect of the beneficent power of 'moral government', reflecting the evangelical quest to instil godliness into the community. Significantly, Stow initially developed his ideas through involvement with the Sunday School movement, which had expanded briskly in the aftermath of the Napoleonic Wars to become Glasgow's largest religious voluntary organisation by mid-century.

The missionary rhetoric was taken up by passionate propagandists like Robert Buchanan, who in yet another raw exposé of life in the wynds linked 'deplorable education destitution' with the high incidence of pauperism and crime in the city.[34] He argued that better schooling would be cost-effective to the community by creating responsible and self-reliant citizens. Buchanan cited the example of his own Tron parish in the inner city, where successful day schools had been set up during the 1840s under Free Church auspices. Significantly, one of the schools was allowed to stay open in the evening so that adults could enjoy 'the rational entertainment of reading periodicals and the news of the day in a comfortable apartment'.[35] Yet despite such initiatives, the sheer scale of educational deficiency in Glasgow could not be remedied by individual enthusiasts like Buchanan. It was claimed by an official government investigation during the 1860s (the Argyll Commission) that only a third of children between the ages of three to fifteen years attended school in the city.[36] For those who did receive education, the number of school buildings was insufficient and standards varied enormously. Church-run schools, Protestant and Catholic, were generally praised for the quality of their teaching. Conversely, the Commissioners roundly condemned privately-run schools in working-class districts, their defining characteristics predominantly 'noxious smells' and gross overcrowding. These were the conditions that helped to secure the state system of elementary education for Scotland in 1872, with Glasgow under the co-ordinating control of an elected School Board.

During the early nineteenth century the Glasgow Sabbath School Union had said much about the missing moral dimension in the lives of city children. It expressed particular unease about the exposure of young people to alcohol, claiming that parents often set a bad example and that drink was too readily available under lax licensing laws. With spirit consumption reaching unprecedented levels by the 1830s, public drunkenness was perceived by reformers as the most visible manifestation of personal indiscipline and a potent symbol of the city's deterioration. A municipal investigation of 1839 into 'Intemperance and Sabbath Desecration' was partly triggered by mounting concern about delinquent behaviour by the young during the traditional New Year festivities, an occasion that was similar to the Fair in providing for the release of pent-up energies through drinking. From the beginning there was a sharp evangelical edge to Glasgow's temperance movement, launched in 1829 by lawyer John Dunlop and publisher William Collins senior. However, many political radicals were also outspoken advocates of total abstinence, in an effort to encourage self-improving impulses among the working population. From the 1830s, radical temperance campaigner Edward Morris entertained audiences with colourful rhetoric about the evils of alcohol, which he suggested was part of an insidious upper-class plot to 'gull the people'.[37] Similarly, there was a solid corps of teetotal Chartists in Glasgow, who formed their own temperance society during 1841.

However, temperance priorities were by no means restricted to the identification of drink and its negative influence. Alcohol-free forms of recreation featured prominently in the movement's agenda, to demonstrate its healthy and motivational outlook. During the early 1840s, the Glasgow-based Western Scottish Temperance Union ardently promoted the establishment of coffee-houses, 'where a cheap and useful beverage might be obtained, instead of the pernicious stuff retailed in dram-shops'.[38] Thereafter, the city's coffee-houses were overwhelmingly connected with the temperance cause. Members of the Cranston family (erstwhile Chartists) made considerable success of such outlets. Ironically, tea was an expensive commodity during the first half of the nineteenth century, but the removal of heavy government duties helped to promote its popularity. The Cranstons opened the first of their Glasgow tea-rooms in 1875, and three years later Kate Cranston set up her own establishment. She proved to be a formidable businesswoman who set exacting standards. Her tea-rooms eventually became famous well beyond Glasgow because of their intricate and innovative interior design, with Cranston an enthusiastic champion of such home-grown artistic talent as George Walton and Charles Rennie Mackintosh.[39]

Glasgow's coffee-houses and tea-rooms were one significant offshoot

37. Cranston's tearooms, 1890s.
Temperance culture reached a high level of sophistication in nineteenth-century Glasgow, tangibly illustrated in Kate Cranston's elegant tearooms. This interior is part of her Buchanan Street enterprise, opened in 1896 and reflecting the arts and crafts influences of designer George Walton. (*T. and R. Annan & Sons Ltd.*)

from temperance culture, albeit combined with shrewd awareness of the commercial potential. Similarly, musical performance became another flourishing area of activity. From the 1840s, Joseph Mainzer's pioneering system of 'singing for the million' was enthusiastically encouraged in the forum of temperance soirées throughout Scotland, in the belief that choral music was elevating and 'soul-stirring'. The rise of evangelicalism lay behind much of the musical passion, with vocal harmony serving as a powerful metaphor for social harmony. However, like the theatre there was insatiable demand for larger-scale performance, which encouraged the erection of substantial venues like Glasgow's City Hall in 1841 and the lavishly-decorated Queen's Rooms in 1857. The City Hall was the venue for popular concerts inaugurated by the Abstainers' Union during the 1850s as a conscious alternative to 'the squalid public-house and the low-down music-hall'.[40] Music was also a prime attraction of the Band of Hope, the juvenile wing of the temperance movement, which built up a strong follow-ing in the city. The success of *The Crystal Fount*, a children's song-book published in 1860, reflected the power of music in alerting youngsters to the perils of alcohol and the redemptive power of abstinence. Probably the best-known of the songs was 'The Drunkard's Raggit Wean', a sentimental evocation of child neglect in Glasgow, which for decades afterwards retained enormous appeal for its tear-jerking qualities.

Increasingly within the temperance movement, total abstinence was promoted as an antidote to urban problems, with crime, poverty and disease attributed emphatically to the corrupting influence of alcohol. At times there was a millenarian dimension to such conviction, with the quest for sobriety representing reassurance against insecurity and uncertainty. In Glasgow this was powerfully demonstrated in August 1842, when Father Theobold Mathew came over from Ireland to promote the temperance crusade. Thousands participated in the proceedings, and the heady revivalist atmosphere was reinforced by the tendency of many prospective teetotalers to indulge in one last bout of drinking ('the farewell to whisky') before pledging themselves to abandon alcohol for ever. To add further emotional intensity, Father Mathew distributed temperance medals which were popularly regarded as having extraordinary powers, especially to heal the sick. While the *Glasgow Herald* disdainfully dismissed this practice as evidence of Roman Catholic superstition, it was supportive of the huge following for temperance among the city's Irish community.[41] In 1844 efforts to alter the 'bacchanalian' image of St Patrick's Day in Glasgow were especially welcomed, with 2,000 attending a special temperance soirée in the City Hall.[42] The aim was to show that the Irish had as much moral resilience as anyone, although the gathering was by no means a solemn occasion. Providing the entertainment gratuitously was David Prince Miller and his company from the newly-established Royal Adelphi Theatre; an enterprise that had evolved, ironically, from the penny drama at Fair-time.

Such efforts to reorientate popular culture in Glasgow demonstrated the concern of a wide range of social groups to harness the momentum of change in the rapidly growing city. Reflecting such priorities, municipal government was becoming increasingly involved in efforts to improve the deteriorating urban fabric. This was, of course, nothing new in a city where civic leaders had long promoted their abilities; on the other hand, the boundary extension of 1846 allowed greater scope for their activities. By this time a more modern identity had been established for Glasgow. In addition to the traditional territory of the old burgh, the city now incorporated developing suburbs, especially to the west of the city, and industrial areas, predominantly to the south and east. Yet as the nineteenth century progressed Glasgow came to represent far more than the designated area of administrative jurisdiction. The next chapter shows how success came to focus on the development of the River Clyde, both within the city and beyond, and the implications this had for the urban economy.

Notes

1. Brenda Collins, 'The origins of Irish immigration to Scotland in the nineteenth and twentieth centuries' in T. M. Devine (ed.), *Irish Immigrants and Scottish Society in the Nineteenth and Twentieth Centuries* (John Donald: Edinburgh, 1990), pp. 5–8.
2. Charles W. J. Withers, *Urban Highlanders: Highland-Lowland Migration and Urban Gaelic Culture, 1700–1900* (Tuckwell Press: East Linton, 1998), pp. 144–5.
3. Robert Graham, *Practical Observations on Continued Fever* (John Smith: Glasgow, 1818), p. 58.
4. Quoted in James E. Handley, *The Irish in Scotland* (John S. Burns: Glasgow, 1964), p. 187.
5. Charles Withers, 'The demographic history of the city, 1831–1911', in W. Hamish Fraser and Irene Maver (eds), *Glasgow, Volume II: 1830 to 1912* (Manchester University Press: Manchester, 1996), p. 147.
6. John Strang, *Report on the Vital and Economic Statistics of Glasgow for 1857* (James Macnab: Glasgow, 1858), pp. 8–9.
7. British Parliamentary Papers, *Reports of the Assistant Handloom Weavers' Commissioners*, 1839, XLII, p. 51.
8. Quoted in George Elmslie Troup, *Life of George Troup, Journalist* (Macniven and Wallace: Edinburgh, 1881), p. 69.
9. W. Hamish Fraser and Irene Maver, 'The social problems of the city' in Fraser and Maver (eds), *Glasgow, Volume II*, p. 364.
10. *Glasgow Examiner*, 10 May 1845.
11. Robert Buchanan, *The Waste Places of Our Great Cities; or, The Voice of God in the Cholera* (Blackie: Glasgow, 1853), p. 28.
12. Quoted in John F. McCaffrey, 'Thomas Chalmers and social change', *Scottish Historical Review* 60 (1981), p. 47.
13. Laurance James Saunders, *Scottish Democracy, 1815–1840* (Oliver and Boyd: Edinburgh, 1950), p. 210.
14. *Glasgow Herald*, 1 January 1819.
15. W. G. Beaton, *Glasgow Our City* (Glasgow Corporation: Glasgow, 1957), p. 154.

16. A. K. Chalmers (ed.), *Public Health Administration in Glasgow* (James Maclehose: Glasgow, 1905), pp. 18–20.

17. James Denholm, *The History of the City of Glasgow and Suburbs* (A. McGoun: Glasgow, 1804), p. 136.

18. Frank Arneil Walker, 'The Glasgow grid', in Thomas A. Markus (ed.), *Order in Space and Society* (Mainstream: Edinburgh, 1982), p. 184.

19. *Glasgow Herald*, 14 May 1830.

20. Andor Gomme and David Walker, *Architecture of Glasgow* (Lund Humphries: London, 1987), pp. 91–2.

21. Quoted in Miles Glendinning, Ranald Macinnes and Aonghus Mackenzie, *A History of Scottish Architecture: From the Renaissance to the Present Day* (Edinburgh University Press: Edinburgh, 1996), p. 252.

22. Irene Maver, 'Glasgow's public parks and the community: a case study in Scottish civic interventionism', *Urban History* 25 (1998), pp. 328–9.

23. *Glasgow Herald*, 14 March 1851.

24. Glasgow City Archives A2.1.2, *Glasgow Town Council: Reports, Memorials, &c, 1794–1813*, p. 298.

25. Richard B. Sher, 'Commerce, religion and the enlightenment in eighteenth-century Glasgow', in T. M. Devine and Gordon Jackson (eds), *Glasgow, Volume I: Beginnings to 1830* (Manchester University Press: Manchester, 1995), pp. 317–18.

26. *Glasgow Herald*, 1 May 1815.

27. Robert Reid ('Senex'), *Old Glasgow and Its Environs* (David Robertson: Glasgow, 1864), pp. 273–4.

28. *Glasgow Herald*, 8 January 1810.

29. Elspeth King, 'Popular culture in Glasgow', in R. A. Cage (ed.), *The Working Class in Glasgow, 1750–1914* (Croom Helm: Beckenham, 1987), p. 155.

30. Constance Pole Bayer, *The Great Wizard of the North: John Henry Anderson* (Ray Goulet: Watertown, 1990), p. 38.

31. John Breckenridge, 'The Humours o' Gleska Fair', in George Eyre-Todd (ed.), *The Glasgow Poets* (Alexander Gardner: Paisley, 1906), pp. 204–8.

32. *Glasgow Herald*, 12 July 1844.

33. W. Hamish Fraser and Irene Maver, 'Tackling the problems', in Fraser and Maver (eds), *Glasgow, Volume II*, pp. 397–400.

34. Robert Buchanan, *The Schoolmaster in the Wynds; or, How to Educate the Masses* (Blackie: Glasgow, 1850), p. 15.

35. Ibid. p. 30.

36. BPP, *Second Report by Her Majesty's Commissioners Appointed to Inquire into the Schools of Scotland*, 1867, XXV, pp. xlv–lxii.

37. Edward Morris, *The History of Temperance and Teetotal Societies in Glasgow from their Origin to the Present Time* (City of Glasgow United Total Abstinence Association: Glasgow, 1857), p. 56.

38. *Glasgow Herald*, 26 February 1844.

39. Perilla Kinchin, *Tea and Taste: the Glasgow Tea Rooms, 1875–1975* (White Cockade: Wendlebury, 1991), pp. 80–124.

40. Walter Freer, *My Life and Memoirs* (Civic Press: Glasgow, 1929), p. 34.

41. *Glasgow Herald*, 19 August 1842.

42. Ibid. 22 March 1844.

Second City of the Empire, 1860–1918

CHAPTER SIX

The Mature Industrial Economy

Between 1860 and 1918 Glasgow was distinguished as the shipbuilding capital of the world. The city's fortunes were bound up inextricably with the Clyde. Its shipbuilding output, although only a part of Glasgow's extensive industrial profile, created an enduring identity that blended masculine skill, cosmopolitanism and entrepreneurial flair. This chapter focuses on the success and status of shipbuilding, and examines why it came to symbolise so much about Glasgow achievement by the early twentieth century. That the image often ran counter to the reality of an industry prone to cyclical fluctuations and job insecurity will also be considered. Nor was shipbuilding proportionately a large employer of Glasgow labour, although a number of substantial city industries were intimately connected, notably steel from the 1870s. The river represented continuity as well as change, with ongoing commitment to open out the rapidly-expanding port of Glasgow. Technical developments in shipping helped to consolidate long-standing commercial impulses, and substantial fortunes were made in the flourishing import and export business. This extended consumer choices, and higher living standards from the 1860s stimulated demand for more exotic and specialised produce. In turn, the changing quality of life raised workers' expectations, reflected in the growth of trade unionism in the city. The Clyde embodied Glasgow's outward-looking aspirations up to 1914, and the river's industrial base became a crucial component of the national war effort after this time.

Shipbuilding Capital of the World

In the course of presenting his *Vital Statistics* of Glasgow for the years 1863 and 1864, City Chamberlain William West Watson enthused:

> In no department of industry is the lively enterprise of Glasgow more strikingly exemplified than in the progress of the Shipbuilding trade. The material now almost exclusively used is iron; and when it is borne in mind that by far the greater proportion of this iron is dug, smelted, rolled, and finished within a few miles around the City, it is not difficult to recognise a reason for the remarkable success of the Glasgow Shipbuilders.[1]

Iron steamers constituted by far the largest component of shipbuilding output at this time, with 172 such vessels out of a total of 242 constructed in Clyde shipyards during the particularly successful year of 1864. The majority were relatively small-scale, less than 1,000 tons, but some Admiralty and overseas naval vessels were of much grander proportions. The *Black Prince* was a frigate of 6,040 tons commissioned by the Admiralty in 1859 and subsequently described as 'one of the largest and finest vessels in our iron navy'.[2] The focus of activity for much of this prolific iron output during the mid-nineteenth century was Robert Napier & Sons, an enterprise built up with considerable flair by the proprietor after arriving in Glasgow from his home-town of Dumbarton in 1815. The son of a blacksmith, Napier created his own masterful legend by claiming to have been born with a hammer in his hand.[3] He moved part of his marine engineering operations to the aptly-named Vulcan Foundry in 1830, then expanded his business to riverside sites at Lancefield in 1836 and Govan five years later. His range of iron ships extended from coal barges to steam yachts and warships, and his prestigious Admiralty contracts helped to establish the 'Clyde-built' reputation for sturdy excellence by mid-century.

As Watson had indicated, the abundance of coal and iron supplies in the

38. Troopship *Malabar*, 1867.
The troopship *Malabar* docked at Robert Napier's Lancefield yard. This iron steamer was bound for service in India, showing how much the imperial connection was bolstering Glasgow's economy in the mid-nineteenth century. Note the presence of sails, which helped to speed such vessels on long-haul voyages. (*Glasgow University Archives and Business Records Centre.*)

39. Napier foremen and families, 1850s.
Robert Napier & Sons was a pioneering and innovative marine engineering concern, which served as a training ground for a generation of Clyde shipbuilders. This group of Napier foremen and their families, photographed in the 1850s, conveys a sense of the confidence that was emerging in the industry. (*Glasgow University Archives and Business Records Centre.*)

west of Scotland was a crucial factor in the rapid rise of Clyde shipbuilding, although it was not the sole reason for the success of firms like Napier's. Developments in marine engineering since at least the pioneering days of Henry Bell's *Comet* in 1812 had given local shipbuilders a considerable advantage over rivals elsewhere. Robert Napier came from a family of innovators, who were determined to achieve economies of scale in the initially expensive business of steam navigation. His cousin David, also a marine engineer, refined the efficiency of boilers and engines, thus saving on fuel costs and allowing for ever-more extensive sea-going voyages. The iron hull, developed in the 1820s, was a technical leap forward in the size, speed and durability of vessels. Like the railways, iron steamships became a potent metaphor for Glasgow's expanding commercial horizons, which helped to elevate the name of Napier into heroic status. Moreover, the family's creative influence was apparent in the number of ex-employees who set up business on their own. For instance, David Tod and John McGregor were former foremen of Robert Napier, whose yard specialised in the construction of iron vessels from the 1830s. John Elder, an erstwhile engineering apprentice at Napier's Lancefield yard, co-produced the first successful compound marine steam engine in 1853. The effect was revolutionary, as fuel consumption was cut by a third, thus allowing for regular long-haul voyages by steamships.

During the 1850s and 1860s Clyde shipbuilders produced 70 per cent of all the iron tonnage launched in Britain, thus consolidating their reputation for innovation. Yet while Glasgow was emphatically the centre of control for the industry, the growing scale of operations meant that it was more profitable for firms to settle outside the city, where there was deeper water and not the same competition from the Clyde Navigation Trust for harbour space. Tod & McGregor's was based in Partick, Napier's partly in Govan, and as was explained in the previous chapter, the population profile of these two districts altered profoundly with the arrival of shipbuilding. The year 1864 was significant in two respects for Govan. Not only was it erected into a Police Burgh, with its own elected local representatives, but John Elder laid out a new shipyard, having decided to expand his successful engineering business. He purchased Fairfield, a riverside estate of twenty-four hectares, and eventually the new enterprise became known as the Fairfield Shipbuilding & Engineering Company. After Elder's unexpected death in 1869, aged forty-five, his widow dedicated part of the estate as a public park, which was opened with much ceremonial in 1885. Govan's prominence in shipbuilding success was evident from the effusive thanks of the Burgh Commissioners to Isabella Elder. Locally-produced vessels were lauded as 'the active pioneers of civilisation and commerce, the intermediaries of human intercourse, and messengers of peace and goodwill throughout the world'.[4] The rhetoric indicated that a sense of cohesive civic identity was being encouraged by those who had helped to create the new industrial community. The pace of change was extraordinary, as between 1864 and 1885 Govan's population rose from 9,058 to 55,463, with four shipbuilding and engineering yards established within the burgh, plus Alexander Stephen's yard in close proximity at Linthouse.

However, the bravura that characterised Govan's achievements masked the disturbing fact that the seemingly inexorable progress of Clydeside shipbuilding was prone to serious reversals. James Nicol, who had taken over as City Chamberlain in 1882, wrote of the 'suddenness with which depression follows a great boom' as unemployment spread within the industry during the black year of 1884.[5] From over 404,000 tons of shipping produced on the Clyde in 1883, output dropped precipitately to 262,000 tons and did not increase again until 1888. Glasgow Trades Council, which was the co-ordinating forum for trade unions in the city, voiced apprehension about the impact of 'dull trade' on shipyard workers and their families, while in Govan employers and union representatives debated the appropriate rate of wage cuts to ensure continuity of employment.[6] Some groups of workers went on protest strike, as Nicol disdainfully reported, the riveters especially dogged in their stance against loss of earnings. Yet for all the

40. John Elder statue, 1888, Elder Park, Govan. The park was opened in 1885, in tribute to the deceased founder of the Fairfield yard, and the statue was erected three years later. A celebratory poem of the time (written by local bard, 'Rab the Riveter') effused: 'Where'er the giant steam-ships sail, on river, sea, or ocean, / John Elder's name and Govan's fame is wafted far and wide.' (*Glasgow City Council Corporate Graphics.*)

cyclical uncertainties, the concentration of shipbuilding expertise on the Clyde meant that technical progress continued to be made, notably in marine engineering, thus bolstering market opportunities during times of prosperity. In contrast to 1884, the year 1913 was golden. The *Glasgow Herald* summed up results in a glowing editorial:

> The figures are astonishing. The Clyde yards have launched 374 vessels with a tonnage of 764,784 and an indicated horse power of 1,117,400. Our twenty miles of river have produced more than a third of the whole

tonnage built in the United Kingdom in 1912, and more than a fifth of the whole new tonnage of the world in that year. There are a few yards in England and Germany that are larger than any to be seen on the Clyde, but we have a greater number of large and busy yards than are to be found in any other part of the world.[7]

The fluctuations in Clydeside shipbuilding up to 1914 reflected extraordinary patterns of demand and then the debilitating impact of global recession. Workplace loyalty, as encouraged by paternalistic employers like Elder, was thus an important device to counter the periodic downswings that bedevilled the industry. Allegiances were reinforced by local patriotism, which identified Glasgow with global interests and a dynamic economic focus. Sir William Pearce, who became the dominating influence at Fairfield's after Elder's death, used imaginative devices to ensure that the yard maintained a high profile at home and overseas. In 1879 he was the originator of the Blue Riband, the accolade bestowed on the swiftest liner crossing the Atlantic, which was regularly won by Fairfield-built vessels. In 1880 the launch of Czar Alexander II's steam yacht *Livadia*, known as the 'Floating Palace' because of its ostentatious luxury, did much to arouse international curiosity about Fairfield's and the Clyde. There was a masculine edge to all this emphasis on competitive achievement, which was compounded by the assertively imperialist climate of the times. Author James Hamilton Muir expressed strong feelings in 1901, using shipbuilding to reflect the quality and scale of Glasgow industry in relation to other British cities:

We believe, every Glasgow man of us, that our shipbuilding is a thing to be talked of, and a most honourable and dignified business to have for the chief industry of a city. Sheffield is known to the world for cutlery, Birmingham for pedlars' wares and nails and bullets, and Manchester for 'Manchester goods'. But Glasgow is the maker of ships, and her sons are proud of their seemly product.[8]

The river was identified inextricably with the city's productivity and prosperity by the early twentieth century, but the allure of the Clyde must be placed in perspective. The volatility of market forces meant that there could be a struggle for survival during times of depression. Yards often undertook unprofitable contracts to stay working, and there was even a reversion to sailing ships during the late 1870s to tide over the crisis. While the Clyde had an enviable reputation for commercial output ranging from quality passenger liners to less glamorous merchant ships, the most reliable source of orders was for military vessels. Ironically, for all the lofty claims of the Govan Commissioners in 1885 about peace and goodwill, war and imperial rivalry served the Clyde shipbuilders very well. Early iron success had been encouraged by the circumstances of the Crimean War and

American Civil War. Sir William Pearce was an Admiralty-trained naval architect who used his former connections to secure orders for Fairfield's as the government sought to match foreign fleet expansion.[9] The Naval Defence Act of 1889 intensified warship production, as did wide-ranging Admiralty reforms from 1904 which heralded the era of the Dreadnoughts.[10] In 1906 the shift of Yarrow & Company from London to Scotstoun, just outside Glasgow, underlined the Clyde's suitability for naval construction, as the company specialised in torpedo boats and destroyers. Although the industry was still prone to serious fluctuations in demand during the 1900s, the increase in armaments' production immediately prior to the First World War decisively restored employment fortunes.

41. Britannia looking out to the Clyde, 1909. By the 1900s the success of Clyde shipbuilding had become intertwined with British global interests, commercial and military. Here a sturdy-looking Britannia surveys the glowing horizon, amidst signs of healthy productivity. The drawing is from *Glasgow Today*, published in 1909 to promote city trade and industry. (*By courtesy of the Mitchell Library, Glasgow City Libraries and Archives.*)

Significantly, from the 1880s shipbuilding technology had altered fundamentally as iron hulls gave way to steel. James Nicol illustrated the extent of progress by 1890, when 347,807 tons of steel ships were produced on the Clyde in contrast to 4,317 tons of iron.[11] There were assorted reasons why iron was displaced. Steel had the practical advantages of being lighter and more flexible. Moreover, iron ore was disappearing from the west of Scotland, as the early success of the industry had taken its toll on local supplies. Pig iron was increasingly imported from England and Spain, which meant that consumers had to pay more for the product. In an effort to circumvent the deficiency, the Steel Company of Scotland was founded in 1871 and set up production at Hallside to the south-east of Glasgow. A wealthy combine which included locomotive builders, engineers and the ubiquitous Tennant's of St Rollox, the proprietors aimed to pool resources in the quest for a cheaper alternative to pig iron. After considerable experimentation the problem of resources was not solved, but in the interim a promising market had been secured for boiler plates and ships' plates, processing imported 'acid' ore which was suitable for steel. By 1880 a close connection between steel and shipbuilding had been forged, quite literally, and thereafter the number of steel producers expanded rapidly in the west of Scotland.

In Glasgow the largest firm was William Beardmore & Company, operating from the former textile district of Parkhead in the East End. The foundry, which dated from the 1830s, had been acquired by Robert Napier. William Beardmore came north from London to work with the illustrious engineering family, and took over the business under his own name in 1871. His son, also William, identified the potential of steel during the 1880s, and diversified into the production of armour plate. The younger Beardmore ran his business on the grand scale, extending the works and spending £250,000 alone on new buildings at Parkhead.[12] During the 1900s he laid out a shipyard at Dalmuir, Dunbartonshire, for the construction of naval vessels and acquired additional steel plants in Lanarkshire to maintain production levels. Another eventual focus of activity was the emerging automobile and aircraft industries. David Kirkwood, future Labour MP and Parkhead-born in 1872, evocatively described the impact of the vast Beardmore steel complex, which 'changed our village into a forge and our weavers into the black squad'.[13] An appropriate symbol of Beardmore omnipotence was the mighty steam-hammer known as 'Samson', which according to Kirkwood set Parkhead quivering as it pounded relentlessly on the metal plates.

Shipbuilding itself employed a small percentage of Glasgow's industrial workforce by 1911, less than 2 per cent, although these figures do not include Govan and Partick, which remained administratively separate from the city until 1912. Engineering and metal-working were much more substantial Glasgow employers, at 17 per cent.[14] There was a range of industries that

42. Beardmore steelworkers and steam-hammer, 1900.
Workmen pose before one of the famous Beardmore steam-hammers. This prodigy resonated noisily throughout the East End community of Parkhead as the steel was processed. The illustration graphically conveys the scale of operations in the enterprise. (*Glasgow University Archives and Business Records Centre.*)

supplied the needs of shipbuilders, with Beardmore's one of the largest concerns. Brassfounders, coppersmiths, boilermakers and assorted machine-tool manufacturers were based in Glasgow, their prosperity intertwined with shipbuilding fortunes. On the other hand, the expansion of the iron and steel industries did not arise from shipbuilding alone. For example, in 1869 Walter Macfarlane relocated his Saracen Foundry to the Possil district and specialised in elaborate wrought-iron work, notably for embellishing streets, gardens and public parks. Concern about the environment was purely commercial, as Possil was notorious for its industrial pollution by the end of the century. Also to the north of the city, in Springburn and Cowlairs, were railway workshops. The opening of the Edinburgh and Glasgow line in 1842 had been the stimulus to activity, and early output was geared towards local needs. In 1865 the German-born Henry Dubs extended Glasgow's locomotive interest when he established engineering works at Polmadie, to the south of the river. By the 1900s Glasgow had secured a substantial overseas market, especially in the British colonies. The North British Locomotive Company, formed in 1903 as a combine of the existing companies, was the largest railway manufacturing firm outside the United States, employing over 8,000.

Ships, Trams and Communications

The volume of trade in the port of Glasgow continued to expand from the mid-nineteenth century, technological developments in steam-shipping opening out market opportunities for the supply of goods and materials to and from the city. The Clyde Navigation Trustees remained acutely aware of harbour deficiencies, not least because of the vocal complaints from Glasgow's shipowners about congestion and delays in loading and unloading cargoes. By the 1850s 1.5 million tons of shipping and over one million tons of cargo were being handled by the port, 50 per cent more than London, Liverpool or Hull in relation to available harbour space.[15] During this decade thorough explorations were made with a view to extending quay accommodation off the river's main channel, and a major phase of development was initiated when Kingston Dock opened in 1867. Even this project could not meaningfully ease congestion problems, because the dock was intended for ships of only 500 tons and larger vessels were still not sufficiently catered for. However, dock expansion proceeded apace up to 1914, and the completion of the first phase of the monumental Queen's Dock in 1877 was marked with much civic ceremonial. As a tribute both to the monarch and the growing scale of Clyde navigational achievements, the 2,080 ton steamer *Victoria* was selected as the first vessel to enter the new basin. Thereafter Queen's Dock accommodated many of the more majestic vessels that plied distant routes such as those for Australasia, the Far East and the Americas, serving as testimony to Glasgow's exotic trade connections as well as the importance of shipowning to the city's economy.

Only gradually did Glasgow become established as a shipowning port, after vessels could be registered in the city from 1810. Greenock and Port Glasgow still accounted for the lion's share of larger ships registered up to the 1830s, but navigational improvements steadily increased the volume of city-based ownership. Understandably, shipping and shipbuilding were often closely connected. The growing number of shipyards from mid-century supplied the diverse demands of Glasgow's shipping companies, from state-of-the-art iron steamers to advanced sailing vessels, notably 'clippers' for the tea trade. For example, in 1851 the Tayside firm of Alexander Stephen & Sons established their first Clyde yard at Kelvinhaugh in Glasgow, specialising in swift and sleek sailing ships for long-haul voyages. George Smith & Sons traded predominantly with Far Eastern ports, and commissioned several of these vessels from Stephen's during the 1850s and 1860s.[16] The Smith brothers, George and Robert, were noted for their shrewd management and reliable service, and ultimately made a fortune. Another Glasgow business with healthy profit margins was Burrell & Son, which diversified from a shipping agency into shipowning during the 1860s, operating from a modest base on the Forth & Clyde Canal. William Burrell senior even established a shipyard at Hamiltonhill, by Port Dundas, which produced small 'puffer' vessels for canal and coastal trade.[17] However, Burrell's greatest success was from the 1880s, under William junior and his brother George, who inherited the company while still in their twenties. They built up a global network of trade, with an especial focus on the Mediterranean, shipping supplies of iron ore from Spain for the new steel industry.

43. Anchor Line poster, 1914. An exotic poster, for the Glasgow-based Anchor shipping line. Although the company originated in the 1830s, its heyday was during the late nineteenth and early twentieth centuries, under the shrewd management of the Henderson brothers. East India trade was stimulated by the opening of the Suez Canal in 1869, but the Anchor Line was also renowned for its lucrative transatlantic routes, conveying thousands of emigrants from Europe to the New World. (*Glasgow University Archives and Business Records Centre.*)

Along with shipbuilders, shipowners became a potent symbol of entrepreneurial success in late nineteenth-century Glasgow. George Burns was
depicted retrospectively as one of the heroic pioneers, who in the early
steamer days had built up the Belfast and Liverpool trade routes and in 1839
was one of the original Cunard partners.[18] His son and grandson, both
Lord Inverclyde, continued the tradition as chairmen of the formidable
Cunard's. The company's vessels plied the transatlantic routes, as did the
Allan Line, established in Glasgow by Alexander Allan in 1846. From the
1860s Allan ships transported increasing numbers of emigrants to the New
World, in a thriving passenger business stimulated by steam-ship speed and
efficiency. The Allans and the Smiths were personally related, reinforcing
the intimate family ties that characterised Glasgow shipowning. James
A. Allan was Robert Smith's grandson, who ardently continued the long-
standing reputation of both families for pro-temperance commitment and
radical politics. Indeed, while still head of the business Allan went so far as
to join the Independent Labour Party and created a controversial identity
as Glasgow's 'socialist millionaire'. Another wealthy shipowner with a social
conscience was Sir James Bell, although his politics (like William Burrell's)
were Liberal Unionist. Bell Brothers came to specialise in the lucrative coal
export market, although Sir James was far better known for being the only
post-1833 Lord Provost to be elected for two periods consecutively, in 1892
and 1895.

The Clyde was Glasgow's trade route to the world, yet the river had a
multiplicity of identities which could reflect the different images of the city
being promoted by the end of the nineteenth century. In 1894 Andrew Aird
shared the predilection of contemporary historians for tracing Glasgow's
rise and progress through the story of the Clyde, 'the source of the greatness
of our "sea-born city"'.[19] Glasgow was frequently referred to as the 'Venice
of the North', the abundance of prestigious Italianate buildings suggesting
an affinity with the great mercantile city of the Adriatic Sea. Between 1889
and 1892 James Templeton & Company went so far as to rebuild their
world-famous carpet factory on Glasgow Green in emulation of the Doge's
Palace in Venice. While the river represented the success of Glasgow commerce and industry, it also had a more mellow profile, steamers transporting
travellers to the scenic Firth of Clyde during the summer months. Here
Glasgow's merchant princes indulged their passion for yachting, a pastime
that had the advantage of conspicuously displaying Clydeside craftsmanship.
Sir Thomas Lipton, the flamboyant Glasgow grocery millionaire and celebrated yachtsman, patronised William Fife of Fairlie, the most fashionable
of the Clyde yacht-builders. The status of sailing for the Glaswegian man of
property was summed up by James Hamilton Muir in 1901:

> He owns a steam yacht, and his sons compete at regattas in those sensi-
> tive little model racers which Mr Fife (like a skilful gardener) produces

44. Sir Thomas Lipton, 1920s. Glasgow's internationally famous grocery tycoon, around 1920. A tall, distinctive, stylish figure, Lipton is wearing his signature polka-dot bow-tie and sailing cap. His great passion was yachting, and Lipton's personal (and unfulfilled) quest was to win the prestigious America's Cup. (*By courtesy of the Mitchell Library, Glasgow City Libraries and Archives.*)

in new varieties every year. At present the fashion is all for the 23-footer, which will stand you anything between £300 and £500.[20]

If yachting regattas paraded the social pretensions of the 'Venice of the North' during the 1900s, a quite different mode of transport reinforced Glasgow's image as the city state, self-sufficient in a range of public services that were provided for citizens. In yet another Venetian analogy, the trams were known as 'the gondolas of the people', cheap, accessible and (from 1894) municipally-owned. In his monumental survey of civic achievements by the 1890s, Lord Provost Bell explained that the tramways constituted a 'natural monopoly', and to preserve the integrity of city streets and ease the flow of traffic councillors had resolved to work the system on behalf of the people.[21] Private omnibuses had been running in Glasgow from mid-century, but the tramways era was inaugurated in 1871, when a twenty-three years' lease was granted to the Glasgow Tramway & Omnibus Company to operate the new system. It was a highly significant point in time, given the inauguration of the City Improvement Trust in 1866. Chapter 8 provides more detail about this ambitious civic project, which included the creation of thoroughfares in central districts and beyond. To maintain control over land use, the Town Council owned the tram-lines from the outset, and thus had considerable say in company strategy. Apart from the East End, the two main routes during the early days extended to Kelvinside and Queen's Park, both suburbs containing the residences of wealthy commuters. These were the most profitable routes, although additional tram-lines to working-class districts opened from the 1880s.

Wholesale municipal ownership was depicted as a vast improvement over the existing service, offering greater comfort and cost-effectiveness, although there were complex reasons for the acquisition. Horse-drawn cars were being superseded by electrification, and councillors did not want to yield their monopoly position in electricity supply (approved in 1890) to

45. Corporation horse-drawn tramcar, 1894.
William Graham photographed this newly-municipalised Springburn tramcar round about 1894. The driver and conductor pose with a smart pair of matching horses, while inquisitive youngsters look on in the background. Significantly, there were no advertisements on Corporation tramcars, a policy which was intended to emphasise civic commitment to public service. (*By courtesy of the Mitchell Library, Glasgow City Libraries and Archives.*)

46. Tramwaymen under training, 1912.
The image of the 'model municipality' is captured in this photograph of Corporation tramwaymen under training. Up to the First World War the department was an all-male preserve, with the workforce presenting an almost military appearance, under the strict controlling influence of Tramways Manager, James Dalrymple. (*By courtesy of the Mitchell Library, Glasgow City Libraries and Archives.*)

any rival. After thorough investigation of mechanical traction in Europe and North America, the first electric cars were introduced on the Springburn route in 1898. Thereafter Glasgow Corporation entered its tramways' golden age, establishing an enviable reputation for the excellence of its public transport during the years before the First World War. The tramways was certainly the largest Corporation department, employing approximately 5,000 prior to boundary extension in 1912. Projecting a discreet but distinctive corporate identity, the tramwaymen were smartly attired in bottle-green uniforms. Advertisements were conspicuously absent from the cars, emphasising that service rather than the profit motive was the prime consideration. Directing the system were energetic and outspoken managers, most notably James Dalrymple, who headed the department from 1904. One of the city's best-known public figures during the early twentieth century, Dalrymple's expertise was esteemed throughout the world, with the Glasgow system held up as an exemplar for others to follow.[22] As tramways profits accumulated, the Dalrymple regime added forcefully to the image of municipal efficiency associated with Glasgow at this time. In 1913 over £33,000 was paid into the common good fund as tramways 'surplus', out of record car receipts of over £1 million.

Glasgow's tramway network eventually reached well beyond the city boundaries and route extensions were continually being constructed, fuelling accusations (notably from railway companies) that the Corporation was empire-building. While the service was far from perfect, with persistent complaints from travellers about overcrowding during peak periods, the tramways became an inextricable part of the city's identity, even after the motor omnibus began to make passenger inroads during the 1920s. Whatever the reality, the tramways were long associated with an era of pre-war confidence and prosperity in Glasgow, and shrewd Corporation emphasis on the benefits of municipal ownership directly related this to the collective interests of the community. Yet a cheap and reliable public transport system was of invaluable benefit to business, as councillors (as prominent businessmen) were aware. There was a two-fold advantage in extending the tramways, as more commuters could be conveyed to their workplace and greater opportunities for city shopping were allowed. In 1896 Glasgow even inaugurated an underground railway service, albeit of modest proportions compared with London or Paris. The circular route of 10.5 kilometres proved to be especially convenient for transporting workers to Govan and Partick, as many Glasgow men commuted to shipyards down-river. Unlike the tramways, the underground was not municipally-owned, although the system was eventually acquired by the Corporation in 1923.

Commerce and the Consumer City

Consumer demand generally was booming in Glasgow towards the end of the nineteenth century. Despite fluctuations in the trade cycle, incomes had increased while prices of food and consumer goods remained stable. During the period 1860 to 1895 real wages rose by 1.5 per cent annually.[23] With more purchasing power, a range of commodities became readily available for those with a reliable income. Moreover, inner-city clearance and improvement from the 1860s had opened out thoroughfares, and created the space for a variety of new shops, stores and warehouses. For example, William Bow's Emporium commenced business in High Street during the 1870s and specialised in household goods, offering a wide choice to 'the judicious house-wife' or couples setting up home for the first time.[24] Copland & Lye was founded in 1873 and soon made an impact with their Cowcaddens warehouse. By 1891 the business had shifted to more commodious premises on Sauchiehall Street, described in publicity material as 'one of the most extensive, most architecturally elegant, and most perfectly equipped drapery emporiums to be met with in the kingdom'.[25] A particularly effective master of advertising was Walter Wilson, proprietor of the Colosseum warehouse in Jamaica Street. He had started off in the millinery trade in 1869, but quickly expanded his sphere of operations to the extent that he was employing 500 staff in twenty-three departments by 1889. From the outset he boldly advertised the allure of the Colosseum. 'Go where you

47. Copland & Lye's Caledonian House, 1930s. A promotional view of Caledonian House in Sauchiehall Street. Established in 1873, the firm was originally based in Cowcaddens, but moved to more central premises in 1878. One of Glasgow's leading drapery stores, it was advertised to its predominantly female patrons as unrivalled for the quality of merchandise and efficiency of service. (*By courtesy of the Mitchell Library, Glasgow City Libraries and Archives.*)

will MR WILSON'S name stares you in face', was one critical assessment of the 1880s.[26] Such was Wilson's success that in 1904 he opened another warehouse in Sauchiehall Street, Glasgow's shopping Mecca by the turn of the century. Les Grands Magasins des Tuileries belied its impressive French title by being run on the lines of an American department store, complete with the city's first bargain basement in 1913.

Sir Thomas Lipton, 'King of the Dairy Provision Trades', was also profoundly influenced by American marketing techniques.[27] The son of working-class Ulster immigrants, Lipton spent four formative years in the United States, learning much about sales showmanship in Stewart's New York department store. On his return to Glasgow he made an almost immediate success of the first 'Lipton Market', opened in the Anderston district in 1871. He specialised in butter, cheese, eggs and ham, the Irish family connection standing him in good stead as a source of supply. He sold his own brand of tea and coffee, acquiring extensive plantations in Ceylon for greater cost-effectiveness. Lipton provided staple fare for working-class consumers, although he allowed for personal touches in service that distinguished his stores from competitors. He was careful to select prime, centrally-located sites and fitted his premises to exacting standards. It was a corporate image that blended a shrewd Glaswegian sense of commercialism with theatricality. During the 1880s Lipton extended the business to branches south of the Border, and his fertile imagination generated ever-more elaborate publicity stunts. In 1881 he pulled off what he later described as 'the cleverest piece of advertising which had been successfully attempted by any British trader'.[28] He ordered two monster cheeses, each weighing over 1,500 kilograms, from the United States. One of the cheeses was exhibited in his Jamaica Street store, the other was despatched for display in London and then Edinburgh. During the festive season Lipton informed the press that his Glasgow prodigy, like a lucky Christmas pudding, would be stuffed with sovereigns and half-sovereigns, cut into portions and offered for sale. Inevitably, purchasers flocked to Jamaica Street, and for years afterwards a succession of bountiful 'Jumbo' cheeses ensured that Lipton's name remained embedded in the public consciousness.

Lipton was by no means alone in carving out a niche in the expanding grocery and provision market. A number of similar firms were established during the 1870s and 1880s, their consumer base predominantly in working-class districts. Andrew Cochrane, Alexander Massey and the Templeton brothers were among the most enduring enterprises. Consumer choice was increased by the development of refrigerated shipping from the 1870s, ensuring plentiful supplies of foodstuffs from as far away as Australasia. Moreover, the port of Glasgow long had been a major importer of North American wheat and grains, stimulating the growth of flour-milling and bakery concerns within the city. By the 1900s technical innovation had vastly increased the scale of operations in bread and biscuit manufacture, with Bilsland Brothers' Anderston bakery producing 270,000 loaves per week.[29] Another practitioner of mass production was the United Co-operative Bakery Society, founded in 1869 at a time of considerable activity in the growth of the co-operative movement in Glasgow. Co-operation appealed to working-class shoppers not only because it was cheap, but because of the regular returns from the 'dividend', based on the quantity of purchases. Following on from the establishment of the Scottish Co-operative Wholesale Society (SCWS) in 1868, branches of retail co-operative societies began to appear in the city during the early 1870s. The SCWS supplied the retailers with a range of goods, and production was considerably stepped-up from 1887 when factories were constructed on a five hectare site at Shieldhall, near Govan. In accordance with co-operative principles these provided model conditions for the workforce.[30]

The success of co-operation provoked a hostile reaction from independent traders in Glasgow, who claimed that it was undermining free competition and private enterprise. This was the main reason why the co-operative societies reluctantly allied themselves with the movement for separate labour representation in the 1890s, in order to secure a political platform for their views. There was an irony in the business elite's promotion of civic enterprise while at the same time they repudiated co-operative collectivism, but as will be shown in the following chapter, Glasgow's reputation for 'municipal socialism' contained many contradictions. Individualism, and especially the flamboyant style of marketing and management associated with Lipton, Wilson and others, was seen as a healthy sign of the expanding economy. The corps of city merchants, industrialists and financiers was identified as the force that had made Glasgow a centre of world-wide importance. Institutions like the Royal Exchange and Stock Exchange embodied the potency of the Victorian and Edwardian business ethos, their Classical and Venetian-style buildings unavoidable architectural features of the urban landscape. These were projected as the domain of masculine authority, as was strikingly revealed in a series of publicity photographs taken by Thomas Annan during the 1890s and 1900s. Yet as historian Stana Nenadic has pointed out, for all the manly image women were not absent from the commercial life of the city.[31] They often held major financial assets and ran an assortment of businesses, especially in catering and retailing. Widows and single women usually fell into this category, such as Isabella Twaddle, who after the premature death of her husband in 1883 took over as head of the substantial family plumbing business.[32]

However, there was a dark side to commercial Glasgow that was glaringly exposed in 1878. On 1 October the City of Glasgow Bank ceased trading. A crisis in confidence had been precipitated by indiscriminate overseas investment in land, railway and mining concerns. Glasgow's joint-stock banks were long characterised by risk-taking, with the Western Bank folding in 1857, but there had previously been nothing as shocking as the events of 1878. It transpired that the City of Glasgow Bank was a huge investor in the Western Union railroad company in the United States, where opportunities for speculation had reached fever-pitch in the aftermath of the Civil War.[33] By 1878 the Bank had a debit of over £1 million in the railroad account. This was not the only questionable area of the Bank's business, as there was reckless lending to a number of doubtful firms, notably with East India connections. The debt mounted up, and in the heady economic climate of the early 1870s even more of the Bank's credit was dissipated. The management did not help matters by falsifying the balance sheets to give the impression that all was well. A number of other enterprises failed in the wake of the City of Glasgow Bank, and the effect on the local economy was traumatic. Over 2,000 families suffered severe loss and many small investors were left penniless. The civic leadership was obliged to help out, particularly with public subscriptions and offers of food and sustenance. In total, the Bank accumulated over £6 million in

Members of the Royal Exchange, 1908.
A striking Annan photograph showing the self-confident, emphatically male business elite of Glasgow assembled in the Royal Exchange. Opened in 1829, the elaborate Exchange building was the former Cunninghame mansion, adapted and extended by architect David Hamilton. A gathering point for the city's merchants, it was known as Glasgow's Rialto, after the old commercial centre of Venice. (*By courtesy of the Mitchell Library, Glasgow City Libraries and Archives.*)

debt. The directors were charged with fraud and found guilty after a sensational trial at Edinburgh's High Court of Justiciary, which was followed keenly by the Glasgow press. City businessman and philanthropist Sir Michael Connal summed up the agonised middle-class response to the scandal when he wrote in his diary: 'Oh! what a wreck of character, and what a stain on the city'.[34]

The Workforce, Trade Unions and Wartime Militancy

The Bank's collapse had a searing impact on Glasgow, emotionally and materially, but all was not well in the economy prior to this time. William West Watson described 1877 as a year of 'commercial disasters at home and abroad; crippled manufacturing enterprise; a shipowning interest as well as a shipbuilding interest unsatisfactorily employed'.[35] Globally there had been intense financial speculation followed by a flurry of commercial failures, so the Glasgow story was by no means unique. Yet unprecedented boom conditions, with serious labour shortages, had prevailed in the city until the downswing of 1874. This placed sections of the workforce in a strong bargaining position over wages and conditions, and the decade or so from the mid-1860s brought marked improvements. In particular, hours of work were shortened and the Saturday half-day holiday became more general, albeit initially the preserve of the skilled trades.

It was during this auspicious period that Glasgow Trades Council was revived in 1871, after a fallow phase of activity. Founded in 1858, the organisation attempted to provide a collaborative forum for an assortment of trade societies. Such locally-based initiatives were a distinctive feature of Scottish trade unionism, largely because it had proved difficult to co-ordinate activities at the national level. Moreover, by mid-century the movement had shed some of the stigma that retarded its progress after the 1837 cotton spinners' strike, while the reorientation of the economy towards heavy industry helped to establish a new base of support. Although the textile trades still featured among the early membership of Glasgow Trades Council, craft societies, especially from the building industry, were prominent. So too were groups such as printers, potters and metal workers, as well as the newly formed Scottish Miners' Union.[36] There were conspicuous absences, as women workers and the unskilled were not yet represented, and the influential Amalgamated Society of Engineers at first was reluctant to commit itself to membership. During a period of intense debate over the electoral reform issue, the Trades Council was also bedevilled with political differences that were not conducive to recruitment progress. However, the boom years of the early 1870s encouraged affiliation. For all the economic problems thereafter, by the late nineteenth century the organisation was able to express the aspirations of a considerable cross-section of workers.

Trades Council success at this time was reflected in the growth of unionism among groups like seafarers and dock labourers, demonstrating the wide-ranging impact of the Clyde on employment opportunities. Even the tramwaymen, still working for the Glasgow Tramway & Omnibus Company, formed a union to agitate for shorter hours and higher wages. The 1888–9 Annual Report of the Trades Council commented enthusiastically that 'in no previous year in the history of labour have so many bodies of workers been attempting to organise themselves', and hoped that a co-ordinating body for 'female workers' could quickly be formed.[37] Trades Council leaders went so far as to sponsor the inaugural meeting of the Women's Protective and Provident League in 1888, which for a while became the focal point for female trade unionism in the city. High hopes were translated into numbers, as Trades Council affiliates more than doubled from forty-five in 1888 to 113 in 1895. Prior to the First World War

Glasgow Trades Council was distinguished as 'probably the most powerful' in the British Isles, and as a means of reinforcing its position provided resources to support Labour candidates in local elections.[38] Political activism was an extension of long-standing commitment to protect and advance the conditions of constituent members, conforming to the improving ethos of 'advanced' Liberal elements among the leadership of trade unions. However, as the Independent Labour Party consolidated its base in Glasgow from the 1890s, the Trades Council increasingly became identified with that party's policies, especially following the unemployment crisis of 1908.

Despite the scale of trade union activism, these advances must be set in the context of Glasgow's reputation as a low-wage city where worker organisation had not been noted for militancy, at least since 1837. Even in Clydeside shipbuilding rates of pay lagged behind those offered by English-based employers. An 1872 comparison of the Clyde with the 'silvery Thames' pointed to the wage factor as a prime reason for the former overtaking the latter in shipbuilding success.[39] In 1906 Yarrow's moved from London to Scotstoun partly because of the greater cost-effectiveness of the Clydeside workforce. Moreover, trade unionism was initially weak in a sector that had no sustained craft tradition, unlike the long-established Thames yards. Even by the 1890s the explorations by Sidney and Beatrice Webb into local trade unionism suggested that less than one in four men in the engineering and metal trades were organised.[40] A quite different form of protectionism was apparent in the freemasonry associated with skilled shipyard workers. Again, loyalty was consolidated through this connection, as some employers (like Pearce) were ardent practitioners of 'the Craft'. While Glasgow freemasonry had politically radical roots, apparent in the reverence of adherents for the egalitarianism of Robert Burns, it became an exclusive fraternity in shipbuilding and engineering. Catholics encountered particular difficulties in entering certain trades. An extreme example of such exclusiveness was Harland & Wolff, the Belfast-based shipbuilders, whose yard in Govan was identified as a bastion of Orangeism after it opened in 1912.

There were other areas of employment that remained difficult for the trade union movement to penetrate. Contemporary concern about certain categories of women's work derived from the proliferation of home-based casual employment, especially in the clothing trades, where hours were long and wage rates low. From a different 'home' perspective, the pre-war period was characterised by the number of domestic servants who experienced similarly unregulated conditions, although it should be stressed that Glasgow never had the same high profile as Edinburgh for servant-keeping. None the less, the domestic sector constituted over 10 per cent of Glasgow's workforce in 1911, and was overwhelmingly a female preserve. Conditions could range from the excellent to the appalling, with uneasy relationships often existing between employer and employed. Indeed, during the 1850s and 1860s Glasgow became notorious for a spate of sensational murders in seemingly respectable middle-class homes, where female domestic servants were involved either as victims or accomplices. Madeleine Smith, a wealthy architect's daughter eventually found 'not proven' in 1857 of poisoning her lover, used servant Christina Haggart as a vital conduit of communication in making assignations for her furtive, ill-fated romance.

And what of middle-class employment? One investigation of Glasgow during the second half of the nineteenth century has suggested that three-quarters of middle-class families were headed by business owners, the majority of them either shopkeepers or tradesmen.[41] As already has been shown, commerce had high status in Glasgow and was an important and consistent component of the city's occupational structure. For some, substantial fortunes could be made, as was illustrated by the career of William Burrell junior, who retired from shipowning in 1917 to indulge his prodigious appetite for art collecting. Conversely, the professional sector did not make significant inroads until the 1900s. Compared with Edinburgh, where one in eight male workers were involved in professional pursuits throughout the nineteenth century, the Glasgow equivalent was one in twenty.[42] However, as a city with a prestigious university, the relatively small professional class remained influential, and doctors, lawyers and clergy were well-represented in the community. A major development was the growth of the white-collar sector, author J. J. Bell remembering the 'innovation' of women clerks at his father's tobacco factory during the early 1880s.[43] Glasgow's formidable local government bureaucracy also offered growing opportunities in this sphere. Including manual workers, the Corporation employed over 15,000 by the 1900s, a significant segment of the city's working population. Within their range of enterprises civic leaders were determined to demonstrate commitment to technical progress, and in 1901 pioneered an integrated public telephone service, complete with a corps of 'lady operators'.

For all the progressive image, there was a more equivocal response to the prospect of municipal trade unions, with some councillors and officials claiming that the Corporation did not need such politically divisive organisations to look after employee interests. Nevertheless, by the 1900s a niche had been established in this sector, and in the years immediately prior to the First World War trade union growth and militancy reached unprecedented levels in Glasgow. There were complex reasons for the 'great unrest' which characterised Clydeside industrial relations between 1910 and 1914, not least a profound sense of job insecurity, especially in the shipbuilding, engineering and metal trades. The industrial slump of 1908 was the worst since the 1870s, generating unemployment levels of over 20 per cent in the city, and affecting skilled male workers with unusual force. To compound the crisis, basic food prices had been rising from the late 1890s, and in real terms wages were failing to keep pace with inflation. That an apparently worker-friendly, welfare-focused Liberal government was in power from 1905

49. Corporation telephones, 1901. A promotional illustration, featuring St Mungo and salmon, which celebrates the opening of Glasgow Corporation's state-of-the-art telephone service in 1901. The personnel in the central switch room indicates that new employment opportunities were available for women as operators. This much-vaunted 'municipal enterprise' was controversially taken over in 1907 by the Post Office, at the behest of central government. (*By courtesy of the Mitchell Library, Glasgow City Libraries and Archives.*)

heightened frustrations about the erosion of living standards. The response was a wave of industrial action over wages and conditions, primarily involving mining, shipbuilding, engineering and transport workers. Glasgow Trades Council co-ordinated much of the activity, 'loaning' delegates like its vice-chairman, Emanuel Shinwell, who helped to organise the successful Seamen's Union strike of 1911.

It was profoundly ironic that boom conditions should have returned to Glasgow in 1913, on the eve of war. However, the prospect of such a conflict had impressed itself on the public consciousness before this time. In 1909 the Glasgow-based labour movement newspaper *Forward* had appealed to Scottish Trades Union Congress leaders to consider the option of a general strike to 'prevent any capitalist Government from even dreaming of war'.[44] Yet as has been shown, the Clyde long had been geared for military production, especially warships, while the predominance of engineering and heavy industries provided an important base for munitions output. Initially it was not an easy transition, for although firms like Beardmore's readily adapted to the exigencies of war, a plethora of engineering and machine-shops was brought into munitions work that needed to be re-equipped for specialised production. As a key munitions centre, Glasgow became a city driven by intensive war effort, as one retrospective assessment revealed:

> It was in the night that the war-time life showed itself in the most striking and yet most mysterious manner. Under the general restriction of lighting, the City as far as possible was in darkness. One heard the steam hammers and other sounds of the larger industries. This was the time for specifically Government traffic. Long trains carrying munitions – guns, tanks, and aeroplanes – were sent off. The main incoming traffic consisted of Red Cross trains which were run direct to the sidings at the military hospitals. Meanwhile, the whole Clyde area had become a vast machine for ministering to the insatiable demands of the forces. New factories were constantly being erected, and every place that could hold a lathe was 'on munitions'.[45]

The war effort inevitably pressurised workers to step up output and increased the use of labour-saving mass production techniques. G. & J. Weir's of Cathcart already was a major supplier of warship pumps and condensers to the Admiralty, but William Weir, as head of the business, was determined to move swiftly into shell manufacture and impose tighter efficiency controls. By early 1915 a combative climate was created at the workplace, exacerbated by the employment of imported engineers from the United States, paid at preferential rates. Weir's action was the catalyst for a major engineering strike which spread to other munitions concerns and provoked furious accusations in the press about selfish and subversive behaviour. David Kirkwood, chairman of shop stewards at Beardmore's and one of the strike leaders, subsequently commented that the trade unions had misread the popular mood of patriotism in Glasgow.

A settlement was reached in March 1915, but not long afterwards the Munitions of War Act was passed, to co-ordinate production and control the supply of labour. David Lloyd George was the first Minister of Munitions and under him William Weir became a full-time Ministry offi-cial, with special responsibility for output in the west of Scotland. The two were determined to enforce 'dilution' in Clyde industry by bringing in women and unskilled men to perform tasks hitherto the preserve of groups like the engineers. The aim was to boost productive capacity, especially for round-the-clock working, and ensure that scarce skilled labour was effectively deployed. In response, a series of strikes reflected the strength of anti-dilution feeling. When Lloyd George visited Glasgow on Christmas Day 1915 to rally trade union support at a specially organised meeting, he was greeted with robust heckling and the proceedings broke up in disorder. Leading on from this, the inauguration of the government's Clyde Dilution Commission in January 1916 was projected as a concession to trade union anxieties, with provision for consultation and negotiation. In early 1916 a number of jointly-agreed, single-plant dilution schemes were introduced, notably at the vast Beardmore's works in Parkhead. David Kirkwood explained that consultation was the key to this change of attitude: 'I was in favour of dilution so long as it did not reduce the standard of life of the workers. I believed in the machine'.[46]

Such co-operation was short-lived, as Beardmore's was soon hit by a strike, prompted by the management's revocation of shop steward freedom of action at Parkhead. There were attempts to bring other munitions workers out in support. In March 1916 Kirkwood was one of six prominent engineering shop stewards summarily deported to Edinburgh under the provisions of the Defence of the Realm Act. The deportees arrived by rail at Waverley Station in the midst of a snowstorm, which gave a surreal Siberian quality to what became a fourteen-month exile for Kirkwood. The government's action was intended to place the men outside the Clyde munitions area, where their influence was considered to be undermining the war effort. In particular, the 'self-appointed body known as the Clyde Workers' Committee' (CWC) was accused of fomenting the strikes, and in some government quarters there were lurid, unsubstantiated claims of covert dealings with enemy agents.[47] Whatever the reality about its influence, the CWC was identified as the subversive heart of Clydeside militancy. Moreover, as an unofficial shop stewards' organisation, and thus outside the trade union mainstream, it was relatively easy to suppress. Among its leading lights were the deported Kirkwood and William Gallacher, an ardent Marxist from the Albion Motor Works, who was arrested early in 1916 on the charge of publishing a seditious article in the CWC's journal, *The Worker*.

In the short term the moves against the CWC successfully silenced a vocal critic of government munitions strategy. Gallacher's heavy sentence of twelve month's imprisonment, together with the prolonged confinement of Kirkwood and others in Edinburgh, was a carefully calculated attempt by Lloyd George to display his resolve and restore management authority to the vital Clyde munitions works. The war was heading for a critical and costly phase in terms of manpower, as the Somme offensive commenced its bloody course in July 1916. Significantly, the progress of dilution eased considerably from this time, and women's presence in the munitions workforce rose from 18,800 in October 1916 to over 28,000 two years later. Yet as will be seen, wartime industrial militancy did leave a legacy despite the government clampdown. It helped to shape the post-war political consciousness that came to be characterised as 'Red Clydeside', the river

50. Beardmore's staff victory dinner menu (front side), 1919. A handsome British lion and a sinister-looking German eagle play a curious game of chess or chequers, representing the struggle between the two imperial powers during the First World War. In the background the 'Busy Bees' of Beardmore's collectively harass another eagle. Such allegorical symbolism abounded at the end of the conflict, and is put to telling effect on the cover of this staff victory dinner menu in 1919. (*Glasgow University Archives and Business Records Centre.*)

Staff Victory Dinner
William Beardmore & Co Ltd
at The Grosvenor Restaurant
on April 24th 1919
at 5.30 P.M.

BUSY Bs GATHER HONEY

providing yet another distinctive focus for Glaswegian identity. Nor did the notoriety discourage Kirkwood or Gallacher who went on to forge parliamentary careers, the former as Labour MP for Clydebank, the latter as Communist MP for West Fife.

Throughout the period 1860 to 1918 economic factors profoundly influenced the political direction of Glasgow. As the next chapter elaborates, business elites continued to dominate local government, while trade union influence was reflected in the rise of independent labour politics from the 1880s. Underlying all this was Glasgow's identity as a major industrial centre, where a sizeable segment of the community came to rely, directly or indirectly, on the fortunes of shipbuilding and heavy engineering. The River Clyde was a powerful metaphor for the economic momentum of

51. Beardmore's staff victory dinner menu (reverse side), 1919.
The predatory birds have been vanquished, as is shown on the reverse side of the Beardmore's victory menu. For all the industrial troubles at this crucial munitions centre during the war, not least the introduction of unskilled labour, the partnership of soldier and workman is triumphantly celebrated. (*Glasgow University Archives and Business Records Centre.*)

the city, as it represented the route to vital overseas markets. That the period was characterised by the assertive promotion of British imperial interests gave added emphasis to Glasgow's global role in trade and commerce. In Africa, Asia, Australasia and the Americas new growth areas had opened up for city investment, although the collapse of the City of Glasgow Bank demonstrated that this was not necessarily a positive influence. On the other hand, by 1900 the industrial enterprise associated with the Clyde and its shipbuilding output seemed to give reassuring substance to the claim that Glasgow had become the 'Second City of the Empire'. Whatever the vicissitudes of market forces and the dislocating impact of war, the reputation endured in the popular consciousness well into the twentieth century.

Notes

1. William West Watson, *Report Upon the Vital, Social, and Economic Statistics of Glasgow for 1863 and 1864* (James Maclehose: Glasgow, 1865), p. 39.
2. David Bremner, *The Industries of Scotland: Their Rise, Progress and Present Condition* (David & Charles: Newton Abbot, 1969 edition), p. 71. First published in 1869.
3. J. Stephen Jeans, *Western Worthies: A Gallery of Biographical and Critical Sketches of West of Scotland Celebrities* (Star: Glasgow, 1872), p. 70.
4. Quoted in Archibald Craig, *The Elder Park, Govan* (James Maclehose: Glasgow, 1891), p. 75.
5. James Nicol, *Vital, Social, and Economic Statistics of the City of Glasgow, 1885–1891* (James Maclehose: Glasgow, 1891), p. 192.
6. Glasgow United Trades Council (publisher), *Annual Report, 1883–84* (Glasgow, 1884), p. 7.
7. *Glasgow Herald*, 23 December 1913.
8. James Hamilton Muir, *Glasgow in 1901* (William Hodge: Glasgow, 1901), p. 117. 'James Hamilton Muir' was the pseudonym of three men, James Bone, A. H. Charteris and Muirhead Bone, who collectively contributed to the book.
9. Anthony Slaven, 'Sir William Pearce', in Anthony Slaven and Sidney Checkland (eds), *Dictionary of Scottish Business Biography, 1860–1960: Volume II, the Staple Industries* (Aberdeen University Press: Aberdeen, 1986), p. 229.
10. John R. Hume and Michael S. Moss, *Clyde Shipbuilding* (Batsford: London, 1975), pp. 19–20.
11. Nicol, *Vital, Social, and Economic Statistics*, p. 191.
12. Peter L. Payne, *Colvilles and the Scottish Steel Industry* (Oxford University Press: Oxford, 1979), p. 89.
13. David Kirkwood, *My Life of Revolt* (George G. Harrap: London, 1935), p. 41.
14. Richard Rodger, 'The labour force', in W. Hamish Fraser and Irene Maver (eds), *Glasgow, Volume II: 1830–1912* (Manchester University Press: Manchester, 1996), p. 168.
15. John F. Riddell, *Clyde Navigation: A History of the Development and Deepening of the River Clyde* (John Donald: Edinburgh, 1979), p. 189.
16. J. L. Carvel, *Stephen of Linthouse: A Record of Two Hundred Years of Shipbuilding, 1750–1950* (Carvel: Glasgow, 1950), pp. 54–5.
17. Richard Marks, *Burrell, Portrait of a Collector: Sir William Burrell, 1861–1958* (Richard Drew: Glasgow, 1983), pp. 37–8.
18. James Maclehose (publisher), *Memoirs and Portraits of One Hundred Glasgow Men: Volume I* (Glasgow, 1886), pp. 59–68.
19. Andrew Aird, *Glimpses of Old Glasgow* (Aird and Coghill: Glasgow, 1894), p. 14.
20. Muir, *Glasgow in 1901*, p. 226.
21. Sir James Bell and James Paton, *Glasgow, Its Municipal Organisation and Administration* (James Maclehose: Glasgow, 1896), pp. 292–3.

22. Bernard Aspinwall, 'Glasgow trams and American politics, 1894–1914', *Scottish Historical Review* 56 (1977), pp. 64–84.
23. W. Hamish Fraser, 'The working class', in Maver and Fraser (eds), *Glasgow, Volume II*, p. 325.
24. Stratten and Stratten (publisher), *Glasgow and Its Environs: A Literary, Commercial and Social Review* (London, 1891), p. 209.
25. Ibid. p. 71.
26. *The Bailie*, 1 March 1883.
27. W. Hamish Fraser, *The Coming of the Mass Market, 1850–1914* (Macmillan: London, 1981), p. 111.
28. Sir Thomas J. Lipton, *Leaves from the Lipton Logs* (Hutchinson: London, 1931), p. 122.
29. William S. Murphy, *Captains of Industry* (Murphy: Glasgow, 1901), p. 196.
30. J. A. Flanagan, *Wholesale Co-operation in Scotland: The Fruits of Fifty Years' Efforts, 1868–1918* (Scottish Co-operative Wholesale Society Limited: Glasgow, 1920), pp. 369–70.
31. Stana Nenadic, 'The Victorian middle-classes', in Fraser and Maver (eds), *Glasgow, Volume II*, pp. 269–70.
32. Jack House, *The Plumber in Glasgow: The History of the Firm of Hugh Twaddle & Son Ltd, 1848–1948* (Robert Maclehose: Glasgow, 1948), pp. 24–5.
33. S. G. Checkland, *Scottish Banking: A History, 1695–1973* (Collins: Glasgow, 1975), pp. 469–70.
34. John C. Gibson (ed.), *Diary of Sir Michael Connal, 1835 to 1893* (James Maclehose: Glasgow, 1895), p. 172.
35. William West Watson, *Report Upon the Vital, Social, and Economic Statistics of Glasgow for 1877* (James Macnab: Glasgow, 1878), p. 9.
36. Fraser, 'The working class', p. 313.
37. Glasgow United Trades Council (publisher), *Annual Report, 1888–89* (Glasgow, 1889), p. 7.
38. Robert Keith Middlemass, *The Clydesiders: A Left-Wing Struggle for Parliamentary Power* (Hutchinson: London, 1965), p. 42.
39. Jeans, *Western Worthies*, p. 143.
40. Fraser, 'The working class', p. 333.
41. Nenadic, 'The Victorian middle classes', p. 267.
42. Rodger, 'The labour force', p. 176.
43. J. J. Bell, *I Remember* (Porpoise Press: Edinburgh, 1932), p. 32.
44. *Forward*, 1 May 1909.
45. W. R. Scott and J. Cunnison, *The Industries of the Clyde Valley During the War* (Clarendon Press: Oxford, 1924), p. 181.
46. Kirkwood, *My Life of Revolt*, p. 100.
47. Iain McLean, *The Legend of Red Clydeside* (John Donald: Edinburgh, 1983), pp. 81–4.

CHAPTER SEVEN

Changing Political Directions

During the mid-nineteenth century the legacy of earlier reform agitations was incorporated into a distinctively Glaswegian identification with Liberalism, which determinedly built upon aspirations for social and moral improvement. This chapter will evaluate the strengths and weaknesses of this commitment, especially the contradictions inherent in the broad base of Liberal support. Individualism was a vital tenet of Liberal belief, which often fuelled conflict over strategy. It could also allow personalities to overwhelm collective interests, in an era when successful men symbolised so much about self-motivation. While the presence of eminent and wealthy citizens in the Glasgow party secured a solid organisational and financial base, it also bred resentment as to the concentration of power. As reform opened out opportunities for participation in the electoral process, pressures for change were exerted to remedy the imbalance. This did not necessarily entail a repudiation of Liberalism, although mounting frustration with the party leadership meant that over time new and radical ideas began to be favoured. From the 1880s the forces of Liberal Unionism and Labour represented a tangible break with the old orthodoxy, although significantly both parties were still indelibly influenced by the Liberal roots of many of their adherents. By the new century a diverse range of political influences had emerged in the city. Socialism was making a propaganda impact and influenced the mood of industrial militancy immediately prior to the First World War. The issue of electoral reform could still arouse powerful emotions, with women conducting a particularly vigorous campaign to extend the parliamentary franchise.

The Politics of the 1860s and 1870s

Liberal strength in mid-Victorian Glasgow was enhanced by the inability of the Conservative opposition to sustain meaningful electoral progress. A feature of Liberal hegemony was the common political ground shared by a disparate array of social groups, although this was not necessarily an easy alliance, with underlying tensions about middle-class motivations in cultivating working-class support. However, connecting bonds included the economically liberating influence of free trade and the notion that society inevitably would improve by adhering to upwardly mobile qualities like thrift, self-reliance and respectability. This latter impulse directed the activities of Glasgow Trades Council, whose founding mission statement in 1858 stressed the need for the moral, social and political elevation of labour.[1] The political objective was pioneering among trades councils within the United Kingdom, and represented a desire for further electoral reform in order to exert pressure on parliament to secure more equitable labour laws. While trade unionism was based on mutual strength, the pursuit of individual rights remained important, not least to defend craft interests and fend off intrusive state interventionism in areas like collective bargaining. From this perspective, the labour movement could identify with Liberalism, and the coalescence of interests was an initial stimulus in Glasgow for renewed reform agitation. Indeed, the Scottish National Reform League was founded in the city during the autumn of 1866, as an offshoot of the English-based Reform League. The aim was the enfranchisement of what the contemporary press called 'the working man', although the issue of votes for women was also being considered tentatively at this time, as a consequence of the intense parliamentary debate over the precise scope of reform.

George Jackson, a Glasgow jeweller and watchmaker, was the Secretary of the Scottish League, and ran the organisation with military precision. A young and able protégé of James Moir, Jackson's prominence illustrated how important political continuities were in the city. Moir himself served as the President of the League, his activism provoking the *Glasgow Herald* to respond, 'There's life in the old dog yet!'.[2] There were further parallels with the past in the massive turnout at the League demonstration in Glasgow Green on 16 October 1866, fifty years after Thrushgrove. Some 40,000 participated in the colourful trades' procession through the city, and (according to the organisers) 150,000 assembled at the Green to hear the speakers.[3] On the other hand, not all Glasgow radicals were impressed by the show of strength. The veteran Alexander Campbell, editor of the *Glasgow Sentinel* newspaper, cautioned his readers against identifying too closely with a campaign led and largely financed by the middle classes. It was, he suggested, a diversion, to consolidate the power of commercial interests and mute criticism among industrial workers.[4] Campbell's political credentials were socialist and his view of progress placed little faith in the panacea of the parliamentary franchise. This more independent labour stance did have some resonance, especially within trade union circles, and for a while Glasgow Trades Council became deeply divided over reform strategy.

Meanwhile, at Westminster, members of the Liberal government had been arguing interminably over the fine details of reform, with many forthrightly believing that electoral rights should be granted only to the 'meritorious' working classes as a reward for hard work and self-discipline. The Conservatives, under the prompting of Benjamin Disraeli, astutely exploited damaging divisions within the Liberal ranks. When the Liberal regime fell in 1866, the new minority Conservative government seized the initiative and introduced reform legislation, eventually passed for Scotland in 1868 as the Second Reform Act. The key provision was the extension of the vote to all male householders in the burghs, or rather, those who had paid their rates by the due date. With the £10 franchise limitation removed, the number of Glasgow's electors rose from 18,361 to 47,854, or around one in nine of the estimated population of 450,000. While this represented a significant increase, it was less than the average for England and Wales, estimated at one in five urban inhabitants.[5] Another important change was Glasgow's entitlement to three MPs instead of two, reflecting the city's growing population and commercial status. Again, this was less generous than it seemed, as electors retained only two votes each. The idea was to encourage the return of 'minority' candidates (effectively, the Conservatives) who would have more of a chance in urban constituencies like Glasgow. The Liberals, theoretically, were rendered less omnipotent by restrictions on the choice of candidates.

Despite the complexities of the legislation, it had a profound long-term impact on the direction of Glasgow politics, both at the parliamentary and municipal level. The nature of the franchise prior to 1868 had meant that activism took place within a relatively restricted domain, where the protagonists (candidates and voters) tended to know each other only too intimately. However, the structure that emerged after 1868 required the cultivation of a much bigger and less predictable section of the voting population, which in turn called for greater organisational skills. This was demonstrated by the political success of the temperance movement, which had much middle-class Liberal cash behind it. Similarly, there was growing support for Conservatism, which aimed to protect the Established Church of Scotland and had a strong whiff of populist Orangeism about it. Orangeism was one of the primary influences in establishing the Working Men's Conservative Association in Glasgow after 1868, which eventually metamorphosed into the broader-based Glasgow Conservative Association. There was still a long way to go for the party in the city, but at least a presence had been established that could challenge the Liberal monolith. Indeed, the latter could rest rather too confidently on its laurels, as happened in the general election of 1874 when the Conservative Alexander Whitelaw was sensationally (and briefly) returned as MP.

Conservatism in Glasgow had revived partly in response to the outbreak of Irish Republican violence that flared in the United Kingdom during the late 1860s, the so-called 'Fenian' outrages. This raised religious tensions because of the vocal presence of Irish Home Rule sympathisers and Orangemen from Ulster. However, the bulk of the city's Catholic Irish eschewed Fenian violence, and increasingly identified with electoral politics, especially as the 1868 Reform Act had substantially opened out opportunities for direct participation. The Irish vote could make a considerable difference to

52. John Ferguson, 1898. Belfast-born, he settled in Glasgow in 1859, setting up business as a manufacturing stationer. A dominating and inspiring figure in the west of Scotland Irish Home Rule movement, Ferguson embraced a range of radical causes, most notably land reform. (*By courtesy of the Mitchell Library, Glasgow City Libraries and Archives.*)

results, as John Ferguson observed in 1871, via the columns of the Home Rule *Nation* newspaper. Claiming that the political strength of the Glasgow Irish could be rallied to win at least half a dozen municipal seats and an MP, he motivated his readers with the words 'organisation is an end as well as a means. It is educational and improving, and it indicates life'.[6] A Belfast-born Protestant, Ferguson went on to make an indelible mark on local politics, although his notable term as a town councillor did not commence until 1893. Back in 1871 he was a major influence in establishing a successful Glasgow Home Rule organisation. A Catholic Liberal, Francis Kerr, stood for the city in the 1874 general election and polled 4,444 votes. This represented a sizeable quota of electoral preferences, and served as a positive declaration of political intent from an increasingly assertive section of the community.

The power of Glasgow Liberalism masked a number of contradictions that episodes like Kerr's candidature brought to the surface. There were divisions as to strategy and often bitter ideological differences, which rendered the 'Liberal' designation at election time not always easy to identify. Continuing the controversies that were prominent during the first half of the century, religion was an especial cause for conflict. Politics was perceived by Glasgow's evangelicals as a practical route to furthering the religious crusade, with temperance ardently promoted among electors in the wake of the 1868 Reform Act. The newly-enfranchised working classes were wooed with the rhetoric that repudiation of strong drink represented manly strength of character. The Liberal *North British Daily Mail* was an influential forum for articulating the teetotal message, under Dr Charles Cameron, who was both editor and proprietor. Significantly, Cameron also served as one of the city's MPs between 1874 and 1900. Temperance progress more generally mirrored concern about improving society, at a time when salvation was being projected through a positive agenda of moral regeneration.[7] The rapturous middle-class audiences for the American evangelists Dwight Moody and Ira Sankey during their 1874 sojourn in the city was a tangible expression of missionary commitment, aimed at wholesale reclamation and restructuring of the urban community.

Such fervour was not greeted with universal approbation and some critics suggested that it smacked too much of social control under the guise of the godly imperative. In his idiosyncratic political journal, *Steel Drops*, former town councillor James Steel fulminated against the religious revival, depicting Moody and Sankey as sinister and un-Scottish.[8] That Steel was a brewer and spirit merchant explains the particularly acerbic nature of his attack, although hostility was manifested with equal passion in working-class districts, notably the East End. The tradition of libertarian radicalism still had considerable clout, and for all that followers could readily identify with the Liberal individualist ethos, the intrusive nature of evangelical activism seemed to run counter to this stance. Of course, Liberal evangelicals claimed that there was no contradiction, that encouragement of abstinence was a preventative cure to social problems, which would offset the need for state interventionism by removing the conditions that nurtured ignorance and anti-social behaviour. However, the tendency for temperance to be depicted as the absolute and only remedy led to accusations of inflexibility. The connection between evangelical Liberals and the Free and United Presbyterian churches was a further alienating factor, especially for the city's Catholic Irish community. When Irishman James Lynch was put forward (unsuccessfully) as a municipal candidate in 1872, his sponsors included the Glasgow Beer, Wine and Spirit Trade Association, showing the complex nature of political alliances that were being formed following franchise reform.[9]

For much of the 1870s the revivalist momentum appeared to be sustained in Glasgow, especially at the municipal level. William Collins junior, the wealthy publisher, became a driving force within the Town Council, pursuing a zealous policy of licensing restriction (for public houses) and consolidating city improvement strategy. In 1877 he became the city's first declared teetotal Lord Provost and promptly banned the consumption of alcohol at civic receptions.[10] At the wider political level he was also

53. City of Glasgow Bank cartoon, 1878.
A barbed cartoon from 1878, which conveys the sense of revulsion aroused by the collapse of the City of Glasgow Bank. Those stern Scottish patriots, Robert the Bruce and John Knox, predict a dire future for the disgraced directors. Two of them, Robert Stronach and Lewis Potter, are depicted here, together with former director, James Nicol Fleming, the recipient of a £250,000 loan from the bank. (*By courtesy of the Mitchell Library, Glasgow City Libraries and Archives.*)

instrumental in forming the Glasgow Liberal Association during 1878, as a forum for evangelical radicals. Yet there was, of course, a murky side to 1878 which fundamentally altered perceptions of the prevailing political power-base. The collapse of the City of Glasgow Bank not only eroded economic faith in the city, but the trial and conviction of the directors for fraud seriously tarnished the image of evangelical probity, given the religious persuasion of certain of the accused. From their exalted position as 'pillars of commercial integrity', they had been exposed as 'rotten props of a decaying and worthless concern', as one assessment witheringly put it.[11] The subsequent depression did little to restore confidence in the moral solution to the city's problems. While the evangelical impulse did not dissolve in the wake of 1878, from this time Glaswegians became particularly receptive to new ideas and the 1880s proved to be of major significance for ideological realignment.

Challenges to Late-Victorian Liberalism

The sharp economic downswing of the late 1870s intensified politics in Glasgow, although influences did not just relate to domestic concerns. Along with urban unemployment came agricultural depression, which hit the west of Ireland especially hard. This led to the foundation of the National Land League for Ireland in 1879, which under the guidance of Michael Davitt vigorously publicised the land reform campaign throughout the British mainland, especially in those areas with large Irish communities. Understandably, Glasgow was fertile ground for Davitt's ideas, although some of his most prominent adherents came from a non-Irish background. James Shaw Maxwell, for instance, joined the local branch of the Land League after hearing a stirring address from Davitt in the City Hall, a route that led him to radical Liberalism and eventually into the fledgling Independent Labour Party. Another seminal influence on the same generation was Henry George, the American land reformer, whose best-selling book, *Progress and Poverty*, was published in 1880. George's solution to the land problem was the 'single tax', or taxation of land values, which was intended virtually to expropriate the property of landlords and restore it to the community. Like Davitt, George was not a socialist, although many mistakenly construed his theories as such. Glasgow was the British city most receptive to Georgeite ideas, and during the 1890s a sizeable body of 'single taxers' was returned to the Town Council, including Maxwell and John Ferguson, the Irish Home Ruler.

The land debate was a politically radicalising factor, with the economic depression generally provoking much food for thought about the conflicting role of capital and labour. Such concerns permeated debate within Glasgow Trades Council, which concluded in 1884 that the sluggish state of industry had been triggered by 'undue speculation, unequal production, and unjust and oppressive Land Laws'.[12] That the land agitation had spread to the crofting areas of the Scottish Highlands brought the issue closer to home, and linked urban and rural problems in a package of reform, expounded energetically by adherents to the radical wing of the Liberal Party. Yet although a ready reception was given in Glasgow to Joseph Chamberlain, the Birmingham screw magnate who had projected himself into the leadership of the radicals, he could by no means command a solid working-class following. There was considerable support for the moderate Glasgow Liberal Working Men's Electoral Union, whose leading light was George Jackson, of Reform League fame. Jackson consciously distanced his organisation from the radical Glasgow Liberal Association, distrusting its overwhelmingly middle-class orientation and ardent claims to represent the political soul of the city.[13] Between such groups the identity of 'true' Liberalism became cause for vigorous competition. However, if the priorities were often markedly different, loyalty to the broad ideal still remained.

All this meant that initially the appeal of socialism was limited in Glasgow. As historian John McCaffrey has pointed out, the city's nine-teenth-century electoral politics were generally shaped by cultural forces and ideologies rather than class antagonisms.[14] Socialism was identified as alien and divisive, although the movement had a vocal presence in the city and ideas were influential. Robert Owen's visionary brand of co-operative socialism won adherents from the 1830s, and in 1843 the *Glasgow Herald* denounced the activities of 'this noxious sect', which had attracted a gathering of some 3,000 on the Green.[15] Mention has already been made of the role of the Owenite journalist, Alexander Campbell, who was a tireless propagandist for trade union and political causes. However, as an organised movement socialism remained negligible. Even the conducive climate of the early 1880s created only a fragile base for the Social Democratic Federation, one of the first British organisations to espouse Marxism. Liberalism, in all its manifestations, still seemed to strike a chord among the majority of politically-aware Glaswegians. Hopes continued to be pinned on the par-liamentary solution and the honourable intentions of Liberal leaders. Support for the Liberal route to reform was apparent in yet another 'monster' Glasgow demonstration during September 1884, this time calling for the franchise to be extended to the rural working classes.[16]

The Third Reform Act of 1884–5 related to the counties rather than the burghs, although in Glasgow the accompanying redistribution of constituencies crucially affected political organisation. The city was split into seven self-contained constituencies, each returning its own individual member. They also had a distinctive local character, ranging from the bourgeois College division in the West End to proletarian Bridgeton in the East End. There were those who felt that the city was still under-repre-sented in relation to its fast-growing population, although the parliamentary profile prevailed until 1918. While candidates appealed across the entire voting community prior to 1885, the new constituency arrangements necessitated a far more individual focus on localities and encouraged keen rivalry to secure nominations. In the 1885 general election the city dutifully returned seven Liberal MPs, but the reviving Conservatives performed creditably, taking full advantage of changed electoral conditions and the simmering tensions within the opposition ranks. The extent of Liberal differences was demonstrated by James Shaw Maxwell's candidature on a 'Radical and Labour' platform in the working-class Blackfriars and Hutchesontown division. Standing against the official Liberal, Maxwell openly declared his allegiance to Chamberlainite radicalism and made much of anti-landlord feeling in a district which contained a large Irish community.[17] He secured over 14 per cent of the vote, denting the Liberal majority and demonstrating that a significant section of the electorate was not going be taken for granted.

The Irish crisis followed on from the 1885 election, with Prime Minister

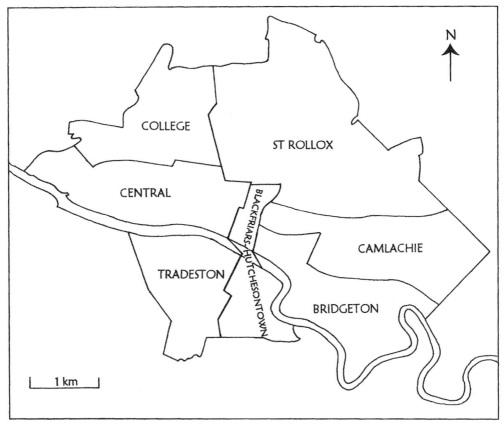

54. Parliamentary divisions, 1885–1918.
Electoral reform in 1885 brought about a major redistribution of Westminster seats. Glasgow was divided into seven constituencies, which had the effect of focusing parliamentary politics much more towards individual localities. (*The author.*)

Gladstone sensationally announcing his conversion to Home Rule and splitting his already factious party. In Glasgow there was considerable following for the new political organisation that was speedily established to accommodate disaffected Liberals, anxious to retain the union between Britain and Ireland. The Liberal Unionists were an eclectic group, made up partly of moderates who were alarmed about Gladstone's constitutional challenge over the Irish issue and the rise of radicalism. Another alienating factor was the vexed question of disestablishment; that is, severing the formal connection between the Church of Scotland and the state. This was pursued with particular vigour by evangelical Liberals like Charles Cameron. Yet paradoxically, the Unionists' national leader was Joseph Chamberlain, who for complex reasons to do with his own burning political ambition was making common cause with elements he had previously disparaged. This brought a significant radical presence into the Liberal Unionist ranks, although the leading activists in Glasgow tended to come from a middle-class background. The class profile was important, because it reflected continuing concern about the fluctuating state of the economy and faith in the imperialist solution to bolster national prestige. Liberal Unionists emphasised the integrity of the British Empire, which was deemed essential for maintaining the United Kingdom's global position in face of assertive competition, notably from Germany. In Glasgow, where the export base depended so much on the imperial connection, Unionism began to make particular inroads among manufacturing and industrial elites.

From a left-wing perspective, the events of 1885 and 1886 also intensified frustration with the Liberal leadership and dramatically raised the profile of independent labour politics. The most famous influence in this direction was undoubtedly James Keir Hardie, whose place in the pantheon of Labour Party luminaries was to reach stellar proportions. Active in the west of Scotland as a full-time trade union organiser for the miners, Hardie came to look upon Liberalism as decadent and middle-class. Renouncing his fervent early attachment to the party, Hardie's 'independent Labour' candidature in the 1888 Mid-Lanark by-election was given much publicity in the Glasgow press as a serious challenge to the Liberal machine. Mid-Lanark related directly to Glasgow's politics because of the boost Hardie's determined (if unsuccessful) stance gave to the idea of forming a separate Labour Party. Indeed, within a month of the by-election, in May 1888, the first meeting for this purpose had taken place in the city.[18] The personnel involved in forming the Scottish Labour Party (SLP) was, like the Liberal Unionists, eclectic in composition, reflecting the broad coalescence of Irish interests, land reformers, radicals and socialists who had campaigned for Hardie. The party's ideological identity was initially unclear, although Hardie's own developing socialist commitment came to be reflected more forcefully. In 1894 the small and localised SLP formally merged with the newly-founded, nationally-based Independent Labour Party (ILP), an organisation which slowly at first then steadily thereafter constructed a powerful base in Glasgow.

For all that the disparate strands of Labour and Liberal Unionism disentangled themselves from the parent party during the 1880s, Glasgow Liberalism doggedly stood its ground. For a while the organisation was fractured, and the cash and commitment of influential Unionist defectors represented a serious loss. In the 1886 General Election one Glasgow seat was taken decisively by the Conservatives and two by the Liberal Unionists. These parties worked increasingly amicably together, Unionism injecting the Conservative cause with more populist appeal, revolving around the dual themes of imperialism and social welfare. As historian Michael Fry has succinctly put it in the Scottish context, 'a Unionism still rather Liberal absorbed Conservatism'.[19] Leading on from this, a formal merger took place in 1912 under the aegis of the Scottish Unionist Association. The hybrid organisation had a unique local identity, with particular emphasis on 'union' within Empire to maintain Scotland's status and prosperity. For decades thereafter Glasgow Conservatives were generally described under the broad Unionist appellation, which aimed to project an image of progressivism while at the same time promoted constitutional integrity.

However, back in the 1880s the depleted Liberals began to pick up the pieces after the Home Rule rupture. The party still remained a broad church that could accommodate a diversity of ideas, including an imperialist wing identified with the patrician Scot, the fifth Earl of Rosebery. There were also erstwhile Liberal Unionist defectors like Glasgow MP Sir George Trevelyan, who could not bring himself to collaborate with Conservatives and so returned to the old party. Glasgow's Liberals laid forthright claim to the Gladstonian heritage, well aware of its continuing emotional impact in the city. The radical objectives of Home Rule, land reform, improved labour conditions, church disestablishment and pro-temperance legislation underpinned an ambitious programme, intended to attract the working-class vote. There was still considerable financial support from wealthy backers, and party activists still had considerable electoral standing, notably in the Town Council, which had long been a bastion of strength.

Local Government and 'Municipal Socialism'

Glasgow became emphatically identified with 'municipal socialism' during the late 1880s, in recognition of the broad range of public services and utilities that were on offer to citizens. Indeed, the city began to attract considerable international attention at this time because of the efficiency of civic administration. The American urban reformer, Albert Shaw, was bedazzled by the way seemingly intractable problems were being tackled and effusively lauded Glaswegian efforts.[20] Of course, Glasgow was not unique in this identification with the municipal socialist ideal. The term was most readily associated with Birmingham during the 1870s when Joseph Chamberlain rose to prominence, serving as the city's mayor amidst a whirlwind of reforming activity before embarking on his meteoric parliamentary career. Birmingham's municipal renaissance was swift and spectacular; Glasgow's commitment to civic interventionism was of longer-standing and associated with an assortment of councillors and officials who did not cultivate the charismatic appeal of Chamberlain. Indeed, one historian has suggested that the Glasgow 'civic gospel' may have inspired the Birmingham reformers, given Scottish evangelical influences on at least two of Chamberlain's mentors, George Dawson and H. W. Crosskey.[21]

It was Birmingham style rather than substance that ultimately made an impact on Glasgow, civic leaders astutely harnessing the publicity that the daring 'municipal socialist' slogan could generate. One of the pioneering practitioners was the ardent Liberal Unionist, Robert Crawford, whose

55. Robert
Crawford, 1887.
Crawford poses for
the Queen's Jubilee
photograph of
Glasgow councillors.
At the time he was
an ardent promoter
of the brand of
'municipal socialism'
popularised by his
political mentor,
Joseph Chamberlain.
Crawford was one of
the most influential
civic personalities of
the period, although
he never became
Lord Provost.
(*By courtesy of the
Mitchell Library,
Glasgow City
Libraries and
Archives.*)

quest for city improvement included the proposal to construct a People's
Palace of Arts in 1891. The previous year he had stated boldly that
'Municipal government as it was realised in Glasgow was pure socialism',
making claims that ran starkly counter to the upright business image of
his civic colleagues.[22] However, at this time there was no actual socialist
presence on the Town Council, and so Crawford could afford poetic licence
as to the motivating impulse behind municipal strategy. The intensification
of national politics during the 1880s gave a far sharper edge to civic affairs,
and exposed the divisions that had emerged in the Liberal ranks.
Councillors like Crawford were determined to take the initiative, appealing

to the electorate with progressive policies that would set Glasgow on a par with other cities, not least Birmingham. Glasgow's municipal socialism was thus deemed eminently safe and responsible in the appropriate hands, with Unionists and Liberals competing over the degree of emphasis rather than any point of principle.

Practical and directly local influences also led to the city's enviable reputation for municipal government towards the end of the nineteenth century. 'Greater Glasgow' was another slogan devised by civic leaders, to reflect long-standing aspirations for the incorporation of populous outlying districts. The Police Burghs were an especial target for territorial expansion, because it was recognised that these districts would augment the civic coffers by providing lucrative rates revenue. There were numerous reasons why the suburbs initially resisted the siren call for amalgamation, including a fierce determination to withstand Glaswegian aggrandisement. However, during the 1880s opposition receded, with economic stringencies after 1878 creating difficulties in the administration of some Police Burghs.[23] 'Greater Glasgow' became the heart of an assertive public relations campaign to finally win over the suburbs, on the basis that union represented collective strength and financial security. Significantly, the 'union' dimension was subtly played upon by the key architect of extension strategy, James D. Marwick, Glasgow's formidably efficient Town Clerk, and himself a Liberal Unionist sympathiser.

Marwick assiduously cultivated the image of civic excellence, with the monumental edifice of the new City Chambers (opened in 1888) representing the purposeful direction town councillors were taking. For decades there had been heated debate about acquiring suitable custom-designed premises to accommodate the ever-expanding bureaucracy, and there was ultimately the added factor of maintaining Glasgow's status. The completion of Manchester's imposing Gothic Town Hall at a cost of £1 million in 1877 was a spur to action, despite the inauspicious economic climate following soon afterwards in the Scottish city. Indeed, the Glasgow building was consciously intended to inspire 'a feeling of assured permanency and stability in our system of local self-government', as Lord Provost John Ure explained during the elaborate ceremony to lay the foundation stone in 1883.[24] The City Chambers eventually cost £590,000, the Italianate structure dominating the centrally-located George Square.[25] Architect William Young's sumptuous interior included corridors of Carrara marble and reception and meeting rooms richly inlaid with wood from all over the world. Glasgow's global position was on display as well as local achievement, a blend of history and progress that appealed to the city fathers and shrewd publicists like Marwick. As a statement in stone about the lofty pretensions of 'Greater Glasgow', the City Chambers could not fail to make an impression on citizens and suburbanites alike.

The civic showpiece was operational by the time a Government

56. Sir James
D. Marwick, circa
1903.
Marwick round
about the time of
his retirement as
Town Clerk, aged
seventy seven, in
1903. He had the
distinction of being
the highest-paid
civic official in the
United Kingdom,
and the city's
reputation as a
'model municipality'
owed much to his
shrewd grasp of
public relations.
(*By courtesy of the
Mitchell Library,
Glasgow City
Libraries and
Archives.*)

Boundaries Commission recommended Glasgow's territorial expansion in 1888, with the requisite legislation implemented three years later. The city more than doubled in size to incorporate overwhelmingly middle-class residential areas, such as Crosshill, Hillhead, Kelvinside and Pollokshields. As has already been noted, the shipbuilding communities of Govan and Partick remained outside Glasgow until 1912, their sizeable populations considered viable for continuing self-government. As well as fundamentally altering the city's geographical identity, 'Greater Glasgow' also allowed the opportunity for unprecedented administrative reorganisation, creating a far more professional base for municipal activities. As a sign of changing times, the Town Council formally became 'The Corporation of the City of Glasgow' in 1895. Moreover, the additional revenue accruing from the wealthy suburbs provided for substantial expenditure on new projects. The idea of municipalising the electricity supply and the tramways system had

57. City Chambers, 1990s.
A winter view of the City Chambers from George Square. Designed according to the exacting specifications of Town Clerk Marwick, the building remains a tangible expression of Glasgow's civic self-confidence towards the end of the nineteenth century. Note the snowy Cenotaph lion, which guards the war memorial, dedicated in 1924. (*Glasgow City Council Corporate Graphics.*)

been long under consideration, but boundary extension gave added incentive to controlling these prime utilities, which respectively became publicly owned in 1893 and 1894. At a different level, there was renewed determination to enhance the urban landscape, in order to live up to 'Greater Glasgow' rhetoric. Plans for Robert Crawford's People's Palace on Glasgow Green represented one aspect of this strategy, although the new Art Galleries and Museum in Kelvingrove Park was altogether grander, costing £257,000 by the time it opened in 1901. Most of the money came from the Corporation's common good fund.

'Greater Glasgow' immediately increased the number of municipal voters to 113,270, of whom 18,307 (16 per cent) were women enfranchised as ratepayers by the 1881 Municipal Elections Amendment (Scotland) Act. The political effect of the added areas was to boost the number of Liberal councillors; a welcome development for the party, as municipal ground had been lost following the débâcle of 1886. Liberals remained loosely the largest grouping on the Corporation, which now had seventy-five elected representatives, but the more committed activists were uncomfortably

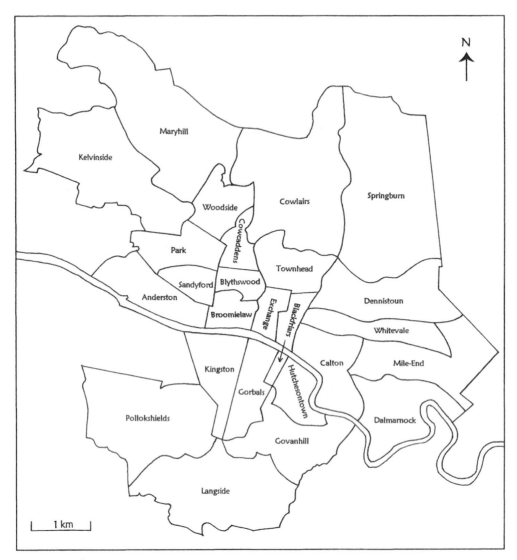

58. Greater Glasgow, 1896.
'Greater Glasgow' was achieved in 1891, after an intense civic campaign co-ordinated by Town Clerk
Marwick. This map shows the division of the city into named municipal wards, arising from major
redistribution arrangements in 1896. (*The author.*)

aware of the need to assert themselves, particularly as a high local profile served as a useful
showcase for parliamentary intentions. In this latter context there were ominous signs of a
shrinking electoral base, with party fortunes plummeting in the 1895 General Election. Only
two Liberals were returned, as opposed to three Conservatives and two Liberal Unionists. This
did not signify a wholesale lurch to the right in the city, as growing support for Labour
candidates was also challenging the Liberal base. Thus, in 1895 Labour's Robert Smillie polled
11 per cent of the vote in the Camlachie constituency, contributing substantially to the defeat
of the Liberal, Samuel Chisholm. The latter was a zealous pro-temperance councillor – indeed,

he was a protégé of William Collins – who disparagingly attributed Smillie's success to covert funding from the drinks trade.[26]

While Labour candidates were attempting the daunting task of winning parliamentary representation, the civic achievement was altogether more tangible. Two ILPers, George Mitchell and P. G. Stewart, were successful in the 1895 municipal elections, and although not a party member, John Ferguson had espoused 'Labour' policies after his return to the City Chambers in 1893. During the summer of 1896 the Workers' Municipal Elections Committee was formed under Trades Council auspices to campaign for broadly designated Labour candidates. In addition to the trade unionists, the Committee included representatives of the ILP, the Irish National League and the Co-operative movement. Ferguson was the pivotal force in holding this diverse organisation together, the veteran activist ensuring that a coherent programme was collectively endorsed, with taxation of land values topping the agenda.[27] Other issues like fair rents, free libraries, civic control of the drinks trade and the minimum wage for municipal workers reinforced the radical appeal, with the result that nine Committee-backed candidates were returned in November 1896. The 'Stalwarts', as they came to be known, had harnessed their energies for the so-called 'General Election' of that year, whereby all the municipal seats were contested. The ward boundaries had been redrawn for the first time in fifty years, remedying the gross electoral imbalance which previously favoured middle-class and business districts to the detriment of far more populous working-class communities.

The Liberals also rallied in the 1896 elections, with the newly-inaugurated Progressive Union used as a vehicle to promote radical policies. Among the leadership was Samuel Chisholm, who was rising in public prominence because of his determination to extend the Corporation's housing commitment. The term 'Progressive' was taken from the London County Council (LCC), where a left-of-centre coalition had been implementing a range of municipalisation policies, with particular emphasis on social welfare. The Glaswegians were attempting to emulate LCC achievements, and in this respect there was room for Progressives and Stalwarts to make common cause, despite rankling doubts among men like Chisholm about the Labour agenda. In 1897, bolstered by Stalwart support, Chisholm was instrumental in obtaining parliamentary authorisation for the Corporation to purchase land and build dwellings for the 'poorer classes'.[28] At the same time a free branch libraries service was being promoted, the campaign led with considerable flair by the radical Liberal, Daniel Macaulay Stevenson. These and other successful causes raised the public consciousness, although not necessarily in a positive way. There were critics who cautioned against financial extravagance, while the prospect of municipal housing provoked fury among private property interests. As with the LCC, accusations of 'faddism' began to be directed at the City Chambers, the socialist proclivities

59. Daniel Macaulay Stevenson, 1900s. A prominent figure in Glasgow Liberal circles, Stevenson came from a politically radical background and was proud of his roots. He served as Lord Provost between 1911 and 1914, and in later years was a noted philanthropist, bequeathing part of his substantial fortune to educational and international causes. (*By courtesy of the Mitchell Library, Glasgow City Libraries and Archives.*)

of certain Stalwart activists encouraging blanket condemnation of measures thought to have overstepped acceptable limits.

There were complex political influences underlying municipal affairs by this time, despite the absence of overt party labels in elections. The state of ideological flux prevailing in the city meant that the former unstated link between civic identity and Liberalism was fast eroding. Progressive hopes of containing the assertive Stalwarts proved to be unrealistic, with the two groups sometimes bitterly hostile to each other. Divisions were glaringly apparent in the contest for the Springburn ward during the 1897 elections. That Patrick O'Hare, one of the successful Stalwart candidates, was both Catholic Irish and a spirit merchant confirmed the worst fears of many evangelical Liberals. A direct result of the Springburn victory was the creation of the Citizens' Union, a pressure group whose prime rationale was to eliminate the disreputable Stalwart presence from the City Chambers. An enthusiastic supporter was Robert Crawford, who in the columns of the *Glasgow Herald* was now describing socialism as 'the worst enemy of municipal progress'.[29] The Citizens' Union was the forerunner of several organisations which aimed to preserve the Corporation for practitioners of moderate and 'businesslike' government. During the 1900s it also helped to encourage a declared 'anti-socialist' grouping of councillors, at a time when the ILP began to consolidate support and project itself as the legitimate voice of Labour in Glasgow.

However, local grievances were only one aspect of the changing perception of municipal socialism. At the national level, various vested interests were encouraging intense debate about the merits of civic interventionism. Municipal control of electricity was particularly controversial, the money-making potential of the new power source recognised by entrepreneurs who were anxious to cash-in on mounting demand. Pressure was exerted to initiate a parliamentary Select Committee on Municipal Trading, and during 1900 Corporation spokesmen made a prominent contribution to proceedings. Samuel Chisholm, who was by this time Lord Provost, strongly refuted claims of empire-building at the expense of the private sector.[30] While the outcome of the deliberations was inconclusive, Chisholm found himself at the centre of a concerted campaign to discredit his Progressive ideas, particularly plans to increase civic expenditure on housing. During 1902 the London *Times* ran a series of critical articles about municipal socialism, suggesting that Glasgow councillors had adopted an over-ambitious and authoritarian approach.[31] The scare was exploited to the full by an alliance of Liberal Unionists, Conservatives, the drinks trade, landlords and property interests, who brought about Lord Provost Chisholm's sensational defeat in the 1902 municipal elections. The irony of this particular local drama was that although the proposed housing programme did not proceed, the reforming momentum initiated by Glasgow's business-dominated civic leadership during the mid-nineteenth century could not easily be halted. For all the sustained criticisms, the deeply-ingrained image of Glasgow as a 'model municipality' did not dissolve.

The Working Classes, Women and War

It was unfortunate for Chisholm that his controversial term as Lord Provost should have coincided with the South African War, which ran its bitter course between 1899 and 1902. The conflict was deeply divisive among Liberals, although the tribulations it wrought were in the long term cathartic for the party. At one end of the Liberal spectrum was an imperialist wing, which endorsed the Conservative government's mission to bring the strategically important Boer Republics into the colonial orbit. At the other end was a committed group of opponents, disparagingly labelled 'pro-Boers',

60. Samuel Chisholm, 1901.
Lord Provost Chisholm in full ceremonial attire at the time of the 1901 International Exhibition. An outspoken temperance crusader and unswerving Liberal, Chisholm was a controversial figure, portrayed by his political enemies as dogmatic and authoritarian. This imposing photograph captures his magus-like qualities. (*By courtesy of the Mitchell Library, Glasgow City Libraries and Archives.*)

who challenged both the morality of the war and the huge cost (in cash and manpower) of sustaining it. Glasgow's Conservatives and Unionists made the most of Liberal differences, and there was initially considerable popular support for the government, given the welcome stimulus to the local economy as the war machine geared into action. Indeed, a wave of pugnacious imperialist sentiment hit the city during 1900, with pro-Boers inside and outside the Liberal party obliged to stand ground against sometimes violent attacks.[32] 'Jingoism' helped to obliterate Glasgow's Liberal representation at

Westminster in the general election of that year, when four Conservatives and three Liberal Unionists were triumphant. National unity was the basis of their appeal, the polarisation of Liberal loyalties cited as evidence of the party's unfitness to govern. The 'khaki' election represented the worst Liberal performance in the city since the onset of parliamentary reform in 1832 and seemed to bode disastrously for the future.

However, one eminent Glaswegian rallied to the defence of Liberalism, and made a dramatic impact on the apparent slide of the party into electoral obscurity. Sir Henry Campbell-Bannerman had stepped into the breach as national Liberal leader, largely because there was nobody else of sufficient standing who could hold the disparate ranks together. Displaying unexpectedly gritty qualities as the war deteriorated into a desperate struggle of attrition, Campbell-Bannerman began to decry the negative power of imperialism. He became the nemesis of Lord Rosebery, who as Rector of Glasgow University was using the city to make rousing statements about the need for Liberals to embrace the Empire.[33] In response, Campbell-Bannerman resurrected the slogan of 'peace, retrenchment and reform', consciously invoking the Gladstonian glory days and inspiring new radical groups like the Young Scots Society. He proved to be far more adept than the self-absorbed Rosebery about building bridges within the party. As the war ended, Rosebery and his imperialists became marginalised, the clash of egos among leading adherents weakening their potency as a campaigning group. Then, in 1903, the Liberals were gifted a gleaming propaganda weapon by Joseph Chamberlain, who announced his commitment to tariff reform. Glasgow was the Scottish centre of Liberal Unionism, but Chamberlain's repudiation of free trade caused immediate consternation among influential supporters, and there were ominous signs of a split within the party.

Tariff reform was the dominant issue in the 1906 general election, which resulted in a landslide Liberal victory. The party won back four seats in Glasgow, with Liberal Unionists holding on to two. Significantly, both the Unionists stood on a free trade platform and both eventually returned to the Liberal fold. Perhaps most sensationally, in Blackfriars and Hutchesontown Labour's candidate George Barnes won a famous victory, with the Irish community giving him strong support. The General Secretary of the Amalgamated Society of Engineers, Barnes defeated Conservative and Liberal candidates to share the distinction (along with Alexander Wilkie of Dundee) of becoming Scotland's first Labour MP. Labour also polled strongly in Camlachie, showing a solid base in those constituencies the party chose to contest. In the two General Elections of 1910, called in the wake of the constitutional crisis over the power of the House of Lords, the pattern was broadly repeated. The Liberal Party maintained its Glasgow position and Barnes was again returned, although his support for the government ensured that this time there was only a Liberal Unionist candidate against him. Radical electoral promises had buoyed local Liberals and restored considerable confidence. That the nature of city politics had changed was emphasised by Samuel Chisholm in 1912, who looked forward to the fruits of Liberal reforms. Going beyond the sphere of municipal socialism, he was now ardently campaigning for 'Scottish affairs to be managed by Scotsmen in a Parliament of their own'.[34]

Such radical Home Rule sentiments might well have been resented by those who felt that Scotswomen also deserved recognition. During the 1900s the militant women's suffrage movement had been consolidating a base in Glasgow, although the vexed question of political equality had a much longer pedigree. As has been seen, electoral rights became a keenly-debated issue at the time of the Second Reform Act, and although the parliamentary vote remained a male preserve, over time women were granted the franchise for certain representative bodies. After 1872 they could vote and stand for the newly inaugurated Scottish school boards, their role in the sphere of children's welfare identified as a wholesome influence. From 1882 women also secured the municipal franchise, although in practice the right extended only to those who were unmarried or widows. Nevertheless, women came to matter at election time, with Liberal strength in the incorporated districts after 1891 attributed to the cultivation of the female vote on issues like temperance. Further opportunities came in 1895, with the right to vote and stand for parish councils and county councils, and in 1907 women could become town councillors. Marion Blackie and Margaret Ker were Glasgow's pioneers in the 1911 municipal elections, although both were unsuccessful. Indeed, it was not until 1920 that the first five women entered the City Chambers as elected representatives.

All these concessions had stopped short of the prize objective of the parliamentary vote. A number of organisations had emerged in Glasgow from 1870 to agitate for electoral parity, the working-class Women's Co-operative Guild arguing forcefully that 'men cannot be free while women remain slaves'.[35] However, by the turn of the century the traditional campaigning tactics, with much emphasis on petitioning, were seen by many as outmoded. In 1903 the Women's Social and Political Union (WSPU) was formed in Manchester by Emmeline Pankhurst, and three years later established a Glasgow base. The WSPU aimed to raise awareness of the suffrage issue by whatever means possible, in the belief that pressure for change had to be relentless. The return of Campbell-Bannerman's Government in 1906 stepped up the crusade, given the declared commitment of so many leading Liberals to radical causes. Yet the government's repeated failure to respond to the women's demands swiftly hardened attitudes. Two Glaswegians who embraced militancy were Frances and Margaret McPhun, who came from a prominent Liberal family. In 1912 both served sentences in London's Holloway Prison after a vigorous bout of shop-window smashing: a highly symbolic display of subversion, that reflected the intensity of feeling over Government betrayal. Significantly, the McPhun sisters brought the appeal

61. Women's suffrage activists, 1912. This unlikely-looking group of Glasgow subversives are, from left to right, Helen Crawfurd, Janet Barrowman, Margaret McPhun, Mrs Wilson, Frances McPhun, Nancy John and Annie Swan. (*Glasgow Museums: The People's Palace.*)

of their movement onto socialist platforms, at a time when there was mounting unease among the left in Glasgow over the erratic progress of Liberal reform.

From the outset there was a strong ILP presence in the Glasgow WSPU. Indeed, as one historian has written, 'the office-bearers had difficulty in convincing the more conservative ladies of the non-militant Association for Women's Suffrage that the WSPU was not in fact an ILP organisation'.[36] The involvement of leading suffrage activists like Janie Allan (of the shipping family) and Helen Crawfurd reflected the growing strength of the ILP in Glasgow, which was further assisted by the launch of a radical weekly newspaper in 1906, *Forward*. Thomas Johnston was the editor and gave room in his columns to a host of worthy causes which were not necessarily in support of the ILP. Thus, the ardent suffragist 'Lily Bell' sternly cautioned her readers in 1907 that the ILP was no exemplar of equal rights, as women were still struggling to assert themselves within the party hierarchy.[37] Johnston himself had a wry turn of phrase, which was evident when he explained the founding of *Forward* in his 1952 memoirs: 'We would have no alcoholic advertisements: no gambling news, and my own stipulation after a month's experience, no amateur poetry'.[38] In addition to the suffrage militants, left-wing luminaries like H. G. Wells, Ramsay MacDonald and James Connolly were *Forward* correspondents, indicating the diversity of its appeal. Closer to home, John Wheatley and others penned a regular column about the activities of the Catholic Socialist Society, while Marxist socialism was expounded by John Maclean of the Social Democratic Federation.

Reflecting a global phenomenon, there was thus a ferment of political ideas in Glasgow during the years immediately prior to the First World War, which in the local context was compounded by growing disenchantment with the Liberal government. The sharp economic downswing that hit the city during the winter of 1908 had created a climate of hardship and insecurity. While there was a Lord Provost's Relief Fund to dispense financial and other support to those who were out of work, the civic leadership could not quell a mounting sense of frustration, which resulted in protests and skirmishes outside the City Chambers.[39] Labour movement activists were prominent in organising the unemployed, which had the result of pushing into prominence a younger generation of ILP members. The high local profile improved electoral prospects, notably at the municipal level. The uneasy Stalwart alliance had finally fractured after the death of John Ferguson in 1906; however, from 1909 Labour candidates, overwhelmingly identified with the ILP, began to make renewed inroads. The housing issue, in particular, came to dominate the Labour agenda. It was promoted in the 1911 elections, largely under the prompting of councillor James Stewart, who was anxious that the Corporation should take advantage of powers under recent government housing legislation.[40] From 1912 a new Labour voice on the Corporation, John Wheatley, reinforced Stewart as a powerful propagandist for housing action.

The progress of Glasgow's municipal housing at this time is explained in the following chapter. However, from a political perspective the issue was crucially important for crystallising the ILP's identity in the years immediately before and after the outbreak of the First World War. This was based on more than the appeal of visionary planning and design ideas, as outlined in Wheatley's famous '£8 Cottage' scheme of 1913. The party was also to the fore in the controversial rents' issue, which became intense after changes introduced by the 1911 House Letting and Rating (Scotland) Act appeared to be favouring the landlords. There had, of course, been long-standing hostility in Glasgow to landlords, which was demonstrated by the support for radical solutions to the power of property ownership such as the 'single tax'. However, the vocal ILP commitment to pressurise for official investigation into excessive rents had considerable attraction for the city's substantial tenant population. The movement was in place prior to the war, but reached flashpoint in the rent strikes of 1915. The demand for housing in Glasgow's booming munitions districts had led to spiralling rent increases and an outraged response from the community. The protests were notable for the pugnacious contribution of women and the astute role played by ILP activists in directing strategy. As will be elaborated, these events were decisive for the introduction of rent restrictions by the Government in 1915.

ILP campaigning successes could not, however, mask divisions in the party over the legitimacy of a war that had struck the city so forcefully. Within the party were pacifists, like John S. Taylor, and those who enlisted as soldiers, such as Alexander Turner. Both were town councillors who had made their names as leaders of the unemployment and housing protests. The Liberal Party was also divided. Daniel Macaulay Stevenson was Lord Provost when war was declared, and experienced a difficult time because of alleged pro-German sympathies. An avowed radical and internationalist, Stevenson had encouraged influential Germans to visit Glasgow prior to 1914 as a means of fostering friendship.[41] His efforts were subsequently construed as collaborationist, especially as he was associated with the Union of Democratic Control, which was a forum for Liberals and socialists to campaign for a negotiated peace. The introduction of conscription in 1916 was another dividing factor, as compulsory military service ran counter to deep-rooted Liberal tradition. At the national level, the bitter antagonism between Herbert Henry Asquith and David Lloyd George was most damaging of all to Liberal unity, with the latter taking over the premiership in 1916 at the head of a cross-party coalition in defence of national interests. At Westminster there was a stark cleavage between Asquith Liberals and Coalitionists, which, as Chapter 10 explains, had disastrous long-term consequences for the Glasgow party. Similarly, the 1916 Easter Rising in Ireland and the cataclysm of the 1917 Russian Revolution polarised attitudes. These direct challenges to the power of the state were either laudable or treasonable, depending on perceptions of patriotism and personal freedom. Glasgow politics were indelibly scarred by the emotions aroused by war, and tensions continued long after the Armistice in 1918.

The political challenges of the early twentieth century indicated that in the electoral sphere and beyond, Glasgow's power-base was altering. Up to the 1880s Liberalism had retained its dominant position partly because it embodied a potent ethos that linked past reform struggles with economic progressivism. The generational continuities were strong even after this time, as was shown by Campbell-Bannerman's buoyant campaign to rehabilitate radicalism during the early 1900s. Yet Glasgow Liberalism had become caught in the conundrum of projecting a broad appeal while at the same time accommodating groups which often had conflicting ideas about the political way forward. Such tensions helped to precipitate the Liberal Unionist split of 1886 and the rise of independent Labour, which in turn fundamentally reorientated the city's politics. While Liberalism at first survived these challenges, the party's uneasy unity was glaringly exposed after the outbreak of the First World War. The next chapter explores Glasgow's experience of the war in greater detail, and explains how the conflict changed political expectations in the city. However, the war forms part of a broader analysis of social developments from 1860, which represented the era of 'Greater Glasgow' expansionism and local government interventionism on an unprecedented scale.

Notes

1. W. Hamish Fraser, 'Trade unions, reform and the election of 1868 in Scotland', *Scottish Historical Review* 50 (1971), p. 139.
2. *Glasgow Herald*, 8 October 1866.
3. Scottish National Reform League, *Great Reform Demonstration at Glasgow* (Thomas Smith: Glasgow, 1866), p. 3.
4. W. Hamish Fraser, *Alexander Campbell and the Search for Socialism* (Holyoake Publishing: Manchester, 1996), pp. 163–6.
5. John F. McCaffrey, 'Political issues and developments', in W. Hamish Fraser and Irene Maver (eds), *Glasgow, Volume II: 1830–1912* (Manchester University Press: Manchester, 1996), p. 200.
6. Quoted in Alan O'Day, 'The political organisation of the Irish in Britain, 1867–90', in Roger Swift and Sheridan Gilley (eds), *The Irish in Britain, 1815–1939* (Pinter: London, 1989), p. 189. The item originally appeared in the *Nation*, 3 June 1871.
7. Irene Maver, 'Politics and power in the Scottish city: Glasgow Town Council in the nineteenth century', in T. M. Devine (ed.), *Scottish Elites* (John Donald: Edinburgh, 1994), p. 118.
8. *Steel Drops*, March 1874.
9. *Glasgow Herald*, 5 November 1872.
10. David Keir, *The House of Collins: the Story of a Scottish Family of Publishers from 1789 to the Present Day* (Collins: London, 1952), p. 187.
11. William Wallace (ed.), *Trial of the City of Glasgow Bank Directors* (William Hodge: Glasgow, 1905), p. 2.
12. Glasgow United Trades Council (publisher), *Annual Report, 1884–85* (Glasgow, 1885), pp. 11–12.
13. I. G. C. Hutchison, 'Glasgow working-class politics', R. A. Cage (ed.), in *The Working Class in Glasgow, 1750–1914* (Croom Helm: Beckenham, 1987), p. 112.
14. McCaffrey, 'Political issues', p. 207.
15. *Glasgow Herald*, 4 September 1843. See also, W. Hamish Fraser, 'Owenite socialism in Scotland', *Scottish Economic and Social History* 16 (1996), p. 84.
16. *North British Daily Mail*, 8 September 1884.
17. Ibid. 14 November 1885.
18. David Lowe, *Souvenirs of Scottish Labour* (W. and R. Holmes: Glasgow, 1919), pp. 1–5.
19. Michael Fry, *Patronage and Principle: A Political History of Modern Scotland* (Aberdeen University Press: Aberdeen, 1987), p. 113.

20. Bernard Aspinwall, *Portable Utopia: Glasgow and the United States, 1820–1920* (Aberdeen University Press: Aberdeen, 1984), pp. 167–8.
21. W. Hamish Fraser, 'From civic gospel to municipal socialism', in Derek Fraser (ed.), *Cities, Class and Communication: Essays in Honour of Asa Briggs* (Harvester Wheatsheaf: Hemel Hempstead, 1990), p. 64.
22. *Glasgow Herald*, 27 May 1890.
23. Maver, 'Civic government', pp. 465–6.
24. Robert Anderson (publisher), *Description of the Ceremonial on the Occasion of Laying the Foundation Stone of the Municipal Buildings in George Square, Glasgow* (Glasgow: 1885), pp. 59–60.
25. Sir James Bell and James Paton, *Glasgow, Its Municipal Organisation and Administration* (James Maclehose: Glasgow, 1896), p. 85.
26. Irene Sweeney, 'Local party politics and the temperance crusade, Glasgow 1890–1902', *Journal of the Scottish Labour History Society* 27 (1992), pp. 50–1.
27. James J. Smyth, 'The ILP in Glasgow, 1888–1906: the struggle for identity', in Alan McKinlay and R. J. Morris (eds), *The ILP on Clydeside, 1893–1932: From Foundation to Disintegration* (Manchester University Press: Manchester, 1991), pp. 38–9.
28. W. Hamish Fraser, 'Labour and the changing city', in George Gordon (ed.), *Perspectives of the Scottish City* (Aberdeen University Press: Aberdeen, 1985), p. 170.
29. *Glasgow Herald*, 25 October 1898.
30. Ibid. 11 July 1900.
31. *Times*, 30 September 1902.
32. Stewart J. Brown, '"Echoes of Midlothian": Scottish Liberalism and the South African War, 1899–1902', *Scottish Historical Review* 71 (1992), p. 168.
33. Robert Rhodes James, *Rosebery* (Phoenix: London, 1995 edition), pp. 419–20. First published in 1963.
34. Introduction to the Young Scots Society, *60 Points for Home Rule* (Alexander Maclaren: Glasgow, 1912), p. 6.
35. Leah Leneman, *A Guid Cause: the Women's Suffrage Movement in Scotland* (Aberdeen University Press: Aberdeen, 1991), p. 35.
36. Elspeth King, *The Scottish Women's Suffrage Movement* (Glasgow Museums and Art Galleries: Glasgow, 1978), p. 15.
37. Elspeth King, *The Hidden History of Glasgow's Women: the Thenew Factor* (Mainstream: Edinburgh, 1993), p. 95.
38. Thomas Johnston, *Memories* (Collins: London, 1952), p. 32.
39. James H. Treble, 'Unemployment in Glasgow, 1903–1910: the anatomy of a crisis', *Journal of the Scottish Labour History Society* 25 (1990), pp. 8–39.
40. *Forward*, 7 October 1911.
41. Aspinwall, *Portable Utopia*, p. 182.

CHAPTER EIGHT

Living in the 'Second City'

Glasgow was known as Scotland's 'Second City' from the late seventeenth century, but commercial and industrial success during the nineteenth century extended the designation into 'Second City of the Empire'. From the 1860s civic leaders consciously attempted to live up to 'Second City' pretensions by giving practical substance to plans for urban regeneration. In the heart of the old city living conditions had deteriorated drastically as slum-dwellers continued to cluster in the warren of wynds and closes that had long been identified as a serious hazard to public health. It came to be realised that a co-ordinated solution under municipal control was the most practical means of reversing further decline. Making a virtue out of social necessity, plans for city improvement were depicted as progressive and life-enhancing. They were related directly to contemporary models of enlightened urban planning, to emphasise Glasgow's place among world communities. Aspirations for 'Greater Glasgow' became a vital component of civic rhetoric, combining slum-clearance and central restructuring with a concerted campaign to absorb the suburbs surrounding the city. Such was the speed of developments that by 1912 Glasgow had become truly the 'Second City of the Empire' in population terms, accommodating over a million inhabitants. This chapter examines the success (and contradictions) of this forward-looking image and its impact on the multi-faceted social life of the city. Particular emphasis is given to the experience of the First World War, which so starkly cut across the confidence that had directed the unprecedented pace of expansion.

Public Health and City Improvements

Glasgow's population grew from 395,503 in 1861 to 784,496 in 1911, the territorial expansion of the city during this period accounting for a significant segment of the increase. The boundary extension of 1891 incorporated 53,000 suburban dwellers, while the 1912 inclusion of Govan, Partick and other outlying districts boosted the 1911 figures by 224,000.[1] Newspapers proudly proclaimed that the city was over a million strong because of the latter addition, well ahead of Birmingham, Liverpool and Manchester in population terms. Less impressively, it remained the most congested city in the United Kingdom, the density of persons per acre calculated in 1912 at fifty-three for Glasgow as opposed to forty-five for Liverpool, the nearest in terms of overcrowding.[2] However, the quest for 'breathing space' had long been a priority of public health reformers, and from the 1870s there was a significant decrease in Glasgow's inner-city population, with ambitious slum clearance programmes helping to disperse the inhabitants. The suburbs were the major growth area from this time, particularly the developing shipbuilding districts. Between 1871 and 1911 Partick expanded from 17,707 people to 68,848 and Govan from 19,800 to 89,725. Conversely, the pace of immigration to Glasgow slowed during the second half of the nineteenth century, with Irish-born inhabitants constituting only 6.73 per cent of the population in 1911 as opposed to a peak of 18.7 in 1851. Increased European immigration, notably from the Russian Empire and Italy, did however add a more cosmopolitan dimension to the city, although numbers remained less than two per cent of total inhabitants.

Extraordinary population density was considered to be the scourge of nineteenth-century Glasgow, and by the 1860s it was recognised that existing mechanisms for controlling overcrowding were inadequate. In 1862 a new Police Act was passed for the city, 'policing' legally interpreted in Scotland as covering a range of environmental obligations. The legislation continued directly from the pioneering work of John Ure during the 1850s, and formalised an administrative structure for sanitary control under a Medical Officer of Health. Almost immediately the first incumbent to the position, William Gairdner, was confronted with a typhus epidemic; the louse-borne disease that was a telling indicator of the fluctuating immunity of the poorer population. In response to the crisis a fever hospital was constructed in the St Rollox district, opening in 1865. Typhus was also the incentive for introducing Glasgow's unique practice of 'ticketing', whereby the sanitary authorities were empowered to inspect domestic dwellings and determine the maximum number of inhabitants. A metal disk was fixed to the door proclaiming the legal limits, and spot checks were made, day and night, to ensure that these were adhered to. By no means all of Glasgow's overcrowded dwellings were labelled, showing that ticketing was used only for the worst cases, such as the notorious Drygate 'Rookery' near the cathedral. That ticketing represented an intrusion of privacy was refuted by Gairdner, who claimed that it discouraged the dangerous concentration of 'a class having lower pecuniary means and less scrupulous habits of living'.[3] He also pointed out the concentrated nature of the crisis in Glasgow, with the worst areas having an incredible density of over 1,000 inhabitants per acre.

The 1862 Police Act was revised in 1866, and extended the remit of the Medical Officer of Health and his staff, particularly their powers of enforcement. Together with the Public Health (Scotland) Act, passed the following year, this allowed for the co-ordination of hitherto disparate functions for combatting fever and controlling insanitary 'nuisances'. The basis was laid for a centralised Public Health Department, whose first full-time Medical

Officer of Health, James Burn Russell, was appointed in 1872. Accompanying this flurry of activity was the 1866 City of Glasgow Improvements Act, a measure that came to be of crucial importance for progressing the sanitary crusade. The idea for a major slum clearance project had been evolving since at least the 1840s, although the early proposals had depended on the availability of private funding.[4] However, repeated failure to raise the necessary capital for combining philanthropy with such a 'profitable speculation' meant that by the 1860s a solution had to be sought through civic initiative. Under the terms of the 1866 legislation the Town Council was authorised to form a Trust on behalf of the community, which could purchase and clear congested areas deemed to be particularly hazardous to health. For this purpose, borrowing powers of £1.25 million were granted. Over 50,000 people, approximately an eighth of the total population, inhabited the thirty-six hectares targeted as the Trust's sphere of operations. They were mostly clustered in the grossly overcrowded wynds and closes around Glasgow Cross, but also concentrated in districts to the east and immediately to the south of the River Clyde.[5]

As with the Loch Katrine water project, the need to reintegrate a seemingly dislocated society was put forward as a prime motivating factor for launching the City Improvement Trust in 1866. Yet it had a fiery baptism, which was not helped by defensiveness over accusations of self-interest on the part of certain councillors. Doubts were forcefully expressed by James Leitch Lang immediately after the 1866 municipal elections when he caused a major political upset by defeating (by a whisker) the Lord Provost, John Blackie junior. A wealthy publisher, Blackie had been passionate in his attempts to convince a sceptical public of the urgent need for 'fresh air, and open spaces, and cleanliness'.[6] Lang suggested that this was a cynical smokescreen; that the true motive was to clear the way for railway terminals and boost company profits. It was doubly damaging that leading councillors like Blackie and his colleague James Watson were identified as participants in a private enterprise known as the 'Philanthropic Company', which from 1861 had been purchasing available property in the slum heart of Glasgow in order to ease the redevelopment process. For the Trust's critics this was not philanthropy but thinly veiled property speculation, and until 1872 an uncomfortable atmosphere prevailed about civic claims as to the benefits of city improvements. However, that year the *North British Daily Mail* published what Charles Cameron, its ambitious editor, claimed was an exposé of the Philanthropic Company. The allegations were eventually withdrawn after Lord Provost James Watson sued the newspaper in a highly public showdown.

There were complex political reasons for the opposition to Blackie, Watson and their close-knit circle, who were regarded by many in Glasgow as in too entrenched a position of power. Moreover, Blackie had been inspired by developments in Paris, where from the 1850s Emperor Napoleon

62. John Blackie junior, 1860s. Blackie round about the time he served as Lord Provost. A key influence on the city improvement programme, he was profoundly influenced by contemporary developments in Paris. However, his ambitious plans to open out and restructure central Glasgow provoked prolonged and often acrimonious debate. (*Glasgow University Archives and Business Records Centre.*)

III and Georges Haussmann, his Prefect of the Seine, had cleared slum quarters, created broad thoroughfares, established parks and open spaces, and embellished the city with buildings such as the new Opera House. A civic delegation headed by Blackie visited the French capital in June 1866, the brilliant summer sunshine heightening the Glaswegian regard for Napoleonic urban planning. In their subsequent report the visitors starkly contrasted the 'neatness and self-respect' that seemed to typify Parisians with 'those loathsome types of utterly degenerate human nature that abound to such an appalling extent in our own closes and wynds'.[7] It was suggested that Blackie was suffering from delusions of imperialist grandeur in his subsequent plans to transform Glasgow, and there can be no doubt that his cheerful evocation of continental street habits, including the relaxed attitude to open-air eating and drinking, damned him among temperance radicals like his adversaries, Lang and Cameron.

Despite Blackie's abrupt departure from office in 1866, the French example was largely adopted in Glasgow, with City Architect John Carrick laying out wide and straight thoroughfares in emulation of Classical Parisian style. In this respect, the Glasgow improvements differed markedly from parallel developments in Edinburgh, where from 1867 the trustees had taken care to recognise the historic character of streets and buildings, and constructed them with due regard to 'the old Scotch style'.[8] However, Edinburgh's sensitivity to the spirit of place was at odds with much of the European experience at the time, where the process labelled 'Haussmannisation' was leading to the wholesale restructuring of city centres.[9] In consequence, comparatively little of Glasgow's old town was preserved as a result of Trust operations, and this conscious break with tradition was symbolised by the demolition of the College buildings on High Street, which have been described as 'probably the most distinguished collection of seventeenth-century architecture in Scotland'.[10] The metamorphosis of the College site into a central railway goods depot said much about contemporary priorities, although there was more than purely economic interest behind the relocation. The city fathers were anxious to depict Glasgow as a bustling and businesslike urban entity, where the free flow of trade and commerce would not be impeded by disconcerting reminders of the past. Streets around the High Street and Glasgow Cross were substantially improved to accommodate traffic, while the monumental restructuring of Main Street transformed the principal thoroughfare of the Gorbals from its village-like appearance.

In Glasgow, as in Paris, the regeneration of the urban landscape was used to reflect the beneficence of the ruling authority. Order was being created out of the chaos of the slums, tangibly demonstrating the positive impulse behind the clearance programme. Yet given the sheer scale of the Glasgow initiative, practical problems inevitably began to unravel. Demolition began in earnest during 1870, but it soon became clear that there would be difficulty in finding suitable alternative accommodation for displaced slum dwellers. This posed a dilemma for the trustees, who, in the words of one retrospective assessment, 'did not then contemplate the erection of dwellings for the working population, being of opinion that such was the function of private enterprise'.[11] Nevertheless, there were some pioneering initiatives. The Trust constructed family tenements in the Drygate and other deprived areas, in order to provide an example of 'model' design. John Carrick laid out municipally owned ground at Oatlands and Overnewton, which was then feued to builders for specifically working-class dwellings. In emulation of Paris, model lodging houses for single people were constructed, the first in the Drygate in 1869. However, these were isolated efforts rather than sustained attempts to resolve a mounting problem. Rents in new properties tended to be beyond the means of the poorest tenants, who

63. City improvement operations, Gorbals, 1870s.
Main Street, Gorbals, during the 1870s, as city improvement construction began to transform the landscape. To the foreground is 'The Old Gorbals Wine, Spirit and Malt Liquor Vaults', by then an antique property which originally formed part of the seventeenth-century mansion built for Sir George Elphinstone. (*By courtesy of the Mitchell Library, Glasgow City Libraries and Archives.*)

moved into cheaper peripheral districts like Cowcaddens. The activities of railway companies, anxious to establish a city-centre base, compounded the crisis. They purchased land from the Trust, often to its considerable profit, with the result that half of the 30,000 Glaswegians displaced by 1885 had been moved out by railways.

Finance was to bedevil the Trust's progress, especially after the collapse of the City of Glasgow Bank in 1878, which caused general building developments to grind to a halt. As a result, the integrated plan of slum clearance and reconstruction became skewed, with tracts of vacant ground remaining conspicuously empty. Councillors were forced to embark on a damage limitation exercise, and from 1886 authorised the construction of dwellings in the central Saltmarket district. The Trust's changing direction helped to stimulate intense discussion as to the best way forward for the city's most intractable social problem. In 1888 James Burn Russell, a prolific pamphleteer, contributed one of his most famous indictments of housing conditions, *Life In One Room*. By this time a quarter of all Glaswegians lived in a profusion of claustrophobic single-ends, with the average density for the city calculated at eighty-four persons to the acre. Russell focused on the deteriorating health of the young, with 'exhausted air and poor and perverse feeding' producing rickety children.[12] Infant mortality rates were such that one in five slum babies never saw the end of their first year. Diseases of the lung, including tuberculosis, bronchitis and pneumonia, had become the primary cause of death among all ages, overwhelmingly attributable to the corrosive slum environment.

Professionals like Russell as well as politicians like Samuel Chisholm believed that housing action was necessary not just to improve the quality of life, but to prevent contagion from undermining the well-being of the entire community. It was, as one campaigner put it, 'a measure of public safety and public progress', which cut across claims that the free market should regulate housing.[13] There was often a strong religious impulse behind such commitment, with Chisholm, a devout United Presbyterian, firmly believing that slums were 'the masterpiece of the drink traffic'.[14] It was largely under his prompting as Improvement Trust convener that building momentum was maintained during the 1890s, with the construction of thirty-four city-centre tenements, containing 1,184 dwellings. This was, however, only minor progress compared with the dearth of appropriate working-class accommodation. As explained elsewhere, resistance to municipal house-building by organised property interests abruptly halted the expansion of the Trust's operations from 1902, and thereafter much of the propaganda initiative passed to the Labour Party. John Wheatley's 1913 pamphlet, *Eight-Pound Cottages for Glasgow Citizens*, outlined an innovative scheme for model dwellings, which was couched in language that forth-rightly blamed poverty rather than drink or ignorance for bad housing. It was a philosophy that had widespread popular appeal with the onset of the First World War, when Glasgow's housing crisis became an issue of urgent national concern.

'Greater Glasgow' and the Suburbs

Wheatley claimed that his housing proposals would create a 'Greater and Grander Glasgow', where the city would be transformed by the efforts of the 'common people' to win electoral power.[15] He was, of course, adapting the long-standing civic slogan of 'Greater Glasgow' which had re-emerged forcefully in 1912, when the incorporation of Govan, Partick, Pollokshaws and other districts considerably boosted the city's territory and population. Indeed, Wheatley was intimately associated with one of these new districts. Although Irish-born, he had spent much of his life in Shettleston, a community mainly of miners and steel-workers to the east of the city. After 1912 Wheatley became a dedicated Glaswegian, recognising that the city's administrative structure was of sufficient scale to allow for the implemen-tation of ambitious social projects, like municipal housing. For the outlying communities the services of Glasgow Corporation were in any case nothing new; 'municipal socialism' had spread well beyond the city limits, with the supply of such vital public utilities as gas, water and sewerage, plus the world-famous tramways. The official rationale for boundary expansion was to retain Glasgow's position as the Second City of Empire, an appeal blending patriotism with improved efficiency in civic management. There was not uniform acceptance of the need for extension and the anti-municipal lobby was especially hostile. On the other hand, socialists like Wheatley were firmly supportive, and the ILP by this time had considerable popular support in communities like Govan, Partick and Shettleston.

The achievement of 1912, which expanded Glasgow from 5,251 to 7,763 hectares, was the culmination of years of determined effort on the part of civic leaders to absorb the plethora of Police Burghs surrounding the city. As Chapter 5 explained, by 1880 nine had been created: Crosshill, Govan, Govanhill, Hillhead, Kinning Park, Maryhill, Partick, plus the dual entities of Pollokshields East and West. Some were of mixed residential profile, although Govan and Partick became more proletarian as shipbuilding took root. However, the majority were almost entirely middle-class. Hillhead, for example, was a West End residential district, which journalist J. J. Bell recalled wryly (if affectionately) in his 1932 memoirs. He described his comfortable childhood during the 1870s and 1880s, pointing out the high regard of inhabitants for their prestigious address. He elaborated: 'Many of them did not wish to be identified with a common Street, and nearly every street was divided up into Terraces, Places, Buildings'.[16] The burgh developed according to a grid plan, predominantly terraced houses and tenements, with the latter considerably more spacious than their inner-city counterparts. There were also abundant amenities, with residents in close proximity to the gardens of the Royal Botanic Institution and Kelvingrove Park. Most heads of household commuted to Glasgow. Like Bell's father, they took advantage of the service operated by the Glasgow Tramway & Omnibus Company from 1872, whose main routes reached beyond the city to the middle-class districts of Kelvinside in the west and Crosshill in the south.

The Police Burghs had their own magistrates and commissioners, as elected representatives were known. Responsibilities revolved around maintaining a safe and wholesome environment, with an important public health remit. With the exceptions of Govan and Partick, their populations remained small, and the scale of operations could provoke Glaswegian derision. At worst, they were perceived as 'parasitic', taking full advantage of city amenities (such as public parks) without paying for their upkeep. During the 1870s and 1880s Police Burgh pretensions were gleefully satirised by *The Bailie*, a humorous Glasgow magazine, where the fictional Provost of Strathbungo, Jeems Kaye, penned a regular column about the affairs of his community. Strathbungo actually existed; a middle-class district adjacent to Queen's Park that was too small to merit Police Burgh status. However, the name and all that it represented allowed author Archibald Macmillan much scope for parody. He depicted Jeems (a Scots diminutive of James) as a worthy exemplar of middle-class prosperity: a coal merchant, a church elder, a devoted family man and supremely self-opinionated. Eventually in his elevated position as Sir Jeems Kaye he was called upon to represent Strathbungo on the 1888 Boundaries Commission, set up by the government to probe the case for 'Greater Glasgow'. One Strathbungo resident had been well-briefed by Jeems to respond to questions about the proposed merger with the neighbouring city. His words reflected much genuine feeling in the suburbs: 'Annexed tae Glesca? I should think no. The Glesca folk come rinnin' oot tae us looking for hooses. Ye never hear o' Strabungonians wanting tae flit intae Glesca'.[17]

The sense of fierce local pride exhibited by the Police Burghs infuriated Glasgow's civic leaders in their missionary commitment to expand the city. For all the lofty claims made in the 1860s about creating a more attractive city through Improvement Trust operations, the suburbs still remained the most desirable residential address. Indeed, the building upheaval in the city centre provided one major asset for the West End, which boosted the amenity value of the area enormously. This was the transfer of the university in 1870 to the present site in Gilmorehill, some six years after the Union Railway Company had persuaded the academic authorities to part with their strategically important land and properties. Despite the destruction of the old College buildings, the university authorities believed that they were acting in the best interests of progress. The Principal, the Revd Dr Thomas Barclay, summed up the feelings of many eminent contemporaries when he claimed that the prime reason for the College's shift was because of its unsavoury slum surroundings. There apparently had been dangers in holding evening classes, with students habitually pestered by prostitutes soliciting outside the main entrance. Although the College was noted for the high number of home-based students, incomers often sought convenient lodgings in notorious areas like the Vennel and Havannah, darkly depicted as a resort of the criminal fraternity.[18]

The university's new location at the crest of Gilmorehill displayed a showpiece for the city that could be seen to advantage for miles around. The architect Sir George Gilbert Scott designed the buildings according to an eclectic Gothic style, which he blended with Scots Baronial influences as a concession to local criticism that the style was too English.[19] Nevertheless, it was regarded during the 1870s as the most splendid edifice in Glasgow, legislation having been passed speedily in 1872 to incorporate the grounds into the city boundaries. The university enhanced an area situated between the exclusive Park district and the burgeoning suburb of Hillhead, altogether more appropriate terrain for educating the aspiring doctors, lawyers and clergymen of Glasgow. Quite clearly, its transfer to the West End had symbolic as well as practical implications. Although the city centre remained a vitally important sphere of architectural activity, Glasgow style was being reflected over a much wider area. Transport developments helped

64. Glasgow University, circa 1890.
The new University sometime after the spire was added in 1887. The estate of Gilmorehill was the location for Sir George Gilbert Scott's quasi-Gothic edifice, set in verdant surroundings beside the River Kelvin. This venerable institution, dating from 1451, became a potent symbol of 'Greater Glasgow' expansion when it moved from its central location to the suburbs in 1870. (*Glasgow University Archives and Business Records Centre.*)

considerably in shaping the new consciousness. With expanding rail and tramways networks, the outlying districts were now within easy reach. Accordingly, the acquisition of the Police Burghs and other prestigious districts was perceived as doing more than adding lucrative rates revenue; they would help forcefully in boosting the city's public relations profile.

Such imposing structures as the university were intended deliberately to emphasise Glasgow's prominence among urban communities. However, in May 1888 the urge to display the city took a qualitatively different direction when the Glasgow International Exhibition of Industry, Science and Art was formally opened by the Prince and Princess of Wales. Held in Kelvingrove Park, the event attracted almost 5.75 million visitors by the time it closed in November. The city was following the fashion inaugurated in 1851 with London's Great Exhibition in Hyde Park. As the Glasgow authorities were well aware, host cities for exhibitions considerably raised their standing at home and abroad. During the 1880s the attractions of Manchester and Edinburgh had been promoted in this way, which provoked the immediate riposte that, 'Manchester and Edinburgh may *try* it, but Glasgow can *do* it'.[20] In this purposeful spirit, architect James Sellars transformed the Kelvingrove landscape into an Arabian Nights fantasy, the main exhibition building reminiscent of the splendid Moorish edifices in southern Spanish cities like Granada. This was not misplaced theatricality; the exotic and (some would say) ostentatious dimension to Glasgow's famous exhibitions from 1888 had a practical rationale. They were an attempt to create an entirely different image from that of the damp, smoky and slum-ridden inner-city. That the 1888 Exhibition was intended to raise funds for a more commodious municipal Art Gallery and Museum further emphasised the serious purpose underlying the extravaganza.

As has been explained, £257,000 was eventually spent on the Art Gallery, which opened in 1901 as the centrepiece of yet another International Exhibition in Kelvingrove Park. It was an event that gave tangible expression to hopes for the new century, especially in relation to the city's position in Europe and the wider world. By this time Glasgow had become the sixth most populous city in Europe, exceeded only by London, Paris, Berlin, Vienna and St Petersburg.[21] In quantifying Glasgow's status, one contemporary historian went even further with his effusive description of 'the first municipality in the world and the second city of the British empire'.[22] Indeed, the 1901 Exhibition aimed to provide a 'full illustration' of the Empire as part of its ambitious remit, placing Glasgow achievement firmly in the context of imperial expansion.[23] Moreover, the need to demonstrate the bonds of Empire was especially significant because the Exhibition occurred in the midst of the South African War. Glasgow was thus the focus of a patriotic spectacle, which placed positive emphasis on the 'civilising' influences of imperial trade and culture. Canada had a particularly imposing pavilion, which not only displayed an eclectic array of indigenous goods but projected the appeal of the Dominion to prospective emigrants, specifically those of 'British blood'.[24] Canadian links with the city were strong, to the extent that in 1867 the first premier of the newly-constituted Dominion had been a Glasgow-born migrant, Sir John A. Macdonald. On the other hand, the diversity of the imperial connection was illustrated at the 1901 Exhibition by a suitably exotic (if stereotypical) presence from the Indian sub-continent, which included hugely popular entertainment from a colourful corps of snake charmers.

By 1901 the goal of 'Greater Glasgow' had been triumphantly realised, to the extent that 2,377 hectares were added to the city in 1891, almost doubling its size. The propaganda onslaught from the 1860s had impressed Glasgow's cosmopolitan credentials, with a host of international commentators now intrigued by the city's commercial and civic success. Six Police Burghs consented to join with Glasgow in 1891 – Crosshill, Govanhill, Hillhead,

65. International Exhibition, 1901.
Kelvingrove Park was the setting for Glasgow's three international exhibitions between 1888 and 1911, and this photograph conveys the sense of theatricality associated with the 1901 extravaganza. The city's Venetian pretensions are on display with gondolas on the River Kelvin. In the background architect James Miller's Industrial Hall reflects something of the domed splendour of St Mark's Basilica in Venice, although his influences were deliberately eclectic, combining Hispanic with oriental. (*T. and R. Annan & Sons Ltd.*)

Maryhill and the two Pollokshields – all appeased with guarantees of generous rating concessions for five years. Strathbungo, incidentally, was also incorporated, along with working-class communities like Balornock, Possilpark and Springburn. However, it was the middle-class suburbs that were the star prize, especially the West End district of Kelvinside, which had never opted for Police Burgh status. The wealthy inhabitants were anxious to safeguard their health and properties, and so welcomed the Corporation's police protection and the extension of a much-needed sewerage system. The territorial additions meant that population density eased considerably, from eighty-four persons per acre in 1881 to forty-eight in 1891. Of course, in comparative terms Glasgow was still overcrowded and by 1911, just before further boundary extension, density had increased to sixty persons per acre. The Cowcaddens municipal ward, to the north-west of the city, was by far the most congested area, with 223 persons to the

66. Dobbie's Loan, Cowcaddens, 1910. As city improvement clearance gradually eased congestion in central districts, newer slums had emerged by the twentieth century. This photograph shows conditions in a back court at Dobbie's Loan, Cowcaddens. Comparison with the closes and wynds of the 1860s shows that, for some Glasgow residents, very little had altered. (*By courtesy of the Mitchell Library, Glasgow City Libraries and Archives.*)

acre.[25] Ironically, while the overall density of the old city was declining, the overcrowding problem had shifted elsewhere.

Art, Education and Recreation

In 1896 the art critic P. Macgregor Chalmers investigated Glasgow's modern buildings and came to the conclusion that 'there is too much architect in evidence and too little art'.[26] The city was in want of refinement, as the penchant for monumentalism had engulfed expression in design. He suggested that what was needed was an art institution worthy of the claims being made for 'Greater Glasgow', which could train 'craftsmen' to be creative yet functional. Chalmers was doubtless aware that a new School of Art was about to be constructed, according to the design submitted by a young architect and former student, Charles Rennie Mackintosh. The plans took fourteen years to complete, but in the interim the School became famous under the energetic direction of its head master, Francis Newbery. His legacy was more than simply an emphasis on degree results; Newbery nurtured creative individuality. Notably, he encouraged the recruitment of women, both as staff and students. The Art School allowed for a broad approach to design, with technical studios affording a range of opportunities for experimentation in areas like stained glass, metal working and pottery.[27]

67. Charles Rennie Mackintosh, 1893. The epitome of Glasgow style, Mackintosh projects a striking profile for the camera of James Craig Annan. Aged only twenty-five, Mackintosh was at that time employed by the architectural firm of Honeyman and Keppie. (*T. and R. Annan & Sons Ltd.*)

68. Margaret Macdonald, 1900. An Annan photograph of Margaret Macdonald, around the time of her marriage to Charles Rennie Mackintosh in 1900. The sinuous, elongated style of decorative art, inextricably associated with the couple, is displayed in the cabinet behind the sitter. (*T. and R. Annan & Sons Ltd.*)

During the 1890s the Macdonald sisters, Frances and Margaret, were among the first to transpose their distinctive graphic work directly on to artefacts. Margaret Macdonald married Mackintosh in 1900, cementing a relationship that had a profound impact on perceptions of the celebrated 'Glasgow Style'. The extenuated contours that became the hallmark of Mackintosh design were Macdonald-inspired, and much work subsequently labelled 'Mackintosh' was collaborative.

The intensive promotion of Mackintosh from the 1970s as an icon of Glasgow innovation has tended to overwhelm the contribution of his contemporaries to the city's prolific creative output. Indeed, the seeds were sown before his time. The long-standing enthusiasm for art collection by the commercial and industrial elites had already helped to stimulate ideas.

Alexander Reid was a prominent Glasgow art dealer, whose influence was formative in shaping the collecting proclivities of wealthy businessmen like William Burrell junior. A sojourn in Paris in 1887 had brought Reid into contact with the French impressionists, and on his return to Glasgow he exhibited the work of an eclectic range of overseas talent. However, he also found time to support the work of local painters, especially the group that emerged from the 1880s known as the 'Glasgow Boys'. Many previously had studied in France, including such luminaries as James Guthrie, John Lavery and Alexander Roche. Significantly, a number of the 'Boys' turned their attention to decorative art, inspired by the ideas of the Edinburgh-based social theorist, Patrick Geddes.[28] Promoting a visionary view of urban regeneration, Geddes aimed to enhance the quality of life through creative endeavour. In this context, art was seen as a vital expression of the civic community, non-exclusive and embracing technical progress. The connection with ideas prevalent in Newbery's Art School is clearly apparent and, closely connected with that, the Mackintosh blend of architecture with decorative design.

The custom-built School of Art represented more than just a sense of confidence in the city's creative potential; it was also indicative of rapidly improving educational opportunities. The university's relocation to Gilmorehill had allowed for a considerable expansion in higher education, with increased student numbers and a greater choice of subjects. During the 1892–3 session 131 women matriculated, a wholly new development. As for children, much had changed since the Education (Scotland) Act was passed in 1872. The legislation brought the fragmented nature of elementary provision under the control of elected school boards, although the city's Catholic schools remained outside the system until 1918, determined not to lose their religious identity. There were seventy-five schools constructed in Glasgow between 1874 and 1916, a third during the 1870s, when pressure for accommodation was greatest. Board representatives had a daunting task trying to ensure the smooth operation of the system. Tracking down truant children remained a perennial problem, especially in times of economic recession when juvenile employment could support family income. In a bid to provide an incentive for keeping youngsters at school, there was a vigorous campaign in Glasgow during the 1880s for abolishing the small fee that parents required to pay. Free elementary education was eventually achieved in 1890, and in 1901 the school-leaving age was raised by the government from thirteen to fourteen.

The welfare of the young had been a major priority of education, public health and philanthropic agencies in Glasgow. James Burn Russell consciously used children as a polemical device in his impassioned rhetoric about the need to create a purer environment.[29] He was determined to extend the number of Glasgow's public parks, believing that ill-health and anti-social behaviour inevitably resulted from confining children too

69. Garrioch Street School, 1916.
Garrioch Street School, showing scholars at play-time. Built for Maryhill School Board in 1905, this red sandstone building was one of many new educational establishments erected in the city following the 1872 Education Act. Maryhill merged with Glasgow School Board in 1911. (*By courtesy of the Mitchell Library, Glasgow City Libraries and Archives.*)

closely. While his solution was regarded in some quarters as too meagre a remedy for the city's blighting problems, during the 1890s Russell success-fully campaigned for the construction of open spaces in working-class districts like Cowcaddens and Ruchill. Reflecting growing emphasis on health and constructive activity, youthful energies were channelled into organisations like the Boys' Brigade. Founded by William Smith in Glasgow in 1883, the BB derived much inspiration from the Volunteer Force, the part-time adult military movement and forerunner to the Territorial Army. There was a powerful evangelical impulse behind Smith's organisation, which endeavoured to win adherents by using the appeal of sport and robust exercise. Sunday Schools similarly livened their activities to attract youngsters. J. J. Bell evoked the sensuous pleasures of the Sunday School soirée in his hugely popular tales of Glaswegian child-life, *Wee Macgreegor*, first published in 1902. In one episode the eponymous hero (Macgregor Robinson) and his young companions were treated to refreshments, a conjurer, a magic lantern show and, to their great relief, heard only the briefest of uplifting moral addresses from the minister.

Despite the changing focus of church-based activities, the evangelical mission to eradicate corruption from the heart of Glasgow remained relentless. While the expanding number of public parks physically allowed for breathing space, additionally they were intended to provide a moral alternative to dram-shops, dancing saloons and music halls. The public landscape was deemed an important area of evangelical control, which was why much energy was projected into removing the Fair from its prime site on Glasgow Green during the 1860s. Leading the campaign was the aptly-named 'Repressive Committee' of the Glasgow Magdalene Institution, a body that had been inaugurated to rescue the city's prostitutes and redirect them into a more wholesome life-style. Following on-the-spot investigation of the festivities during one July, the Committee evoked a lurid image of the Fair as 'a prolific source of evil' and 'just one huge brothel'.[30] The civic authority was persuaded to act, and from 1871 show-folk were shifted to a less central site at Vinegar Hill in Camlachie. Another device used to regulate the behaviour of Glaswegians was Sabbatarianism, not least to ensure that on Mondays they were fit for work. For instance, Sunday music and sporting activity were banned in the municipal parks, to reinforce the special nature of the Sabbath as a day for calmness and contemplation. Such prohibition endured well into the twentieth century. Indeed, it was not until the 1950s that the harmless and respectable pursuit of Sunday bowling was permitted, in face of continuing Sabbatarian resistance.

70. Children's soirée, Milton Church, 1900s.
Children waiting for admission to a Saturday soirée at Milton Church, in the early 1900s. Such entertainment was hugely popular in an era when religious institutions directed much of the leisure-time activity for young Glaswegians. (*By courtesy of the Mitchell Library, Glasgow City Libraries and Archives.*)

There was an obvious contradiction between the perpetuation of social control and the public relations emphasis on the progressive city, which took stylistic inspiration from the great urban centres of Europe. Daniel Macaulay Stevenson was caught in the conundrum during 1898, when he faced fierce Sabbatarian objections to plans for opening municipal museums on Sundays. Stevenson's cause was successful, but he was vocally accused of pushing Glaswegians down the rocky road to secularism, and worse. Related to this, a sustained campaign to fend off corrosive cultural influences was stimulated by the meteoric rise of the cinema during the 1900s and the growing popularity of Italian-run cafés and ice-cream parlours. The latter establishments were considered dangerous not just because of the foreign dimension; they often did not conform to Sunday trading strictures and allegedly encouraged gambling and unlicensed drinking.[31] In the columns of *Forward* Thomas Johnston was vitriolic about what he claimed to be the intrusive influence of 'the social purity humbugs'. He decried attempts to regulate 'when and how the workers of Glasgow will eat ice-cream, hot peas, and fish suppers, drink lemonade and enter picture shows'.[32] In his withering use of language against the often patronising pronouncements of purity crusaders, Johnston struck a chord with working-class opinion that electorally stood the ILP in good stead.

The strength of feeling about the cinema was evidence of how far the medium had captured the Glaswegian imagination. That it was also profitable business ensured that it retained a high profile. George Green was one entrepreneur who immediately recognised a promising market opportunity in 1896, when films began to be shown commercially in the United Kingdom. Originally a circus proprietor from Lancashire, Green developed his East End showground to accommodate a cinema for 500 people. Like many of the early pioneers, he made short films of local interest, to add to the allure of the entertainment. Green built on this success, eventually establishing a chain of 'Picturedromes' by 1911.[33] However, he was by no means the city's only impresario, with the accolade of Glasgow's 'Barnum' going to another Englishman, Edward Bostock. Descended from a long line of travelling menagerie proprietors, Bostock had first brought his animals to Glasgow during the 1870s. He was dismayed but not deterred by the rowdy behaviour of the audience and eventually settled in the city. Bostock hit a rich commercial seam in 1894 when he opened a zoo in Cowcaddens, and soon diversified into circus and theatre ownership. Appreciating the Glasgow passion for the exotic he offered spectacular entertainment, often featuring his lion-tamer brother, Frank. In his memoirs Bostock regretted that he had not made more of the cinema boom, but noted how closely the success of moving pictures was tied in with the popularity of shows and circuses during the early days.[34] This connection was one reason why the cinema aroused the disdain of the purity lobby, who saw it as an extension of tainted fairground culture.

Organised sport was more acceptable 'rational recreation', although even then the fondness of some Glaswegians for betting could cloud the healthy image. There was increased demand for sport because of rising living standards, which provided more disposable income and a reduction in working hours. By the late nineteenth century there was an explosion of interest in a range of activities, from bowls and billiards through to cycling, tennis and golf, the last three pursued by women as well as men. Rugby and association football were strictly all-male preserves, the latter stirring powerful emotions as competition under the Scottish Football League intensified from 1890. Queen's Park had been formed as the first 'Glasgow' club in 1867, although technically it was a product of the South Side suburbs beyond the city boundaries. Rangers emerged in 1872 and Celtic in 1888, the latter having an important charitable function, raising money for the Catholic poor of the East End.[35] However, with the creation of the Scottish Football Association (SFA) and the introduction of professionalism in 1893 both clubs adopted a ruthlessly businesslike approach to their development. They worked in tandem to ensure that they could get the best and most

71. Football, Glasgow Green, circa 1910.
Football on Glasgow Green during a hazy, damp day. The sport had consolidated its phenomenal popularity by this time, at both amateur and professional levels. While scarcely matching the scale of Hampden Park, Glasgow's premier football stadium from 1903, there is nevertheless serious spectator interest in the games being played. (*Glasgow Museums: The People's Palace.*)

lucrative fixtures. As a large percentage of their revenues came from playing each other, it came to be realised that there was commercial potential in exploiting religious and ethnic differences, with Rangers representing an assertive 'true-blue' brand of Scottish Protestantism and Celtic the Catholic Irish. The bitter sectarianism that scarred the 'Old Firm' image was much more a phenomenon of the 1920s and 1930s, but the roots were there in the 1890s, with the desire of the respective managements to make money.

Another indicator of increased leisure-time was the growth in popularity of excursions and holidays outside Glasgow. J. J. Bell again provided useful commentary on the 1870s and 1880s, when the rule was 'to make holiday within a radius of fifty miles of the city, and mainly on the shores of the Firth of Clyde'.[36] He pointed out that the term 'seaside' was rarely used by Glaswegians, who invariably spoke of going to 'the coast'. The expansion of Scotland's passenger rail and shipping network from the mid-nineteenth century did much to aid travel, and temperance and public health campaigners were especially keen that city dwellers should imbibe the fresher air of coastal resorts. Indeed, temperance excursions, organised by influential groups like the Band of Hope and the Abstainers' Union, could attract parties as large as 1,000 people, primarily from the better-off working classes. Steamer trips had become booming business by the 1900s, whether for short excursions or lengthier holidays, the vessels departing from the Broomielaw and other centrally-located quays. James Hamilton Muir wrote lyrically in 1901 of Glasgow's flourishing 'suburbs by the sea'; resorts such as Dunoon, Largs and Rothesay.[37] Using familiar imagery, he contrasted the profane and polluted city with the tranquillity of the coastal environment. Invigorating, calming and restful, such breaks were intended to restore much-needed energy among the working population and thus keep Glasgow's commerce and industry buoyant.

Glasgow at War

The First World War began militarily on 3 August 1914, with the German invasion of Belgium and northern France. The next day King George V formally declared that Great Britain and the Empire were at war. Throughout the realm thousands immediately volunteered for service, in the widely held belief that the conflict would be short-lived. Glasgow became established as a key recruiting area. Indeed, by the end of 1918 over 200,000 men out of the million-strong population had served in the armed forces. Most of the early Glasgow battalions were attached to the Highland Light Infantry, the largest being the 15th HLI or Tramways Battalion. James Dalrymple, the Corporation's Tramways Manager, took up the recruitment drive with such zeal that he subsequently was described as 'the greatest recruiting agent the war ever produced'.[38] Dalrymple embarked on a whirlwind campaign to rally men to the cause, using decorated tramcars, street parades, open-air

72. The 'Coasting Season', 1880s. A representation of Glasgow's 'Coasting Season', drawn by cartoonist 'Twym' for *Quiz* magazine. Summer excursions to the Firth of Clyde had become booming business by the end of the nineteenth century, as 'Twym' (A. S. Boyd) cheerfully conveys. (*By courtesy of the Mitchell Library, Glasgow City Libraries and Archives.*)

cinema shows and other ostentatious forms of advertising. The symbolism of Glasgow's tramways was crucially important; the city was acknowledged to have one of the best public transport systems in the world, the embodiment of civic efficiency. By using the same energy that built up this formidable peace-time reputation, Dalrymple was deliberately demonstrating Glasgow's commitment to excel in the war effort. Significantly, almost 4,000 men from his department eventually served as combatants.

Historian J. M. Winter has written generally about the social experience of the war in Britain, noting that the recruitment drive tapped powerful sentiments of loyalty felt by men to their home communities.[39] Locally raised battalions were an effective way of encouraging recruits to join-up collectively, in the knowledge that they would not be separated from their friends or work colleagues. Part of the attraction of the Tramways Battalion was the shared sense of camaraderie and a distinctively Glaswegian commitment to the war. From this perspective, the Corporation was important for projecting local identity and boosting morale, with the Lord Provost prominent as the wartime figurehead for the city. This was initially awkward for Glasgow, as from 1911 the incumbent was Daniel Macaulay Stevenson, who personally had close German connections. However, Stevenson loyally played his part in promoting recruitment until he retired in November 1914. His successor was the wealthy shipowner and staunch Unionist, Thomas Dunlop, who was altogether more ebullient about encouraging the war effort. Revealingly, he pitched the benefits of enlistment to potential volunteers as 'for their own credit, for the good name of our city, and the honour and safety of the Empire'.[40] The conjunction of city and Empire was a recurring theme of war rhetoric in Glasgow, patriotism representing both the common good and the greater good of global British interests.

Universal conscription was not introduced until May 1916, a development that marked a change in attitudes to the war in Glasgow, with considerable public unease about the compulsory military element. Prior to this time the enthusiasm of the recruitment drive had been a useful device for rallying popular support. Even Wee Macgreegor, now aged nineteen and employed respectably in the grocery trade, was depicted by his creator J. J. Bell as loyally enlisting in the 9th Battalion of the HLI. The kilted 'Glasgow Highlanders' (as they were known) had romantic appeal for Macgreegor, although he worried that he might be 'ower wee' to be accepted.[41] Needless to say, he made the grade, was sent to Flanders and though wounded, he survived. That the city's fighting forces could be small was collectively demonstrated by the 18th Battalion of the HLI, a 'bantam' unit, below regulation height but still fit for service. Portrayed as fearless, pugnacious and predominantly working-class, the battalion was almost wiped out at the Somme in 1916 and Passchendaele in 1917. Yet on the whole Glasgow's military volunteers tended to come from the more skilled occupations; for instance, the men of the tramways service, who had been employed by the Corporation as fine physical specimens, able to withstand the rigorous routine at the helm of the tramcars. War service was presented to recruits as a healthy and character-forming experience, although as the conflict became prolonged and the casualty list increased, such sentiments eroded.

Of course, the war dramatically altered everyday life for those Glaswegians who remained at home. One of the earliest effects of munitions production in the city was to create a housing crisis, as the influx of extra workers intensified demand for accommodation. Private landlords felt free to charge increased rents because housing was at a premium, thus creating considerable friction in communities near to the centres of production,

notably Govan and Partick. This was the motivating impulse behind the vigorous campaign of the Glasgow Women's Housing Association for freezing rents and instituting fair rents courts. The women adopted such pungent slogans as 'Fight the Huns at Home' to convey the unpatriotic spirit of rapacious landlords, and resistance to rents' increases began to be co-ordinated from the spring of 1915. Threats of non-payment provoked landlords to initiate ejectment proceedings, which only added to their unscrupulous image. The conflict was exploited to the full by able propagandists such as Patrick Dollan, a journalist for *Forward* and a prominent Labour town councillor. The women's militancy was used to reflect the extraordinary circumstances of war, as they defended hearth and home while the men were on active service. Part of their tactics involved setting up 'Aye Ready' brigades to warn of impending attempts at ejectment, and the emissaries of landlords could be scornfully and sometimes violently dealt with when they arrived to serve warrants.

The powerful impact of the campaign fostered widespread public support. The landlords were unable to extricate themselves from accusations of war-profiteering, and their discomfiture was given maximum publicity by strike leaders. Lloyd George, as Minister of Munitions, was placed in a delicate position over the events in Glasgow, well aware of the sympathy for the women's action. He was also under considerable pressure to maintain the momentum of war production, and could not allow the discontent to detract from his single-minded mission to step up munitions output. This related not only to the Clydeside area but other munitions centres such as north-east England and Belfast. Emulative action over rents could well have a drastic nationwide impact, with the potential to provoke industrial unrest and seriously undermine the war effort. Moreover, the issue was casting the government in a particularly bad light over its inaction to confront profiteering allegations. In order to nip the crisis firmly in the bud, the 1915 Rent and Mortgage Restrictions Act was passed, removing the power of landlords to make arbitrary charges and forcing them to restore rents to pre-war levels. This was a crucially important development for Glasgow, as it fatally undermined the status of private landlords and set the government thinking about ways of stimulating municipal housing as part of its post-war reconstruction programme.

The vociferous complaints over high rents was only one aspect of public concern about the spiralling cost of living, especially for necessities such as fuel and food. While 'business as usual' may have been the slogan devised by traders anxious to preserve public confidence, there was suspicion that not a few were taking unfair advantage of manifestly unusual circumstances to charge exorbitant prices. Over the winter of 1915 and 1916 an acute coal shortage elicited the comment from one Glasgow newspaper that 'keeping the home fires burning' was no easy task, given that scarce supplies had been appropriated for munitions production.[42] Glaswegians were warned to be on their guard against exploitative coal merchants, who were charging more than twice the usual rate. Milk, sugar and potatoes were other scarce commodities, and 'lively scenes' were reported by the city's press as wrathful women made their feelings known in well-publicised protests to the City Chambers. Their banners echoed the rent strikes with slogans such as 'Who pinches baby's milk? The Home Huns!', and delegations, organised by groups like the Women's Labour League, demanded 'equality of sacrifice'.[43] The clear implication was that class criteria were operating in the distribution of foodstuffs.

In response, Lloyd George's Coalition government tackled the vexed question of food control more thoroughly than its predecessor, fixing prices and introducing rationing during 1917 for commodities such as tea and butter. An irony striking many Glaswegians at the time was that the control of alcohol had been a much earlier national priority. In 1915 the Central Control Board (Liquor Traffic) was created as the formidable-sounding guardian of abstinence in areas of strategic importance, such as the west of Scotland. Temperance was considered to be a national duty during the war, and in May 1915, during a blistering attack on the drink menace, Lloyd George accused Clyde workers of succumbing all too easily to temptation. Soon afterwards a range of regulations was introduced to restrict the availability of alcohol, with drastically curtailed opening hours for public houses and a reduction of the proof levels for spirits. Some critics felt that these measures did not go far enough. In 1916 Corporation councillors were among the advocates of a total wartime ban on alcohol, wounded that their city should have acquired such a reputation for inebriation. Sir Joseph P. Maclay, a wealthy Glasgow shipowner who became Controller of Shipping in the Coalition government, was a long-standing temperance luminary who vocally decried the corrosive qualities of drink at a time when maximum efficiency was called for. Yet despite such sustained pressure for blanket prohibition, it was felt to be an option that ultimately was too alienating and demoralising.

Nevertheless, the Liquor Control Board did retain considerable powers. It turned its vigilance to the behaviour of Glasgow day trippers in coastal resorts such as Dunoon and Rothesay, and restrictions were imposed on the availability of drink in these areas during the summer of 1916. This was more to impress the need for sobriety, as opportunities for practical indulgence were fast receding. Travel to and from Glasgow was already subject to the exigencies of war, with much-curtailed rail and steamer services. Moreover, the massive munitions drive at the height of the Somme offensive had delayed the traditional July holidays for workers in key areas. The government eventually granted what it called a 'rest period' in August and September, anxious to prevent any sense of holiday frivolity from holding up production. Such restrictions meant that workers tended to remain in the city and sought local entertainment for relaxation. During the Fair holiday of 1917 the *Glasgow Herald* reported that the cinemas and music halls were the most popular recreational outlets.[44] New Year had been spent in similar vein, with pointed references to the unusually abstemious behaviour of citizens. However, the sombre mood began to lift by 1918 and energies were channelled into some novel activities. Edward Bostock generated brisk business when he opened a roller-skating rink in his zoo premises, which had hitherto been used for military storage purposes. The patrons were predominantly munitions workers, described by him as robust skaters and much given to 'horseplay'.

By October 1918 women constituted 56 per cent of the 50,200 workers employed in Clydeside munitions production. A back-handed compliment to their efforts was given in 1924, when it was authoritatively stated:

> In quantity of output they were unrestrained by Trade Union habit and usage, and being temporary workers, they were not influenced by the subconscious harbouring of energy, which is the natural protective attitude of the male worker, with a life-time of industrial work before him.[45]

For the duration of the war in Glasgow the vital role of women was proclaimed as a patriotic virtue, their involvement in supposedly uncharacteristic 'mechanical work' demonstrating commitment during profoundly disjointed times. Similarly, while the recruitment of women in the previously all-male Tramways Department was essential for keeping public transport functioning, it also represented shrewd Dalrymplian advertising for the war effort. By February 1916 there were 1,180 tram conductresses in Glasgow, although only twenty-five women tram-drivers; like the munitions workers, their jobs were strictly temporary.[46] Nevertheless, the propaganda focus on female capability proved to be a double-edged weapon, because in the long term it raised expectations. It contributed to the pervasive notion that the war had blurred definitions of separate social spheres, and that with the onset of peace there would be greater scope for personal mobility, whether in education, career or politics. Government promises of a more egalitarian society fuelled such aspirations, as leaders like Lloyd George attempted to counter war-weariness during the last phase of the conflict.

The euphoria that greeted the Armistice around lunch-time on 11 November 1918 was described by a *Glasgow Herald* reporter, when the city centre became thronged with people:

> Shop girls, office girls, munitions girls, many having the flags of the Allies tastefully draped as head-dresses, paraded in groups; businessmen, tradesmen, apprentice hands, soldiers, women and children intermingled, jostled, shook hands, exchanged greeting with fellow-citizens.[47]

Whatever their concerns about the future, the government remained committed to radical post-war reconstruction, especially in health and housing. While there were genuine welfarist sentiments within the War Cabinet, there was also fear of social dislocation, given the daunting task of dismantling the massive war machine. Glasgow loomed large in shaping strategy, because it was a key munitions area with a legacy of conflict, especially over housing. As one official report put it in 1917, with reference to an identified shortage of 100,000 workers' homes in Scotland: 'The industrial unrest attributable to this cause . . . can only be allayed by the Government taking steps to grapple with a problem which appears to have grown too great for private enterprise now to meet'.[48] This meant providing aid in the form of

74. Woman munitions worker, 1916.
A female munitions worker in Alexander Stephen's shipyard at Linthouse, near Govan. Such images conveyed
the extraordinary conditions of war, as women entered the all-male bastions of heavy industry in Glasgow.
(*Glasgow University Archives and Business Records Centre.*)

subsidies to local authorities and ensuring that land for building houses
was available on reasonable terms. The impact of subsequent enabling
legislation profoundly altered the physical fabric of Glasgow, as state and
municipal agencies combined to create one of western Europe's largest
public housing sectors.

However, if the state stepped in to support post-war health and housing
initiatives in Glasgow, a basis for action had already been established at the
local level. The city improvement programme may have had controversial
origins in 1866 and fluctuating fortunes thereafter, but redevelopment left
an indelible mark on shaping the inner city and beyond. It also visibly
added to the self-promoted image of the 'model municipality', which
formed part of the sustained campaign to extend the boundaries from the
1860s. The climate of pre-war confidence seemed set to continue after the
Armistice, but as will be seen, the rapidly deteriorating economic climate
from the 1920s meant that many ambitious reconstruction promises could
not be implemented. Despite the lessons of the war, the social problems of

the city seemed still to be multiplying, with unemployment generating wholly new grievances.

Notes

1. Charles Withers, 'The demographic history of the city, 1831–1911', in W. Hamish Fraser and Irene Maver (eds), *Glasgow, Volume II: 1830–1912* (Manchester University Press: Manchester, 1996), p. 142.
2. John Wheatley, *Eight-Pound Cottages for Glasgow Citizens* (Glasgow Labour Party: Glasgow, 1913), p. 10.
3. Quoted in A. K. Chalmers (ed.), *Public Health Administration in Glasgow* (James Maclehose: Glasgow, 1905), p. 30.
4. As suggested by the *Glasgow Examiner*, 10 May 1845.
5. Brian Edwards, 'Glasgow improvements, 1866–1901', in Peter Reed (ed.), *Glasgow: the Forming of the City* (Edinburgh University Press: Edinburgh, 1993), p. 84.
6. Quoted in the *Glasgow Herald*, 6 November 1866.
7. Glasgow City Archives DTC 14.2.2, 'Notes of personal observations and inquiries in June, 1866, on the city improvements of Paris, &c', in Glasgow Town Council, *Municipal Reports, 1846–1866*, p. 9.
8. Frank Walker, 'National Romanticism and the architecture of the city', in George Gordon (ed.), *Perspectives of the Scottish City* (Aberdeen University Press: Aberdeen, 1985), p. 151.
9. Leonardo Benevolo, *The European City* (Blackwell: Oxford, 1993), pp. 179–80.
10. Andor Gomme and David Walker, *Architecture of Glasgow* (Lund Humphries: London, 1987), p. 45.
11. Sir James Bell and James Paton, *Glasgow, Its Municipal Organisation and Administration* (James Maclehose: Glasgow, 1896), p. 224.
12. James B. Russell, *Life In One Room: or, Some Serious Considerations for the Citizens of Glasgow* (James Maclehose: Glasgow, 1888), p. 14.
13. William Smart, *The Housing Problem and the Municipality* (N. Adshead: Glasgow, 1902), p. 9.
14. Quoted in the *Glasgow Herald*, 9 October 1902.
15. Wheatley, *Eight-Pound Cottages*, p. 5.
16. J. J. Bell, *I Remember* (Porpoise Press: Edinburgh, 1932), p. 14.
17. *The Bailie* (publisher), *Jeems Kaye: His Adventures and Opinions*, third series, (Glasgow, c.1890), p. 78. The author, Archibald Macmillan, remained uncredited in the *Jeems* volumes.
18. John R. Kellett, *Railways and Victorian Cities* (Routledge and Kegan Paul: London, 1979), pp. 217–18.
19. Miles Glendinning, Ranald Macinnes and Aonghus Mackechnie, *A History of Scottish Architecture: from the Renaissance to the Present Day* (Edinburgh University Press: Edinburgh, 1996), pp. 302–3.
20. Perilla Kinchin and Juliet Kinchin, *Glasgow's Great Exhibitions* (White Cockade: Wendlebury, 1998), p. 17.
21. C. A. Oakley, *The Second City* (Blackie: Glasgow, 1946), p. 149.
22. See the preface to John K. McDowell, *The People's History of Glasgow* (Hay Nisbet: Glasgow, 1899), unpaginated.
23. John M. MacKenzie, '"The Second City of the Empire": Glasgow – imperial municipality', in Felix Driver and David Gilbert (eds), *Imperial Cities* (Manchester University Press: Manchester, 1999), p. 228.

24. *The Exhibition Illustrated*, 27 July 1901.

25. Glasgow Corporation, *Report of the Medical Officer of Health of the City of Glasgow, 1911* (Robert Anderson: Glasgow, 1912), appendix, p. iii.

26. P. Macgregor Chalmers, *Art in Our City: Glasgow 1896* (Chalmers: Glasgow, 1897), p. 22.

27. Daniel Robbins, 'Glasgow School of Art and the Glasgow style', in Wendy Kaplan (ed.), *Charles Rennie Mackintosh* (Glasgow Museums: Glasgow, 1996), p. 71.

28. Duncan Macmillan, *Scottish Art, 1460–1990* (Mainstream: Edinburgh, 1990), pp. 272–6.

29. Irene Maver, 'Children and the quest for purity in the nineteenth-century Scottish city', in *Paedagogica Historica* 33 (1997), pp. 818–23.

30. Linda Mahood, *The Magdalenes: Prostitution in the Nineteenth Century* (Routledge: London, 1990), pp. 130–4.

31. Callum G. Brown, 'Popular culture and the continuing struggle for rational recreation', in T. M. Devine and R. J. Finlay (eds), *Scotland in the Twentieth Century* (Edinburgh University Press: Edinburgh, 1996), pp. 219–20.

32. *Forward*, 15 March 1913.

33. Bruce Peter, *100 Years of Glasgow's Amazing Cinemas* (Polygon: Edinburgh, 1996), p. 7.

34. E. H. Bostock, *Menageries, Circuses and Theatres* (Chapman and Hall: London, 1927), p. 198.

35. Bill Murray, *The Old Firm: Sectarianism, Sport and Society in Scotland* (John Donald: Edinburgh, 1984), pp. 18–19.

36. Bell, *I Remember*, p. 56.

37. James Hamilton Muir, *Glasgow in 1901* (William Hodge: Glasgow, 1901), pp. 214–29.

38. Oakley, *The Second City*, p. 277.

39. J. M. Winter, *The Great War and the British People* (Macmillan: London, 1985), p. 30.

40. Quoted in the *Glasgow Herald*, 25 January 1916.

41. J. J. Bell, *Wee Macgreegor Enlists* (Hodder and Stoughton: London, 1915), p. 18.

42. *The Bulletin*, 14 March 1916.

43. *Glasgow Herald*, 1 December 1916.

44. Ibid. 17 July 1917.

45. W. R. Scott and J. Cunnison, *The Industries of the Clyde Valley during the War* (Clarendon Press: Oxford, 1924), p. 100.

46. *Glasgow Herald*, 29 February 1916.

47. Ibid. 12 November 1918.

48. British Parliamentary Papers, *Commission of Enquiry into Industrial Unrest: No. 8 Division, Scotland*, 1917, Cd. 8661, p. 4.

Glasgow Since 1918

CHAPTER NINE

Industrial Decline and Economic Reorientation

This chapter charts the fluctuations in Glasgow's economic fortunes from 1918, focusing in particular on local responses to industrial decline in the city. Managing the economy came to be a preoccupation in the wake of the war, not just within government circles, but among the beleaguered business community. For all the intensity of wartime production, Glasgow experienced a recession during the early 1920s, when global demand for shipping drastically diminished. Unemployment levels rose, and as the decade progressed there was a mounting sense of insecurity in the city. By the 1930s the world depression had struck Glasgow forcefully, leaving a searing impact on the industrial workforce. While the prospect of the Second World War helped to rekindle the economy through armaments' production, the long-term problems were not resolved and gave corrosive continuity to the city's industrial profile. Despite sustained efforts to introduce new industries and bolster shipbuilding via substantial state subsidies, the scale of Glasgow's structural defects proved impossible to overcome. From the 1970s the emphasis shifted decisively away from the old manufacturing base. The city was channelled towards an overwhelmingly service-based economy, where culture and tourism were promoted assiduously as key components of the post-industrial image.

The Inter-War Economy

What prompted the recession of the early 1920s, and why did deterioration continue through to the 1930s, to generate unprecedented levels of unemployment in Glasgow? Crucially, the dislocation of war had sharply reorientated the global economy, although the effects took time to become apparent. While Glasgow's war machine inevitably slowed down after the Armistice, this did not mean an overnight reversion to peace conditions. Military demobilisation was deliberately phased to ensure that the labour market was not skewed too drastically. Substantial employers, like Beardmore's, were also prepared to adapt their output to changing times. Indeed, technical advances made during the war, notably in aircraft production, seemed to offer abundant opportunities for diversification. Yet the reality for Glasgow proved to be far from optimistic. New rivals were emerging to challenge the old economic order, notably Japan and the United States, which both embarked on an ambitious shipbuilding programme. Trade barriers were set up by several overseas governments, anxious to safeguard their indigenous industries from competitive pressures. While this was a perpetuation of developments long before the war, which had provoked British calls for retaliatory protectionism from the 1880s, the more hostile international climate after 1918 profoundly affected the west of Scotland because the economy relied so much on exports. The outcome of the Washington disarmament conference in early 1922 further dented economic prospects, with formal agreement among the naval powers to curtail their programmes. No new military vessels were allowed for a period of ten years, and contracts that already had been placed were suspended. Clyde shipbuilders were confronted with a drastically declining world market, exacerbated by what some considered to be their reliance on an outmoded form of technology, the marine steam engine, as opposed to the state-of-the-art diesel engine. James Lithgow, President of the Shipbuilding Employers' Federation, was forthright about previous complacency in the industry: 'While we have been cherishing our war ideas of our own value, the world's ideas of the value of our goods have left us in the clouds'.[1] The clear suggestion was that radically new methods of organisation were necessary to compete internationally.

The scale of the crisis was indicated by the fall in Clyde shipbuilding output from over 672,000 tons in 1920 to 175,000 in 1923. Indications of mounting unemployment in Glasgow first became apparent during the summer of 1921 and by the new year 90,000 people were officially out of work. According to one report, the declining fortunes of erstwhile munitions workers were displayed by the unusual number of second-hand 'cottage pianos' and fur coats in city sale-rooms, such luxuries having been sold to make ends meet.[2] A Lord Provost's Relief Fund was inaugurated to help the unemployed pay their rents, and 'rent tickets' were sold on Corporation tramcars as a means of allowing charitably-inclined Glaswegians to donate to the cause. However, despite stagnation in the export market, the sharp downswing of the early 1920s was followed by a period of cautious recovery. Home-based orders maintained sufficient momentum to keep the industry afloat throughout the decade, with a steady rise in production to over 600,000 tons in 1928. There was concern in the city, but not despair, as long-term prospects looked hopeful.

The coal industry, although not so directly important to Glasgow in terms of employment, was much harder hit by the post-war recession. Efforts to impose wage cuts heightened tensions in Scotland's mining communities, and the deteriorating state of relations between the employers and workforce led to flashpoint in 1926. In May the General Council of the Trades Union Congress (TUC) called a nationwide General Strike, to co-ordinate support in defence of miners' conditions. It was an attempt to

75. Father Clyde, 1923. A cartoon from *The Bailie*, depicting a Neptune-like Father Clyde draped in seaweed. The 'scoorie' (blustery) weather represents a metaphor for Glasgow's unpredictable economic prospects. (*By courtesy of the Mitchell Library, Glasgow City Libraries and Archives.*)

A DULL OUTLOOK.

Father Clyde—"Scoorie weather and no sign o' liftin'"!
(The trade outlook for the Clyde is depressing.)

harness a dangerously explosive situation, given the strength of feeling within the labour movement. The activities of the National Minority Movement, formed in 1924 to campaign for a more militant trade union strategy, helped to fuel the combative spirit. Fear of politically-motivated unofficial action pushed the TUC into taking the initiative. Thereafter, the disastrous progress of the strike was due in no small measure to the Conservative government's counter-campaign against the menace of Bolshevism as represented by TUC leaders, who ironically had not wanted to call the strike in the first place.

There was spirited action from some sectors of Glasgow's workforce during the nine days of the strike. Transport was among the first front-line activities to close down on 4 May 1926, with few trains running and Corporation tramcars conspicuously absent from the streets. 'How strange a world wherein the things we have seen and known and have depended on fail us!', was the comment of the *Emergency Press*, a temporary amalgam of the city's daily newspapers.[3] Headlines about the 'cityward trek of the suburbanites' identified that it was middle-class commuters who were most inconvenienced by strike action. More ominously, there was violence as a result of mass picketing, notably outside East End tramway depots, when 500 Lanarkshire miners joined forces with transport workers to stop the cars getting through.[4] This aspect of the strike left an important legacy because it alerted the public to deteriorating conditions within the Tramways Department. Profits had been plummeting since the early 1920s, and privately-run motor omnibuses seemed to be a more cost-effective transport option. A general undercurrent to the strike was the tension between old forms of technology and the new, in an era when there was considerable uncertainty among workers about future prospects. Glasgow's much-vaunted tramways seemed to encapsulate this conundrum; a massive enterprise that was failing to adapt and was thus in danger of obsolescence. It was a disturbing metaphor for the city generally.

Despite the response of the transport workers, the strike did not have the impact that might have been expected from a city with a reputation for industrial militancy. The famous 'Red Clydeside', which had consolidated its pugnacious image during the war, was only marginally involved. Engineering and shipyard workers were in the 'second line' of action, and were not called out until the last day of the strike. Moreover, the sheer size of Glasgow made effective control difficult. While the Scottish Trades Union Congress (STUC) was charged with co-ordinating strike arrangements, lines of communications were poor, especially the supply of essential propaganda and information sheets. As in other British cities, there was a corps of volunteers recruited by the government's Organisation for the Maintenance of Supplies (OMS) to do the work of strikers and ensure that essential services were not undermined. The OMS claimed that it had enrolled 7,000 volunteers in the city; significant enough, but scarcely sufficient to cope in the event of long-term industrial action. Only 300 of the volunteers came from Glasgow University, where over 5,000 students were matriculated. The reluctance of the student body to participate in the OMS has been attributed to the influence of the Labour Club, showing that the university was not quite so patrician as might be imagined during the 1920s.[5] The role of the volunteers was, in any case, part of the government's propaganda onslaught to demonstrate disunity among the population.

The General Strike and the prolonged coal strike thereafter seriously disrupted fuel supplies and destabilised Glasgow's economy, but there were signs of overall improvement towards the end of the decade. In a bid to ease

the anxiety of business ratepayers about spiralling increases in local taxation, the government introduced de-rating legislation in 1929. This allowed
for rates relief to industry, and was intended to restore economic confidence and attract much-needed new enterprises into urban areas. The
timing, however, was less than appropriate. The world depression arising
from the collapse of the New York Stock Market in October 1929 had a
searing impact on Glasgow. Shipbuilding output was decimated, declining
from 529,000 tons in 1930 to the unprecedented nadir of 56,000 in 1933.[6]
Unemployment levels rose to around 30 per cent of the insured population,
although the relative diversity of the economy meant that Glasgow was
not so disastrously affected as the neighbouring shipbuilding community
of Clydebank. However, austerity measures introduced by the National
government in 1931 heightened perceptions of the crisis. Unemployment
insurance benefits were cut by a tenth and a new system of public assistance
was inaugurated, which incorporated the notorious 'means test'. This was a
device which allowed the authorities (Glasgow Corporation) to take into
account entire family income and savings, and then deduct a proportional
amount from the recommended payment. The intrusive nature of the
means test was an incentive for many to support the National Unemployed
Workers' Movement as a tangible expression of concern about rapidly
deteriorating living standards. By May 1933 over 121,000 Glaswegians were
dependent on public assistance.[7]

Civic and business leaders endeavoured to reassure the population that
the crisis was transitory. The Development Board for Glasgow and District
had been formed in 1930 under the auspices of the Corporation and
Chamber of Commerce, and inspired much motivational rhetoric about
the need to turn the tide of Glasgow's fortunes. The city's motto was adapted
from 'Let Glasgow Flourish' to '*Make* Glasgow Flourish' during the
Corporation's high-profile Civic and Empire Week of 1931.[8] Another initiative that brought municipal and business interests closely together was
the promotion of the Scottish National Development Council (SNDC)
during 1931. The idea originated with two *Daily Record* journalists, David
Anderson and William Power, who urged that a co-ordinating body should
be established to work for economic revival. There was a distinctly nationalist dimension to the Council's mission statement, 'To inspire Scotsmen
with a belief in the future of their own country'.[9] This appeal to manly
patriotism was intended to reverse the pervasive notion that Scotland had
become an economic wasteland and that industrialisation had run its
course. The creation of the SNDC was also indicative of the growing
recognition that a more planned approach was necessary in order to
withstand volatile market forces. Significantly, apart from a few Liberal die-
hards, free trade was deemed to be dangerously anachronistic by the 1930s.
Protectionism and rationalisation were now the favoured interventionist
strategies for stemming industrial decline.

Sir James Lithgow (he became a baronet in 1925) was the driving force behind the SNDC, and encouraged economic regeneration with missionary zeal. Appropriately, he came from a Free Church background, and his philosophy was very much a blend of old and new, with a strong streak of evangelical paternalism. The family fortunes derived from the shipbuilding business that dominated Port Glasgow on the lower Clyde, although Lithgow had intimate Glasgow connections. Rationalisation came to be his watchword during the 1920s; the attempt to streamline declining industries, bringing them under centralised control, but strictly within the private sector. To give substance to rationalisation ideas, Lithgow (along with a consortium of banks) formed National Shipbuilders' Security Limited (NSS) in 1930. Almost immediately, NSS acquired and closed Beardmore's ailing Dalmuir yard, just outside Glasgow. Within three years a further half dozen Clyde yards had ceased operations, two had suspended work and three were operating on restricted quotas.[10] The swift contraction of shipbuilding had an inevitable impact on connected industries, notably steel, which went through similar Lithgow-inspired rationalisation. NSS closures and reorganisation were bitterly attacked by the left, who claimed that Lithgow was exploiting the economic crisis to bolster his own position. Indeed, by the outbreak of the Second World War he was scathingly portrayed by one Labour Party critic as 'the uncrowned King of Scotland', his rationalised domain now yielding profitable returns from the armaments' boom.[11]

The scale of the depression in the west of Scotland also compelled the National government to intervene. The 1934 Special Areas Act covered the counties contiguous to Glasgow, but not the city itself, as Corporation councillors had baulked at the label of 'distressed area'. However, the focus on new initiatives, with an increasing role for the Scottish Office, did help to promote Glasgow interests. The Scottish Economic Committee was an offshoot of the SNDC which worked in tandem with the government to create a more dynamic national image. One notable achievement was the 1938 Empire Exhibition, held in Glasgow's Bellahouston Park. As Chapter 11 elaborates, the architecturally innovative Exhibition continued the city's tradition of staging high-profile international extravaganzas to impress confidence in the future. That the Empire featured specifically in the Exhibition's title was an attempt to reinforce Scotland's long-established overseas links, albeit at a time when the the imperial relationship was changing. Significantly, by 1938 Glasgow had shed the status of 'Second City of the Empire' in population terms. Although over a million people still lived in the city, Bombay, Calcutta, Montreal and Sydney each had a greater number of inhabitants.[12] There was thus an element of nostalgia as well as economic purpose in the declaration that the Exhibition should serve as 'a clarion call to the scattered family of the British Commonwealth of Nations to come and talk as a family over the old days and ways'.[13]

More generally, the special areas legislation of the 1930s aimed to attract and foster investment. Near Glasgow the Hillington Industrial Estate was a pioneering venture; a factory and workshop site for the accommodation of light industries, underpinned by government grants and rating incentives. Estates in Slough and Welwyn Garden City had served as role models for the Scots. The new Hillington companies manufactured items like electrical goods, clothes and consumables, the last category including William MacDonald & Sons, whose enduring claim to fame was the Penguin chocolate biscuit.[14] Hillington's success soon encouraged similar estates to be established at Shieldhall and Dalmuir, the latter using the site of Beardmore's defunct shipyard. These developments were small-scale, employing less than 5,000 people by the outbreak of the Second World War. Nevertheless, they were important symbols of modernity, steering Glasgow and its environs away from the traditional industries that had become synonymous with stagnation. They also represented good intentions; a crucial part of government morale-boosting strategy throughout the depression. In September 1934 the Clydebank launch of the great Cunard liner, the *Queen Mary*, visibly reflected the commitment of employers, workers and the state to aid recovery. As David Kirkwood – now Clydebank's Labour MP – proudly put it, 'on that day I felt that the whole nation was built into that ship'.[15] Thereafter the tide really did seem to turn, as international developments further boosted job prospects. From 1936 German remilitarisation stimulated the British armament programme, which increased Clyde output, although it also heightened the prospect of war.

Of course, Glasgow employment during the inter-war period represented far more than shipbuilding and its related industries. By 1933, for instance, the Corporation had almost 34,000 full-time staff, a sizeable proportion dealing (ironically) with public assistance. By this time local authority workers covered a broad range of the employment spectrum, and included chief officials, teachers, the police force, clerks and assorted manual workers. Transport also remained a substantial sphere of Corporation activity, and the sector generally employed a high proportion of the male labour force, constituting 15 per cent in 1931. The census of that year indicated that the metal industries, including shipbuilding, remained the single most important sector for men at 18.5 per cent, but commercial and administrative employment were growth areas. Women also were increasingly likely to be employed in clerical and secretarial work, and as teachers and nurses had a prominent presence in the professional sector. Yet although the First World War had the effect of opening opportunities for women, old patterns re-emerged as the 1920s progressed. There was a 50 per cent increase in the number of female domestic servants in Glasgow between 1921 and 1931, with almost 14 per cent of working women employed in the sector by the later date. This figure was substantially less than the Scottish total of 21 per cent, but nevertheless constituted a significant segment of the city's female labour force at a time when jobs generally were difficult to find.

Shop work was another expanding area of female employment, and the relatively high numbers in Glasgow matched those for domestic service in 1931. The city's depressed inter-war reputation gave a skewed impression of consumer culture in a centre serving the Clydeside region for the supply of retail goods. One English commentator suggested in 1929 that Glasgow shops were 'as fine as any in Bond Street', and many of the pioneering department stores from the late nineteenth century continued to thrive.[16] Copland & Lye's Sauchiehall Street premises were substantially extended in 1934, and aimed to attract shoppers by offering two commodious restaurants, complete with in-store orchestra. Moreover, a new generation of Glasgow entrepreneurs was emerging, notably Hugh Fraser, described by one historian as 'the ultimate drapery tycoon'.[17] From the 1920s he extended the family business to build a substantial chain of retail outlets, under the distinctive House of Fraser trademark. Indeed, the expansion of chain stores at this time was a nation-wide phenomenon, illustrated by the arrival of Marks & Spencer in Glasgow during 1937. On the other hand, for many in the city the multiplicity of shopping outlets represented starkly contrasting life-styles. In his 1935 novel, *The Shipbuilders*, George Blake was being profoundly ironic when he depicted the sumptuously decorated food stores of Union Street as 'a world overflowing with goodness, a city with a healthy appetite and the money to indulge it'.[18] The depression was inextricably bound up with the image of industrial failure in Glasgow, which cut across perceptions of the economically buoyant city. Despite the gradual healing process, the scars remained raw.

War and Industrial Decline

Planning for war began in earnest during 1936, with Clyde industrialists Sir James Lithgow and William Weir (now Viscount Weir of Eastwood) taking a pivotal role in advising the government about the organisation of munitions' supplies. However, in spite of their efforts, the urgent need for military hardware from September 1939 presented awkward problems of matching output with demand. The coal industry was especially slow to respond to the crisis, which inevitably retarded progress elsewhere. All this demonstrated the massive momentum behind the war effort. As the economy reorientated towards maximum production, unemployment fell precipitately because of the need to recruit workers and military personnel. Unlike 1914, conscription was enforced from the outset, the notion of a volunteer army perceived as untenable. Reflecting military and merchant demand, Clyde shipyards launched an average of 493,000 tons annually during the full war years from 1940 to 1944 inclusive.[19] Beardmore's in Parkhead again became the focal point of armaments' production, and expanded into factories outside Glasgow. Additionally, technological developments since 1918 had profoundly altered the nature of warfare, with far more emphasis

76. Copland & Lye, Caledonian House, 1920s.
Female sales staff in Copland & Lye's prestigious Caledonian House department store during the early 1920s.
Display is used to good effect to impress the range and style of merchandise on the consumer consciousness.
(*By courtesy of the Mitchell Library, Glasgow City Libraries and Archives.*)

on air power. As a sign of changing times the government constructed a new factory at Hillington, which from 1940 manufactured Rolls-Royce aero-engines.

The memory of 'Red Clydeside' militancy during the First World War loomed large in the government's industrial relations strategy, and there was determination to avoid confrontation. Cynicism was recognised as pervasive in Glasgow, especially among industrial workers. As a reporter for Mass Observation, the social research group, commented in 1941: 'Quite a lot of the [Glasgow] men still hate their bosses, just about as much as they hate the Fascists. Quite a lot of bosses are hating their men nearly as much as they are hating Hitler'.[20] Yet although tensions existed, there was not the same political gulf as in the previous conflict, with the Labour Party a key participant in the wartime Coalition. The government's Ministry of Information promoted the egalitarian image of 'Jock Tamson's bairns' (a secular Scots version of 'all God's children') to help mute class and sectarian divisions. Glasgow Corporation had a Labour majority, and Lord Provost Patrick Dollan used his persuasive journalist's rhetoric to rally workers in support of the war effort. On the other hand, some wartime disputes did hit the headlines. For instance, women had been recruited for engineering work at Rolls-Royce in Hillington, but were grossly discriminated against in terms of wages and job status. Eventually they were permitted to join the hitherto male bastion of the AEU, and strike action was called in 1943 which secured a satisfactory outcome for the women. As shop steward Agnes McLean later explained, although the settlement stopped short of equal pay, 'A lot of the women's wages were lifted right up and their skills recognised'.[21]

Glasgow's industrial base remained resilient in the immediate aftermath of the war, and positively gained from the Cold War, notably the Korean conflict of 1950–3. At the same time, erstwhile European rivals were trying to reconstruct their fractured economies, so that Glasgow was placed in a particular position of advantage. This meant that employment levels remained stable, wholly reversing the trend of the inter-war period. In December 1938 almost 83,000 Glaswegians had been registered as out of work, in contrast with 17,500 in December 1951.[22] As far as the 'gainfully employed' were concerned during the later period, the largest single category comprised workers in shipbuilding, engineering and metal manufacture, at around 15 per cent of the total. Clerical workers (predominantly women) were the next largest category at 11 per cent, showing the continuing rise of administrative employment in the city. Demonstrating the impact of the war on work patterns, domestic service accounted for only 7 per cent of the female labour force. And, of course, a range of new work opportunities had been created after 1945. The Labour government transferred the utilities of gas and electricity from local government to state control, nationalised the railways and coal industry, created the National Health Service and reorganised the system of national insurance and social security. Glasgow Corporation embarked on one of the most ambitious housing and planning programmes in the United Kingdom. Workers were needed to augment the existing infrastructure of these sectors, given the extended scale of operations.

Despite new growth areas, the seeming buoyancy of Glasgow's economy was based on unusual and transitory global circumstances. Whatever the impressive employment statistics for the early 1950s and the equally impressive fact that over 400,000 tons of ships were being launched on the Clyde each year, the traditional economic base was eroding. Shipbuilding supremacy was emphatically a feature of past history, at 5 per cent of global tonnage as opposed to 20 per cent in the palmy days before the First World War. To compound the process of economic decline, from 1945 there was a brisk outflow of British investment overseas; a phenomenon partly fuelled by fear of nationalisation. Conversely, any inward investment was not directed towards Glasgow. Contemporary planning policies consciously aimed to disperse industry, as there was simply not the space for large-scale initiatives in the congested city. Post-war new towns like East Kilbride offered a healthier working environment, and so attracted the lion's share of investment. Another factor militating against Glasgow was the automotive boom of the 1950s. There was a preference for new industry to be located next to modern motorways; an asset that the city then conspicuously lacked.

It was not so much Glasgow as the Clyde conurbation that was considered to be important for development. This tied in with the government's promotion of regional policy after 1945, as part of an integrated approach to nurturing economic growth. Continuing the pre-war notion of 'special areas', 'development areas' were designated, and the trend continued for creating industrial estates beyond the bounds of Glasgow. Multinational companies, such as the American electronics giants Honeywell and IBM, took advantage of favourable investment opportunities. During the 1950s there were also attempts to create a distinctive regional identity, based on the potential of steel and motor vehicles.[23] The Ravenscraig steel mill at Motherwell became a symbol of modernisation for an old staple industry, economies of scale being profitably demonstrated as existing enterprises pooled their productive resources. The town of Linwood, in close proximity to Glasgow, was targeted as Scotland's Detroit, and in 1963 the British Rootes Group began to manufacture the Hillman Imp motor car. However, the conurbation's shifting industrial profile did not boost job prospects within Glasgow. As Chapter 11 explains, the population was being directed away from the city to new towns and overspill areas. From 1957 unemployment levels began to rise; a trend compounded by the phasing out of compulsory military service ('national service'), showing how long elements of the extraordinary war economy had survived.

At the same time there was also a global recession in shipping, which left the Glasgow economy at an acute disadvantage. For all that successive governments were adopting interventionist strategies, this was nowhere near the cushioning that rivals were experiencing, notably Sweden, the Netherlands, and the reviving nations of West Germany and Japan. Overseas companies also had the benefit of more modern production methods than their Clydeside counterparts, who remained entrenched in older practices and reluctant to commit the investment necessary to update their infrastructure. However, it was not until 1965, under Harold Wilson's Labour government, that there was direct intervention. The Fairfield's yard at Govan was facing financial collapse, and to counter such a devastating prospect a new consortium was initiated, blending public and private sector resources. Liquidation was avoided through joint initiative, which led to careful scrutiny of the deficiencies of British shipbuilding, as outlined in the Geddes Report of 1966. This called for the reorganisation of the industry into larger units, resulting in the formation of two combines on the Clyde. The first, Scott-Lithgow, was centred on the port of Greenock. The second, known as Upper Clyde Shipbuilders (UCS), was based in Glasgow and

Clydebank. From the beginning, the diverse UCS components worked uneasily together, and as time progressed it proved difficult to co-ordinate a cohesive strategy or focus on areas of money-making potential. The much-publicised liner *Queen Elizabeth II* may have seemed a motivational project like the *Queen Mary*, but it was ultimately a mammoth loss-making venture for UCS, directing energies away from more meaningful cost-effective enterprises.

UCS swiftly became wholly dependent on government capital to keep it afloat, and by 1971 the combine was facing bankruptcy. The new Conservative government, under Edward Heath, refused to grant further financial support. Rather than accept the inevitable closure of the yards, the workforce adopted the novel tactic of a 'work-in'. The 1970s was the era of 'sit-ins' and 'love-ins', as expressions of collective strength of feeling, and so the 'work-in' accorded with such contemporary notions. The rationale was to occupy the work premises so that the government liquidator would not be able to enter the yards to dismantle and remove machinery. Leading the work-in were shop stewards Jimmy Reid, Jimmy Airlie and Sam Barr, all Communist Party activists at a time when the organisation still had considerable trade union clout. There were heroic echoes of 'Red Clydeside' in their pugnacious response to the government, with Reid in particular projected by the media as the swashbuckling man-of-the-moment. He declared defiantly: 'The Upper Clyde is being sacrificed on the altar of sheer political dogma. We refuse to accept that somebody sitting in Whitehall is going to kill our industry'.[24] The response was overwhelming, with an industrial stoppage in August 1971 involving some 200,000 west of Scotland workers. In fitting historical tradition, there was also a mass protest demonstration to Glasgow Green, which was given international publicity.

Some commentators of the period have gone so far as to suggest that there was the possibility of civil unrest, again showing comparisons with 'Red Clydeside' during and immediately after the First World War.[25] Whatever the reality, the strength of public feeling against the UCS closures was crucial for influencing the government to abandon its so-called 'lame duck' strategy, and keep the yards functioning. However, all this had a huge cost. Govan Shipbuilders initially received £35 million's worth of government aid, and substantial financial incentives were given to the American oil-rig manufacturer Marathon, which had taken over from UCS at Clydebank. Teddy Taylor, then Conservative MP for Glasgow's Cathcart constituency, was subsequently scathing. In 1991 he told the *Glasgow Herald*, 'We could probably have achieved more by sending an aeroplane to drop £10 notes over the area'.[26] The strategy of the Heath government fended off pressing political problems in the short term, but did little for bolstering the economy of the west of Scotland, as the much-needed modernisation of the yards failed meaningfully to materialise. The £101 million ultimately committed by both Conservative and Labour governments up to 1975 helped

77. UCS demonstration, 1971.
A photograph from August 1971 that conveys the scale of the protest against the threatened closure of Upper Clyde Shipbuilders. An estimated 80,000 people marched through central Glasgow. (*By courtesy of the* Herald *and* Evening Times.)

to harden political attitudes, especially when Margaret Thatcher took over as Conservative leader that year. Moreover, the intervening oil shock of 1973, prompted by the outbreak of the Arab-Israeli war, meant an unprecedented post-war crisis for the United Kingdom economy, with inflation rising to over 25 per cent by mid-1975. This represented a turning-point for Glasgow's old economic base, although deindustrialisation became a process inextricably associated with Thatcher's Conservative government from 1979.

Deindustrialisation and the Post-Industrial City

Scottish local government reorganisation in 1975 had the effect of dissolving Glasgow Corporation, an administrative entity that formally dated from 1895. Municipal functions were divided between the newly created dual authorities of Glasgow District Council and Strathclyde Regional Council. While the political implications are discussed in the next chapter, there was an important economic rationale to this radical reform. The aim was to promote 'efficiency and resource equalisation' and give direct accountability to regional policy implementation.[27] Critics, especially from the Scottish Office, considered that the old structure had become too fragmented and ossified, especially within the Clydeside area. Accordingly, reorganisation aimed to transform the role of local government, making the new authorities more pro-active in development strategy. Regionalisation was useful in co-ordinating collective economic interests and acted as a focus for funding from the European Community, which the United Kingdom had joined in 1973. It was also a device that could cut across local partisanship and create the notion of a wider common good for the west of Scotland. As one publicity feature declared about the new regional administration: 'References to a councillor or a potential official coming from Ayrshire, Dunbartonshire, Renfrewshire or Glasgow are frowned upon as outmoded expressions'.[28] Nevertheless, Glasgow was the major population component of the region, with approximately a third of the 2.8 million inhabitants, and continued to be a resource priority given the city's rapidly declining industrial infrastructure.

In 1975 the new District Council promoted the civic celebration of 'Glasgow 800', ostensibly to commemorate the granting of the burgh charter in 1175, but also to demonstrate continuity with the old Corporation. The theme was the familiar one of a city 'with a historic past and an exciting future'.[29] Linked with that future was the prospect of a Scottish oil boom. Significantly, 1975 was the year when the first supplies from the North Sea were officially landed in Aberdeenshire. The Clyde was identified as having an important role to play in providing the array of hardware needed to keep the oil platforms functioning. If shipbuilding was sliding into terminal decline, the Clyde mode of construction now too specialised to compete internationally, then the skills could be profitably transferred to the promising oil sector. In conjunction, oil research and development had become briskly expanding business. Glasgow benefited directly from this trend, due to the relocation of the government's British National Oil

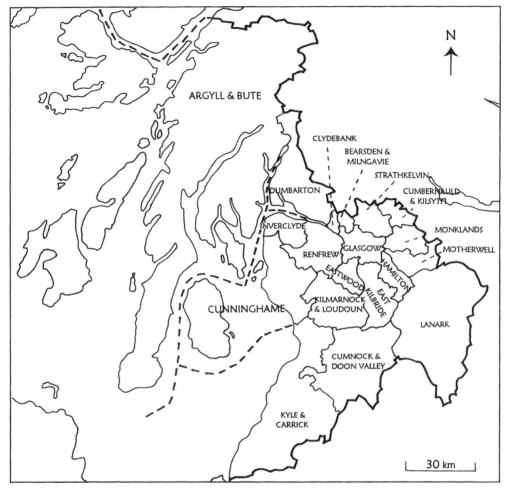

78. Strathclyde Region, 1975–96.
A map showing the extensive boundaries of Strathclyde Region, which served 2.5 million people when it was inaugurated in 1975. Although Glasgow was the administrative centre, regional government was intended to give a more cohesive identity to the west of Scotland. Strathclyde disappeared with the 1996 reorganisation of Scottish local government. (*The author.*)

Corporation to the city. The new oil developments were welcomed by the author of a glossy 'Glasgow 800' publication, who proclaimed that, 'a big new industry, a "he-man industry" of the kind Clydesiders know', was in the process of being established.[30] Unfortunately, this potent vision proved to be elusive. As has been well-documented, British firms conspicuously failed to reap rewards from North Sea oil, with most of the orders for equipment placed overseas.[31] BNOC was metamorphosed into Britoil as part of the Conservative privatisation programme, and after cutting back operations substantially, the company was taken over by British Petroleum in 1988.

In 1981 the number of people employed in shipbuilding on the Clyde had fallen to 12,750. By the 1990s, as one historian wryly commented, the labour force was so small that it did not even merit a mention in the *Scottish Digest of Statistics*.[32] Two yards rather shakily survived the process of deindustrialisation: Yarrow's at Scotstoun, owned by General Electric, and Kvaerner Govan, a Norwegian company. In 1999 public unease intensified over the prospect of Kvaerner pulling out of Govan, placing 1,200 jobs at risk. However, BAE Systems took over both of the Glasgow shipyards, ensuring their survival into the twenty-first century.

The Clyde's radically changing profile was further emphasised by the scaling down of harbour activities from 1966. As the docks ceased operations due to the advent of containerisation, some were filled-in and landscaped. In keeping with past experience, the contraction of shipbuilding had a knock-on effect in related areas. Metal manufacture, especially steel, was decimated. Between 1977 and 1983 the nationalised Clyde Iron, Tollcross, Hallside and Clydebridge works were closed.[33] The once formidable Beardmore's at Parkhead was an earlier casualty, having ceased trading in 1975. As a sign of changing times, its site was developed during the mid-1980s as an elaborate, glassed-in shopping complex. Scottish steel disappeared altogether in 1993 with the closure of the Ravenscraig plant in Motherwell. For many this represented the defining moment of deindustrialisation north of the Border, and was particularly poignant because of the importance of heavy industry in shaping Scotland's economic identity from the late nineteenth century. Linwood, that other wing of 1960s regional redevelopment strategy, had stopped producing motor vehicles in 1981.

One analyst of deindustrialisation has contrasted the 'virtuous circles of growth and vicious circles of decline' that came to characterise the Glasgow conurbation by the 1990s.[34] Glasgow's specific problems reflected both the low rate of job creation as well as job loss in the manufacturing sector. Within the city employment in manufacturing had declined to less than a third of the mid-1960s level. No significant manufacturing company set up business to redress the employment balance, deterred by high costs, the physical constraints of the city and skills shortages. Any that were attracted to the region tended to favour the more dynamic industrial areas, notably the new towns, although some forty hectares of the city had been included in the first enterprise zones created by the Conservative government in 1980. The reluctance of manufacturers to locate in Glasgow was compounded by the steadily ageing profile of the population. As Chapter 11 elaborates, the emigration outflow had gathered momentum from the 1950s as younger residents departed from the city. This was a significant factor in the sharp population decline from 1.1 million in 1951 to 681,228 in 1991. Older industrial areas were especially affected. For instance, by 1981 20 per cent of East End residents were of pensionable age, compared with 15 per cent across Strathclyde Region.[35]

However, manufacturing represented only one part of the complex story

79. Clyde landscape, 1990s. As Clyde industry contracted drastically during the course of the 1970s and 1980s, the river's landscape altered accordingly. The giant Finnieston crane dates from 1931, and thus represents continuity, but in the background new building developments are in progress. The steely edifice of the Clyde Auditorium eventually emerged in 1997 as part of the Scottish Exhibition and Conference Centre. (*Glasgow City Council Corporate Graphics.*)

of the city's economy during the last decades of the twentieth century. Well before the Thatcher era, the service sector had been rising in Glasgow, from 48 per cent of the workforce in 1961 to 68 per cent in 1981. By the 1980s, the profile of the archetypal Glasgow worker was no longer the man in manufacturing but the woman in public services, this category accounting for one in four employees. And here the broad definition of 'service sector' gives a misleading impression, because although the public and business services became substantial employers, distributive and leisure services (such as shops, hotels and restaurants) did not parallel this growth. In stark contrast to the national trend, Glasgow actually lost 13 per cent of such jobs during the 1980s. There was thus a profound twist of irony in the assertive consumer repackaging of Glasgow as the post-industrial city *par excellence*.

This begs the important question as to when Glasgow's image began to alter from a decayed, defensive and deindustrialising urban community to the glittering city of culture that was evolving during the 1980s. The conception of specific ideas is a dangerous speculation in history, as it can steadily lead backwards into the mists of time. However, Chapter 11 attempts to place the much-vaunted 'reinvention' of Glasgow in the broad context of cultural change within the city during the late twentieth century. With specific reference to the economy, the *West Central Scotland Plan* of 1974 undoubtedly was crucial for identifying the scale of deprivation in the corroding city and suggesting that the post-war focus on outward development was draining too much from the centre. One immediate outcome of the *Plan* was the regenerative Glasgow Eastern Area Renewal Project (GEAR), which aimed to revive a locality that was being hard hit by the chilly winds of recession. Aided by the new Scottish Development Agency (the SDA, subsequently called Scottish Enterprise) municipal leaders then began to promote Glasgow with panache. Using his unique status as figurehead for the city, Lord Provost Michael Kelly took on the role of roving international ambassador between 1980 and 1984, his single-minded mission to get Glasgow noticed.[36] Ideas were borrowed and refined from the successful 'I love New York' campaign and the 'Glasgow's Miles Better' legend was born.

Undoubtedly, Kelly's key publicity asset was the benign and beaming cartoon character, Mr Happy, on licence from artist Roger Hargreaves. The slogan of 'Glasgow's Miles Better' that accompanied the nationwide promotion of Mr Happy was the creation of Struthers Advertising & Marketing Limited, who even recruited Prime Minister Thatcher to give authority to the new image. As she put it in the preface of an effusive tribute: 'The people of Glasgow, whose forefathers pioneered trade around the world and engaged in extraordinary feats of engineering in distant countries, are now putting these same qualities to work in successfully transforming Glasgow'.[37] There was a strong whiff of 'Second City of Empire' rhetoric in this retrospective reference to past achievements, even though the designation was now an anachronism in the post-colonial era. Yet, as the 'Miles Better' campaign revealed, the intertwining of history and progress was still a favourite device for infusing confidence in the city. Nor was the overseas connection forgotten in efforts to make Glasgow better known. Civic leaders were acutely aware that an estimated ten million descendants of Glaswegians lived outside Scotland: an extended and influential global community, likely to be receptive to the mother city's self-assured, high-profile image.

Of course, the problem of the inner cities was not unique to Glasgow,

80. City Chambers and Mr Happy, 1996.
The imposing facade of the City Chambers, opened in 1888, is given 1996 embellishment as a suitably bohemian Mr Happy draws public attention to the Festival of Visual Arts running throughout that year. (*Glasgow City Council Corporate Graphics.*)

and regeneration strategies were being addressed elsewhere in the United Kingdom, especially after the rioting that had erupted in English urban centres during 1980 and 1981. Historian Helen Meller has explained how economic growth became tied in with the promotion of culture, and that Glasgow's strong sense of local tradition and civic identity placed the city in a pole position of advantage among the larger British communities.[38] In particular, there was Glaswegian sensitivity to the past (or a perception of the past) that could be used to enhance prestigious new initiatives. The Burrell collection was a celebrated example of the kind of cosmopolitan image that Lord Provost Kelly and his public relations team were anxious to impress. In 1944 Sir William Burrell, the erstwhile shipping magnate, had demonstrated philanthropic spirit by bequeathing some 6,000 items from his extensive and eclectic art collection to the city. For some years after his death in 1958 (aged ninety-six) civic leaders were unsure of what to do with their spectacular windfall. However, from 1970 plans were progressed to build a custom-designed gallery amidst the bucolic setting of Pollok Estate, in the south of the city. The Burrell project thus had a long pedigree, but 1983 proved to be an auspicious year for the grand opening of the gallery, given the intensification of regeneration strategy. Not only did it demonstrate renewed faith within the city, but there were high hopes that it would serve as a tourist attraction, in an area of rapidly growing importance for the city's economy. The potential of tourism had been recognised in 1982 when some £62 million was expended by visitors to the city, helping to sustain 5,400 jobs. Ten years after assiduously cultivating this market, expenditure had almost doubled, generating some 20,000 jobs.

By this time priorities for the city's economic growth were concentrated on business services and tourism, and in 1991 the Glasgow Development Agency was created to facilitate this dual objective. The language of thrusting enterprise was to the fore. The District Council's Director of Planning, James Rae, identified Glasgow internationally as 'one of the first examples of a post-industrial city... regarded in knowledgeable circles as a model for economic regeneration'.[39] The revived inner-city featured forcefully in the post-industrial image. During the early 1980s architect Gordon Cullen had been commissioned by the SDA to produce a strategy for creating a 'vibrant cosmopolitan city centre', accommodating a range of shops and amenities.[40] He focused on Buchanan Street as the heart of a development combining features of the old architecture and the new. There were hopes that a Glasgow equivalent of the Champs-Elysées would emerge, especially as Sauchiehall Street had long lost its reputation for quality retail outlets. The closure of many of the city's long-standing department stores, such as Copland & Lye, indicated the intense competition generated by the arrival of the multiple chains, especially from the 1960s. Accordingly, in Buchanan Street the glamorous Princes Square shopping complex reflected 1980s concepts of marketing, offering patrons a choice of shops and restaurants, mostly originating from outside Glasgow. Building on this success, the Buchanan Galleries opened in 1999 as Scotland's largest shopping centre, housing more than eighty stores. Architecturally, it represented visible testimony that the Glaswegian penchant for the monumental was still very much alive.[41]

Yet as the 1990s progressed, the glossy image became increasingly tarnished. For many Glaswegians the city had become a lively and attractive place to live, but there continued to be intractable social problems, particularly relating to high unemployment levels. The biggest headache was the large number of men out of work over a prolonged period, with limited prospects of finding jobs. In 1991 fewer people were employed full-time in Glasgow than a decade before, and the trend towards temporary, short-term work continued. This meant less job security and eroding levels of unionisation. Moreover, for all the claims that Glasgow had pioneered the post-industrial city, the decline of manufacturing had created a disturbing vacuum in the process of regeneration. Blame, especially from city councillors, was directed towards the Scottish Office prior to the return of the Labour government in May 1997. There were accusations that the economic inducements offered to enterprise zones and new towns meant that it was

81. Prince's Square, 1990s.
The glamorous shopping mall of Princes Square in the 1990s, a decade after it was first developed. It was an early indication of Glaswegian pretensions to create a Champs-Elysées in the central thoroughfare of Buchanan Street. (*Glasgow City Council Corporate Graphics.*)

more cost-effective for existing Glasgow-based firms to relocate. The demise of Strathclyde Regional Council in 1996 also fragmented the base that had been built up to integrate the core with the periphery, and local government reorganisation that year created enormous financial problems for the new single-tier local authority of Glasgow City Council. With dwindling council tax revenues due to the declining population there came to be a funding crisis for the city, with serious implications for local authority jobs and services.[42] The public sector, a mainstay of much of Glasgow's employment, was under threat. Even that enduring talisman of the regenerated Glasgow, Mr Happy, was made redundant in 1997, his copyright costs too steep for the beleaguered City Council.[43]

The vicissitudes of Glasgow's economy after 1918 represented the struggle to sustain the pre-war industrial base in face of drastically changing global circumstances. However, the renewed prospect of war once again served the city's interests by bolstering employment in traditionally important areas like shipbuilding and engineering. Although there were indications that the employment structure was altering during the inter-war period, the shift away from manufacturing and towards the service sector became increasingly apparent during the second half of the century. Of course, economic reorientation had profound implications for Glaswegians, that went beyond immediate employment considerations. The ideological flux of the post-1918 period reflected profound uncertainties about the city's future. As the next chapter explains, this helped to redefine the nature of political power at both the parliamentary and local government level, provoking frequently combative debate over urban strategy.

Notes

1. Quoted in J. M. Reid, *James Lithgow: Master of Work* (Hutchinson: London, 1964), p. 81.
2. W. R. Scott and J. Cunnison, *The Industries of the Clyde Valley during the War* (Clarendon Press: Oxford, 1924), p. 184.
3. *Emergency Press*, 5 May 1926.
4. Ibid. 7 May 1926.
5. Paul Carter, 'The west of Scotland', in Jeffrey Skelley (ed.), *The General Strike, 1926* (Lawrence and Wishart: London, 1976), p. 134.
6. J. Cunnison and J. B. S. Gilfillan (eds), *Glasgow: the Third Statistical Account of Scotland* (Collins: Glasgow, 1958), p. 841.
7. David Stenhouse, *Glasgow: Its Municipal Undertakings and Enterprises* (Glasgow Corporation: Glasgow, 1933), p. 116.
8. Glasgow Civic and Empire Week Committee, *The Book of Glasgow* (Glasgow Corporation: Glasgow, 1931), p. 10.
9. Quoted in Reid, *James Lithgow*, p. 148.
10. Anthony Slaven, *The Development of the West of Scotland, 1750–1960* (Routledge and Kegan Paul: London, 1975), p. 189.
11. Thomas Burns, *The Real Rulers of Scotland* (London Scots Self Government Committee: Glasgow, 1940), p. 11.
12. C. A. Oakely, *Scottish Industry Today* (Moray Press: Edinburgh, 1937), p. 195.
13. Empire Exhibition (publisher), *Official Guide* (Glasgow: 1938), p. 72.
14. C. A. Oakley, *Glasgow Made It: How Glasgow Came Through the 1930s Depression* (Glasgow Chamber of Commerce: Glasgow, 1984), p. 4.
15. David Kirkwood, *My Life of Revolt* (George G. Harrap: London, 1935), p. 262.
16. H. V. Morton, *In Search of Scotland* (Methuen: London, 1929), p. 249.
17. Brenda M. White, 'Distributive trades', in Anthony Slaven and Sidney Checkland (eds), *Dictionary of Scottish Business Biography, 1860–1960, Volume II: Processing, Distribution, Services* (Aberdeen University Press: Aberdeen, 1990), p. 332.
18. George Blake, *The Shipbuilders* (B. & W. Publishers: Edinburgh, 1993 edition), p. 149. First published in 1935.
19. Slaven, *Development of the West of Scotland*, p. 211.
20. Quoted in Seona Robinson and Les Wilson, *Scotland's War* (Mainstream: Edinburgh, 1995), p. 74.
21. Quoted in Neil Rafeek, 'Agnes McLean, 1918–1994', *Journal of the Scottish Labour History Society* 30 (1995), p. 123.
22. Cunnison and Gilfillan (eds), *Third Statistical Account*, p. 923.
23. Michael Pacione, *Glasgow: the Socio-Spatial Development of the City* (Wiley: Chichester, 1995), pp. 141–3.
24. Quoted in John Foster and Charles Woolfson, *The Politics of the UCS Work-In* (Lawrence and Wishart: London, 1986), p. 176.
25. Pacione, *Glasgow*, pp. 136–7.

26. Quoted in the feature by Alan Clements and Kirsty Wark, 'UCS: the lame duck that stood its ground', in the *Glasgow Herald*, 29 July 1991.

27. Michael Keating, *The City that Refused to Die: Glasgow, the Politics of Urban Regeneration* (Aberdeen University Press: Aberdeen, 1988), p. 36.

28. *Scotsman*, 23 August 1974.

29. Ibid. 9 May 1975.

30. Hugh Cochrane, *Glasgow: the First 800 Years* (City of Glasgow District Council: Glasgow, 1975), p. 64.

31. Christopher Harvie, *Fool's Gold: the Story of North Sea Oil* (Penguin Books edition: London, 1995), pp. 144–50.

32. Peter L. Payne, 'Industrialisation and industrial decline', in Anthony Cooke, Ian Donnachie, Ann Macsween and Christopher A. Whatley (eds), *Modern Scottish History: 1707 to the Present, Volume II* (Tuckwell Press: East Linton, 1998), p. 89.

33. Keating, *City that Refused to Die*, pp. 168–9.

34. John Macinnes, 'The deindustrialisation of Glasgow', *Scottish Affairs* 11 (1995), p. 84. This is a concise and readable analysis of a complex subject.

35. Alan Middleton, 'Glasgow and its east end', in David Donnison and Alan Middleton (eds), *Regenerating the Inner City: Glasgow's Experience* (Routledge and Kegan Paul: London, 1987), p. 29.

36. Keating, *City that Refused to Die*, p. 174.

37. John Struthers, *Glasgow's Miles Better: They Said It* (Struthers Advertising & Marketing: Glasgow, 1986), p. 7.

38. Helen Meller, *Towns, Plans and Society in Modern Britain* (Cambridge University Press: Cambridge, 1997), pp. 101–2.

39. James H. Rae, 'Glasgow: a city of change', in *The Planner* 79 (June, 1993), p. 3.

40. Peter Reed, 'The post-industrial city?', in Peter Reed (ed.), *Glasgow: the Forming of the City* (Edinburgh University Press: Edinburgh, 1993), p. 189.

41. Johnny Rodger, *Contemporary Glasgow: The Architecture of the 1990s* (Rutland Press: Edinburgh, 1999), pp. 57–9.

42. See the feature by John McCalman, 'City hopes for rabbit in the hat', in the *Herald*, 19 February 1996.

43. Ibid. 31 March 1997.

CHAPTER TEN

Municipal and Parliamentary Politics

The direction of politics in Glasgow from 1918 was profoundly affected by the opening out of voting rights as a result of post-war legislation. Initially this did not seem so, with the position of the Labour Party uncertain due to disappointing results for candidates in the 1918 general election. However, this chapter focuses on how the phenomenon of 'Red Clydeside' began to make an impact on the public consciousness, the rhetoric and style of activists winning over the electorate from the 1920s. Not surprisingly, Labour success aroused a concerted backlash, although it was Unionists who mounted the most effective political challenge and remained strongly placed in the city until the 1960s. The once mighty edifice of Glasgow Liberalism crumbled in the wake of the war, its appeal drastically undermined by damaging divisions in the party.

Glasgow was, and remains, rich in powerful political personalities. Justice cannot be done in this brief survey to the multitude of individuals who contributed to the often combative political life of the city from 1918. Accordingly, the focus has been on parliamentary and municipal affairs, and the men (mostly) who left their mark in both spheres. It is worth pointing out that although the 1918 legislation legitimised women's involvement as voters and candidates in parliamentary elections, out of 101 Glasgow MPs returned from that time up to 1997, only six were female. Two of the women, Labour's Agnes Hardie and Helen McElhone, were selected to fill the place of their deceased husbands as MPs, although both proved to be highly capable politicians. Hardie was Glasgow's first woman MP, returned in a 1937 by-election. These limitations on female representation symbolise yet another contradiction of Glasgow; that for all the image of progressivism, a large proportion of the population was left politically languishing for much of the twentieth century.

'Red Clydeside' and the Post-War Labour Breakthrough

The general election called in the wake of the November 1918 Armistice seemed to promise much for the socialist movement in Glasgow. Before 1914 the ILP had been carving out an identifiable profile in community politics, and the wartime exploits of leading activists helped to consolidate the image of a dynamic organisation that could articulate the aspirations of working people for a better quality of life. John Maclean's presence among the corps of Labour parliamentary candidates in 1918, standing in the Gorbals constituency, was indicative of hopes that even an unswerving revolutionary socialist could successfully challenge the old political order. The implementation of the 1918 Representation of the People Act further fuelled Labour hopes that substantial electoral inroads could be made. Glasgow's parliamentary constituencies had been fundamentally redistributed to provide a more realistic reflection of the city's population. Govan, Partick and other substantial communities had been absorbed in 1912, and the 1918 legislation boosted the number of designated Glasgow MPs from seven to fifteen, just over a fifth of the total Scottish representation. In tandem, the parliamentary franchise was extended, creating a radically different base for campaigning operations than hitherto. Compared with a total of 87,036 registered voters in 1910, the territorially expanded city had 524,008 in 1918, a large proportion of whom were likely to be Labour supporters.[1]

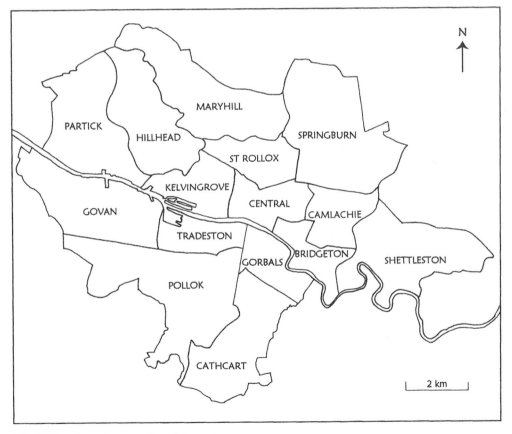

82. 1918 parliamentary constituencies.
The city was divided into fifteen parliamentary constituencies in 1918, when electoral reform fundamentally altered the political profile of the city. (*The author.*)

Yet despite the impressive increase in numbers, mass democracy had by no means arrived in Glasgow or elsewhere in the United Kingdom. Whereas all men aged over twenty-one and with six months' residency were entitled to vote, for women the age limit was fixed at thirty years, with more complicated residential qualifications.[2] Until equal franchises were introduced in 1928, the gender differential tended to exclude single, working-class women from the electoral roll. This strategy demonstrated the insecurity felt at Westminster about major constitutional change during the politically testing period in the immediate aftermath of the war. Glasgow's reputation as the subversive heart of 'Red Clydeside' heightened the sense of unease about the future, especially the unpredictable role the socialists would play under the new electoral system. Lloyd George was intent on maintaining his Coalition government beyond the Armistice, ostensibly for the sake of national unity, but also to safeguard his own position given the chasm that had emerged in the Liberal Party after the rupture with Asquith in 1916. Accordingly, during the 1918 election campaign the Prime Minister was caught uncomfortably between promoting more congenial reconstruction issues, such as housing and social welfare, and jingoistically emphasising the insidious threat of Bolshevism and the need for draconian German war reparations. This set the standard for Coalition candidates in Glasgow, not least George Barnes in Gorbals, who had severed his connection with the Labour Party after refusing to resign from the War Cabinet. Although his opponent, Maclean, advocated a largely conventional Labour programme, the latter's Bolshevik credentials were enough to encourage a disparate array of supporters to rally round Barnes, including local Unionists.[3]

There was ultimately bitter disappointment among Labour ranks over the outcome of the general election, held in mid-December. Only Govan turned socialist, with the victory of Neil Maclean, although in Shettleston John Wheatley came a close second to the Coalition Unionist, Thomas Adair. It should be stressed, however, that overall there was an extremely low turnout at the poll, mainly due to serious deficiencies in the outdated electoral register. The unusual circumstances of the election meant that the Unionists were the clear beneficiaries, fending off the Labour challenge and routing independent Asquith Liberals in working-class constituencies like Springburn and St Rollox. Moreover, while the Coalition had saved three Glasgow seats for Lloyd George Liberals, their dependence on Unionist support gave them a precarious electoral base. Unionist morale was also boosted by the return of their national leader, Andrew Bonar Law, for the Central constituency. Although not noted for his charismatic qualities, this wealthy Glasgow businessman could display a steely streak, notably in 1912 when he outspokenly defended Ulster resistance during the Irish Home Rule crisis. Significantly, the Irish dimension was one of the important nuances to the 1918 election, with Labour candidates pitching a strong appeal to the Catholic electorate in Glasgow and Unionists continuing to defend the integrity of the United Kingdom.

'Red Clydeside', at least in the electoral sense, seemed to have been nipped firmly in the bud. Yet the setback did not dent longer-term ambitions for a Labour breakthrough, especially as it came to be realised that in 1918 so many extraordinary factors had militated against success. As far as Glasgow's ILP leadership was concerned, efforts were increasingly concentrated on parliamentary and municipal representation, in order to penetrate the key citadels of power both at national and local level. The encouragement of community activism consequently played less of a role in ILP priorities and the new emphasis had a damaging effect on the recruitment of women to the party.[4] This helped to create an enduring image of Glasgow Labour as male-dominated; a perception bolstered by the subsequent paucity of women as MPs and councillors, at least until the 1980s. Shifting ILP strategy after 1918 also led to a more ruthless approach in the quest to achieve electoral power. The Communist presence in particular posed a threat to parliamentary nominations, at a time when the broad Labour organisation could still accommodate the revolutionary left. Rivalries intensified as the ILP endeavoured, largely successfully, to monopolise can-didatures. In this respect the party leaders, most notably Patrick Dollan, demonstrated a shrewd understanding of *realpolitik*, which gave rise to the pervasive notion that a formidable Labour 'machine' had been constructed in inter-war Glasgow.

The focus on the parliamentary and municipal road to socialism did not mean that the city lost its reputation for industrial militancy. Within weeks of the 1918 general election Clydeside briefly became the centre of national attention as engineering workers went on strike, their objective to secure the 40-hours' week. Part of the rationale was that shorter working would offset unemployment, believed likely in the wake of mass demobili-sation of troops. However, ministers in the Coalition government identified a dangerous political sub-text, especially as the Clyde Workers' Committee had been revived, and the names of Messrs Gallacher and Kirkwood loomed ominously again. While wider trade union support for the engineers remained patchy, there was still a sufficiently disturbing quality about developments in Glasgow for the government to intervene directly. The return of Lloyd George's Coalition had not diminished concern about civil unrest as a result of post-war dislocation, and events in Europe (notably the Communist-led Spartacist uprising in Germany) were reinforcing fears of emulative action nearer home. The intensity of the government's response in Glasgow was thus intended to prevent any hostages to political fortune. As Bonar Law cautioned his Cabinet colleagues, 'It was certain that if the movement in Glasgow grew, it would spread all over the country'.[5]

In consequence, the strike reached an explosive climax on 31 January

1919. Prominent trade unionists had gone to the City Chambers to discuss the heightening industrial crisis with civic leaders. Emanuel Shinwell, then a town councillor and chairman of Glasgow Trades Council, later recalled:

> About 11 am on Friday a huge mass of people began to assemble in George Square. They brought their brass bands with them. All doors of the City Chambers were locked and a strong force of police guarded the building. My deputation, consisting of eleven members, including David Kirkwood and Neil McLean, struggled through the mass of people in order to meet the Lord Provost. We were taken to the library, when we were told that rioting had broken out. I rushed to the Lord Provost's room with the rest, demanding to know how a perfectly orderly crowd had been transformed in a matter of minutes into an angry mob.[6]

The violence and passion of 'Bloody Friday' came to be the encapsulating image of 'Red Clydeside'. The whiff of near-revolution ever afterwards hovered over the events of that day, despite Shinwell's insistence that it was an incident that got out of hand, with mass panic ensuing as a result of aggressive police action to contain the crowd. The authorities took swift and exemplary action against perceived ring-leaders. Shinwell was one of several labour movement activists arrested and charged with sedition, and along with William Gallacher eventually served a prison sentence. The Jewish and Irish antecedents of the two men fuelled insinuations from Fred Macquisten, newly-elected Coalition Unionist MP for Springburn, about 'non-Scottish' influence underlying unrest in the city. Although the strike ultimately collapsed, the lurid press evocation of Bolshevik machinations by a sinister 'faction bent on mischief' deeply troubled the middle-class consciousness, and helped to consolidate the politics of anti-socialism in Glasgow.[7]

In the long-term the 40-hours' strike did not damage the Labour cause, which continued to grow in electoral strength. During the pivotal year of 1922 the Coalition government had foundered irredeemably, with Bonar Law replacing the discredited Lloyd George as Prime Minister. The subsequent general election was an attempt to gain a popular mandate for the Conservatives and Scottish Unionists, and although Bonar Law's government was returned nationally, Glasgow reflected radically different voting behaviour. Labour triumphantly won ten out of the fifteen constituencies, taking all of the predominantly working-class seats and even attracting support in middle-class districts. Indeed, although he won safely, the Prime Minister had nurtured anguished thoughts during the campaign about losing the Central seat and ignominiously leaving his party leaderless.[8] There were a number of reasons for this striking improvement in Labour fortunes. Crucially, the electoral register was far more accurate than in 1918, allowing for a 75 per cent turn-out of voters and consolidating the ground that Labour had gained with franchise reform. The ten Glasgow representatives came exclusively from the ILP, showing the extent to which party organisation had developed in a relatively short space of time. Catholic Irish support was also less equivocal. The virtual demise of nationalist organisations after the 1921 Anglo-Irish Treaty and the creation of the Irish Free State helped to tip the electoral balance in Labour's favour.

Glasgow's famous Labour victory of 1922 was unprecedented in the United Kingdom, despite sweeping national gains which gave the party the second highest number of MPs at Westminster. The Clydesiders, as they

83. 'Strange Shadows', 1922. A cartoon from the pro-Unionist magazine, *The Bailie*, in the immediate aftermath of the 1922 general election. With ten Labour MPs returned out of the city's quota of fifteen, St Mungo's sinister Bolshevik alter ego demonstrates that for some Glaswegians the times were seriously out of joint. (*By courtesy of the Mitchell Library, Glasgow City Libraries and Archives.*)

The Bailie Cartoon Supplement,   November 22, 1922.

STRANGE SHADOWS.

St Mungo—"I'm no' feared, but that's a queer kin' o' a shadow for a respectable person like masel to throw."
[Glasgow politically is two-thirds Red.]

were quickly dubbed by the press, included such luminaries as James
Maxton and John Wheatley, whose impact on inter-war Glasgow was
profound. Both men firmly understood the importance of a high profile as
well as conviction politics; indeed, one of the features of the Clydesiders
was the personality factor, in an era notable for the growing influence and
competitiveness of popular newspapers. Their pugnacious approach was

84. James Maxton
election poster,
1922.
Labour's favoured
self-image is shown
in this general
election poster. The
gaunt, unmistakable
figure of James
Maxton cradles the
city's future, while
the infant looks
quizzically towards
the camera. Child
welfare was a
central feature of
Labour's
campaigning
strategy in the
1920s. (*Glasgow
Museums: The
People's Palace.*)

VOTE FOR MAXTON
AND SAVE THE CHILDREN.

exemplified by the suspension of Maxton and three others from the House of Commons in 1923 for using ungentlemanly language during a highly-charged debate over child health.[9] Whatever else the incident achieved, it grabbed headlines and endured as a potent symbol of Clydeside iconoclasm. Such individualism proved to be a considerable source of strength in consolidating Labour's popular appeal, as it seemed so tangibly to indicate a flexible approach to politics. Nevertheless, as time progressed, the individualist stance came to have a dangerously double-edged impact, with competing power groups fragmenting party unity.

Inter-War Electoral Politics

In the general elections of 1923, 1924 and 1929 the Labour Party maintained its superior position in relation to the number of MPs returned for Glasgow constituencies. However, with the rapid demise of Liberalism as a parliamentary force, the Unionists became the main focus of opposition. Sir John Collie was the last Glasgow MP with declared Liberal connections, representing the Partick constituency between 1922 and 1923. Demonstrating the deep divisions over the party's post-war identity, he had fought a bruising electoral campaign against Sir Daniel Macaulay Stevenson, standing as an independent Liberal. Although many disenchanted Liberals switched support to the Unionists, others were attracted by the radicalism of the ILP, and in Scotland's urban heartland the haemorrhage of votes to Labour did the Liberal Party considerable electoral damage. Former Bridgeton MP, Alexander MacCallum Scott, who James Maxton claimed as a personal recruit to socialism, blamed an overly mature Liberal leadership for being out of touch with the aspirations of younger voters.[10]

While Labour seemed to capitalise on the Liberal vacuum among the working-class electorate, the Unionists worked diligently to woo the middle classes. Part of this strategy involved a change of image towards an altogether more mellow brand of politics, which espoused social welfarism and distanced the party from the kind of Protestant 'die-hardism' associated with the true-blue wing of Unionism.[11] The female vote was specifically targeted, especially in middle-class districts, where the number of women electors was proportionately high. Walter Elliot, returned in a by-election for the Kelvingrove constituency in 1924, was one of the most famous exponents of the new Unionism, and remained a dominant figure within the Glasgow party until his death in 1958.

On the other hand, it would be mistaken to assume that for all the progressivism of Unionist policies, consensus politics was a feature of inter-war Glasgow. The polarisation between left and right remained acute, as John Wheatley experienced in his Shettleston constituency during the 1924 general election campaign. Both his socialism and Catholic Irish background came under fierce attack from the Unionist candidate, who (notwithstanding the shifting strategy of the party leadership) maintained Orange connections.[12] A convenient focus for anti-Catholic prejudice was the 1918 Education (Scotland) Act which brought denominational schools into the state system, with assurances that their distinctive religious character would be safeguarded. For staunch Protestants this meant the distasteful prospect of subsidising Popery, and appeared to be the thin edge of the wedge in terms of further concessions. Leading on from this, the surge in Labour support was attributed in a large part to Catholic Irish influence. The Glasgow Good Government League was founded in 1920 to co-ordinate 'anti-socialist' strategy in municipal elections, and one prominent activist, William George Black, made his concern quite explicit when he addressed a gathering of supporters. Glasgow, he maintained, had changed character and was no longer 'purely a douce Scottish city'.[13] 'Douce' is a Scots word meaning 'respectable', and Black immediately went on to connect the change with the Irish community and burgeoning political organisations that were 'alien in conception, alien at any rate to our Scottish ways of working'.

Insecurities about the Catholic Irish presence were exacerbated by the social dislocation experienced in the city after 1918, and which became especially marked as the economy began to falter during the 1920s. Nostalgia for the days of pre-war prosperity and Glasgow's forceful role in the imperial mission was based on a misty perception of the past, but served as a suitable yardstick for judging contemporary problems. The post-war city was seen as a much more sinister place, with journalists such as William Bolitho and George Malcolm Thomson contributing to the pervasive image of Glasgow as the 'Cancer of Empire'. Ironically, the crusading zeal of the Clydeside MPs helped to fix negative attitudes, because of their concern to highlight what was wrong with the city, especially the grossly defective state of health and housing. A potent indicator of failing Glaswegian confidence was growing cynicism about the civic authority. That the Labour Party was making considerable headway at the municipal level helped to increase the anxieties of both the press and ratepayers' organisations about the cost to the community of public services. In 1921 the *Glasgow Herald* was forthright in cautioning its readers that they could not afford 'the luxury of a Labour administration and a pampered proletariat'.[14] As the Labour presence multiplied in the City Chambers during the 1920s, it became a ready target for the barbs of opponents about eroding municipal standards.

Yet contrary to its success in parliamentary elections, Labour did not secure a majority of councillors until 1933, and the perception of civic decline was much more complex. In Glasgow there was growing concern about the bureaucratic nature of the municipal machine, which in the wake of the war seemed to have created its own disturbing momentum. The 1926 General Strike brought matters to a head, because Corporation workers were one of the most prominent groups supporting industrial action. Their stance polarised attitudes about the role and responsibility of municipal government. On the one hand, their refusal to operate public services was seen to be subverting Glasgow's much-vaunted spirit of civic co-operation. On the other hand, James Dalrymple's dogged refusal to reinstate striking workers in the Tramways Department, including war veterans, provoked vehement criticism of his management style. Significantly, the municipal elections of 1926 in the wake of the strike yielded significant gains for Labour. This had the effect of precipitating Dalrymple's abrupt resignation after forty-five years' service, his fall from grace a telling symbol of the shifting balance of power within the Corporation.

By the end of 1926, Labour had fifty councillors out of 113 on the Corporation. While this represented considerable progress, the failure to take overall power until 1933 can be partly attributed to the criteria that prevailed for municipal voting, which were more restricted than for parliamentary elections. Although suitably qualified women over twenty-one had the franchise prior to 1928, universal suffrage did not apply. Owner-occupancy determined voting rights, which meant that people defined as 'lodgers' were often excluded from the voters' roll. Comparisons between local and national politics were therefore fraught with difficulty, compounded by the different nature of the municipal opposition to Labour. The 'Moderates' were a loose and often uneasy blend of Unionists, Liberals and non-aligned, who vocally deprecated the intrusion of party politics into civic affairs and relied on declared 'non-partisan' pressure groups like the Glasgow Good Government League to get their message across. Over time they were criticised as too disorganised in their approach, one 1933 *Glasgow Herald* editorial blaming 'slackness and over-confidence' on the declining electoral fortunes of their candidates.[15] In face of mounting pressure the Moderates disappeared from the municipal scene in 1936, to be replaced by the far more forward-sounding (and Unionist-dominated) Progressive Party. Ironically, the appellation associated with radical Liberals before the war was now appropriated to erase discredited Moderatism. The 'socialist menace' still loomed large in Progressive demonology and there was a commitment to monitor public expenditure, but improved health, housing and social provision was also stressed as vital for the well-being of the city.

During the 1930s politics was volatile in Glasgow because the drastic impact of the depression seriously tested the abilities of those in positions of power. The collapse of Ramsay MacDonald's Labour government in 1931 had seismic effects on the party, which fractured as a result of the economic crisis. In the general election called that year to endorse a 'National' Coalition, Glasgow's official Labour representation was reduced from ten MPs to four. That the times were seriously out of joint was reflected by the return of the Duke of Argyll's Unionist grandson (Charles Emmott) for the solidly working-class Springburn constituency. Yet from a different perspective, Labour grimly stood ground in Glasgow, as for the whole of Scotland the party managed to take only six seats. Moreover, in the Shettleston constituency the controversial figure of John McGovern was returned as an independent Labour MP. The successor to John Wheatley after the latter's unexpected death in 1930, McGovern had been promptly expelled by his constituency association over alleged irregularities in the selection process for the by-election.[16] His independent stance was an augury of things to come. In 1932 James Maxton led the disaffiliation of the ILP from the national party, in disgust over the compromising constraints of Labour's parliamentary procedures. Two Glasgow representatives supported him (McGovern and George Buchanan, MP for Gorbals), and with the return of Campbell Stephen for Camlachie in the 1935 general election, the Maxton group assertively projected itself as the uncorrupted soul of socialism at Westminster.

The leftward preference of Glasgow voters was re-established in 1935, when four ILP and five Labour MPs were elected. Of course, by this time Labour had taken control of the Corporation, albeit initially with the support of eleven ILP councillors. Intriguingly, Labour's municipal achievement was made easier by the rise of a new (and transient) political phenomenon, the Scottish Protestant League (SPL). Founded by Alexander Ratcliffe, a former lay preacher, the SPL's eclectic programme ranged from the 'Rome on the Rates' bogey of the 1918 Education Act to quasi-socialist welfarism.[17] Ratcliffe proved to be too idiosyncratic a leader to establish a meaningful electoral base, but during the fateful year of 1933 the SPL's populist appeal still had sufficient potency to take seats from the beleaguered Moderates. Thereafter, Labour's municipal star remained in the ascendant, at least until after the Second World War. Credit for consolidating the party's base has been attributed firmly to Patrick Dollan, called 'the one man who dominates Glasgow Town Council' by a pro-Unionist journal in 1935.[18] Dollan's formidable organisational abilities and persuasive personality helped to mellow the fiery image of 'Red Clydeside' and gave authority to Labour's municipal presence at a time when efforts were being made to improve outside perceptions of the city. He crowned a long civic career in 1938 by becoming Glasgow's first Lord Provost from a Catholic Irish background and, embracing conformity, accepted a knighthood in 1941.

Dollan had emphatically not endorsed ILP disaffiliation from the Labour Party, despite his intimate connection with the former organisation. He considered Labour unity as crucial to withstand assorted challenges, whether from populist groups like the SPL or the revolutionary socialists of the Communist Party. While the Communists never commanded the electoral support that Labour candidates in Glasgow could muster, they maintained a high profile, most notably in the unemployment demonstrations of the early 1930s. Peter Kerrigan and Harry McShane were party

85. Patrick and Agnes Dollan, circa 1938. Patrick and Agnes Dollan pose as Lord and Lady Provost. Dollan was the second Labour politician to be thus honoured, and the first ever to come from a Catholic-Irish background. A journalist, Dollan proved to be particularly adept at projecting the city's image during the late 1930s. (*By courtesy of the* Herald *and* Evening Times.)

activists prominent in the Glasgow District of the National Unemployed Workers' Movement, which ardently promoted the interests of the jobless.[19] The successive hunger marches to London especially caught the public imagination and attracted a broad range of support, although Communists were organisationally to the fore. However, common cause among the left was not so apparent in Glasgow during the 1936–9 Spanish Civil War. While many Catholic socialists struggled to reconcile their faith with the Church's support for Franco, the bitter conflict that developed among the various left-wing groups on the Republican side was reflected in John McGovern's impassioned denunciation of Communism in his 1937 book, *Red Terror in Spain.*

Challenges to Labour from the 1920s to 1950s

Although Glasgow acquired an enduring reputation as a left-wing city, inter-war politics ranged across a broad spectrum, and definitions of 'left' and 'right' were by no means clear-cut. The decline of Liberalism had the effect of fragmenting old allegiances, and both Labour and the Unionists gained significantly from shifting voting preferences. Yet as the core of support for Communism showed, the strategy and ideology of the two main parties did not necessarily accord with the aspirations of all politically-aware Glaswegians. During the 1920s the Scottish nationalist movement also constructed a base in the city, which although not electorally successful, nevertheless made a considerable impact. Of course, the quest for Scottish Home Rule had long formed a central tenet of Liberal and later ILP policy. From 1922 Glasgow's Labour MPs were forceful advocates of self-govern-ment, and in 1924 (during the first brief Labour administration) George Buchanan introduced a Private Member's Bill for a Scottish Parliament. There were recurring references to Glasgow in his argument; that the 'tragedy' of the city's deteriorating health and housing conditions was not because people were 'poor, or Scottish, or Irish, or drunkards', but because the Westminster Parliament was too remote and overburdened to deal effec-tively with such problems.[20] However, despite Prime Minister MacDonald's previously declared commitment to Home Rule, the Buchanan Bill floun-dered. Thereafter the Labour Party turned decidedly lukewarm on the issue.

Law student John MacCormick was an activist in the Glasgow University Labour Club who had been attracted to the ILP because, as he later put it, 'it had inherited much of the old Radical tradition of Scotland'.[21] However, by 1927 he had become disillusioned with Labour back-pedalling on Home Rule, and was instrumental that year in forming the Glasgow University Scottish Nationalist Association. Although it was one of several nationalist organisations in the city, the focus on University politics provided a useful public relations forum for the energetic MacCormick. As one historian has explained, the Association injected much-needed spark and freshness to the nationalist cause, which hitherto had lacked sense of direction.[22] A considerable propaganda coup was scored in 1928 when the nationalist candidate in the University rectorial election (the veteran radical, Robert Bontine Cunninghame Graham) almost topped the poll. Ironically, his defeat was viewed as a victory, because it fuelled momentum and brought together disparate nationalist groups. Later in 1928 the National Party of Scotland (NPS) was founded to co-ordinate strategy and support, with MacCormick as Secretary.

The NPS was identified firmly as left-of-centre, and indeed there were tentative approaches to persuade Maxton and his ILP group to join forces in the early 1930s. However, the socialist emphasis on centralising solutions to economic problems meant that the nationalists became marginalised in left-wing circles, their cause considered to be narrow, impractical and eccentric. Patrick Dollan witheringly described the NPS as 'a mutual admiration society for struggling poets and novelists and of no use to the working class', in a veiled reference to party luminaries like the poet and fellow journalist Hugh MacDiarmid.[23] There was also unease that nationalist parliamentary candidates would, like the Communists, fragment Labour support. In the 1931 general election schoolteacher Elma Campbell jangled Labour nerves in the St Rollox constituency by taking over 13 per cent of the vote, although the Unionists failed to win the seat.

The gulf between Labour and the NPS meant that MacCormick began to seek alliances elsewhere. Acutely aware of the need to broaden the range of nationalist support and construct a more authoritative image, he pitched the appeal of the NPS in a consciously moderate and middle-class direction. With the nadir in Labour fortunes during 1931 and 1932 such a shift in strategy seemed to make sense, especially as popular newspapers like the *Daily Record* were giving unprecedented coverage to the Home Rule option as a meaningful alternative to growing political polarisation amidst the economic crisis. In Glasgow considerable publicity was generated by the exploits of Kevan McDowall, a solicitor (like MacCormick) and Secretary of the Cathcart constituency Unionist Association. Articulating a passionate belief in the pre-war imperial federalist ideal, whereby Scotland would have its own parliament within a strong British Empire, McDowall provoked a hostile reaction from both the Unionist hierarchy and Glasgow business-men, anxious to preserve the economic integrity of the United Kingdom.[24] Eventually in 1933 the heretical McDowall was expelled from the party along with a number of supporters. He immediately joined forces with a small but influential group of right-of-centre nationalists to form the Scottish Party, and after much manoeuvring by MacCormick to win over the NPS Executive, the two organisations merged to form the Scottish National Party (SNP) in 1934.

Initially the new nationalist organisation had limited electoral appeal in Glasgow, with Labour's recovery by 1935 restoring equilibrium to two-party domination. The war was a further focus for unity, exemplified by Lord Provost Dollan's heartfelt appeal to citizens to do their civic and patriotic duty. Yet although there was unprecedented support for Labour south of the Border in the 1945 general election, the Glasgow response was more muted, with only one change in the division of seats. Walter Elliot lost the marginal Unionist constituency of Kelvingrove by eighty-eight votes, the presence of a Liberal and a Scottish Nationalist (Hugh MacDiarmid) indicating the diversity of politics in the wake of the war. Nor was the breach between Labour and the ILP healed in 1945, due to resistance on the part of James Maxton to submerge his party's identity. Returned yet again for Bridgeton, it was a telling indicator of Maxton's popularity that he was not opposed by a Labour candidate. Indeed, personal loyalty had been a major factor in holding the ILP together, and after Maxton's death in 1946 there was no-one of similarly charismatic qualities who could replace him. The Bridgeton by-election was narrowly won by James Carmichael for the ILP, but during the months that followed all three of the party's Glasgow MPs threw in their lot with Labour.

There were inevitable accusations of political opportunism because of this turnaround, although a retreat from the Labour cause generally in the city may have contributed to the closing of ranks. In municipal elections the Labour majority on the Corporation was steadily eroded by Progressive gains during 1946 and 1947, the *Glasgow Herald* attributing declining popularity to 'the ever increasing material inconveniences' of post-war austerity.[25] The Progressives depicted Labour hegemony since 1933 as a stagnating influence, the legendary 'machine' having become too deeply and dangerously entrenched. Ominously, the defeat of the Labour candidate in the 1948 Camlachie by-election, following the death of Campbell Stephen, reflected disenchantment among the committed left as well as growing support for Unionism. A significant blow to Labour morale the following year was the election as Lord Provost of Progressive leader Victor Warren, a former Unionist parliamentary candidate. By this time the political balance on the Corporation was at a knife-edge, with the Progressives eventually edging into overall control. It was not until 1952 that the Labour group managed to reassert its dominant position.

Labour's problems in Glasgow were exacerbated not just by economic stringency but by apparent government insensitivity to Scotland. Prime Minister Clement Attlee and his Cabinet were accused of deliberately playing down the contentious Home Rule issue. Policies of state centralisation were also believed to run counter to the long-standing Labour emphasis on local democracy, the transfer of municipal electricity and gas undertakings to national ownership considered to be 'expropriation' in some socialist circles.[26] The notion that Scotland was suffering under a remote and unsympathetic regime rallied support from a broad spectrum of political opinion, ranging from Unionist to Communist. John MacCormick, who had left the SNP in 1942 after a bitter leadership struggle, harnessed the popular mood with his cross-party, Glasgow-based movement, Scottish Convention. Momentum built up swiftly, reaching a heady climax in 1949, when the 'Covenant' campaign was launched in favour of a Scottish Parliament. Reflecting historical continuity, there were conscious echoes of the 1638 declaration of Covenanting resistance at Glasgow cathedral. MacCormick later recalled one huge public meeting in the city during November 1949, where 'for two hours, a continuous stream of douce Glasgow citizens filed past to proclaim by their signatures their faith in their Scottish nationhood'.[27]

The propaganda success of the Covenant was regarded with cynicism by the Scottish Labour hierarchy, who tried to exploit the movement's profoundly ambiguous political profile. However, the defensive Labour reaction was interpreted as a sign of weakness, contributing towards the party's faltering electoral performance in Glasgow and elsewhere. That there was expediency involved in Scottish Unionist support was shown when the Covenant's meteoric rise declined precipitately after the

Conservative government was returned in 1951. No longer in need of the 'Scottish card' to play against Labour, and with assurances of further administrative devolution via the Scottish Office, the Unionists took speedy steps to steer public sympathy away from nationalism. MacCormick's conviction that the Covenant should transcend party politics had given the campaign a sense of earnest moral mission during the post-war period of reconstruction, but the popular unity engendered by the cause proved to be ephemeral. Neither the Labour nor the Unionist leadership had the heart for dealing with the complexities of constitutional change, which was identified as a low priority compared with implementing the vast housing and planning projects that formed the core of their ambitious election promises.

Nevertheless, Covenant supporters were associated with one episode which burrowed deep into the popular consciousness and lingered long after their movement was all but forgotten. On Christmas Day 1950 the Stone of Destiny (the ancient Coronation stone of Scotland) was sensationally stolen from its controversial resting place in Westminster Abbey, which was no mean feat, considering that it weighed over 200 kilograms. Four self-styled 'reivers' were involved, Ian Hamilton, Kay Mathieson, Alan Stewart and Gavin Vernon. Hamilton, a Glasgow University law student and protégé of MacCormick, was the acknowledged 'brains' behind the plot, designed symbolically to draw attention to Scotland's usurped sovereignty. He later wryly recollected, 'It was naivety as much as faith that took us down that road to London'.[28] Ultimately the precious relic was recovered, and no-one was prosecuted. The careless custodianship of the Stone had caused more than enough embarrassment for the government and publicity for the Covenant campaign.

Political Reorientation from the 1950s

In the 1950, 1951 and 1955 general elections Glasgow returned a quota of eight Labour MPs and seven Unionists, with (as a sign of changing times) the designation of 'Conservative' used much more frequently to describe the latter party's candidates. Constituency boundary changes were implemented twice during this time (in 1950 and 1955) to reflect the city's shifting population base. The new divisional alignment was one reason why the previous Labour stronghold of Govan narrowly turned Unionist in 1950, and adhered to the right for the next five years. Renewed support for the Unionists was also evident in the return of the veteran Walter Elliot to the Kelvingrove seat lost in 1945, his shrewd attack on Labour's Scottish record, especially on housing, hitting hard with voters. Yet despite the successes of the 1950s, the Unionist position was more precarious than that of Labour, which became increasingly entrenched in the predominantly working-class constituencies. Moreover, the redistribution of population as a result of

86. John MacCormick and Stone of Destiny 'reivers', 1951.
MacCormick (centre) poses proudly with the young Ian Hamilton (left) and Gavin Vernon (right). Hamilton
masterminded the audacious removal of the Stone of Destiny from Westminster Abbey on Christmas Day
1950, aided by Vernon and two others. (*By courtesy of the* Herald *and* Evening Times.)

Corporation rehousing strategy was beginning to have a profound effect on
the electoral balance. Although the Conservative government was returned
again in the 1959 general election, Labour made two gains in the city, bringing its representation to ten MPs. Victory in the Scotstoun constituency was
directly attributed to the influx of voters to the new Drumchapel housing
scheme.[29]

Far worse was to follow for Glasgow Unionists in the 1964 general election, when a Labour government was narrowly returned under Harold
Wilson. Unionist representation contracted drastically to the two constituencies of Cathcart and Hillhead, the success of Cathcart's new MP,
Teddy Taylor, partly attributable to his strong local base. On the other
hand, the overall decline in Unionist votes in Glasgow was a severe jolt to
the party leadership. Losing the Pollok seat had particularly symbolic resonance, given that during the inter-war period MP Sir John Gilmour was
repeatedly returned with majorities well into five figures. Pollok was yet
another constituency affected by rehousing, although the solid showing of
the revitalised Liberal Party in 1964 helped to dent the Unionist vote. A

future Scottish Secretary of State, George Younger, recalled the mood of panic the catastrophe immediately wrought within Unionist circles:

> To lose Pollok was unimaginable. The older hands saw very clearly that what was disappearing was the working-class Tory vote, the Unionist vote, and with supreme illogic of course, at that moment we chose to stop being Unionists and became Conservatives.[30]

In order to alter what was thought to be an outmoded image, Glasgow (and Scottish) Unionism was officially given a revamped Conservative identity in 1965. Not just the name but the organisational base underwent a metamorphosis, the centralisation in Edinburgh of hitherto autonomous Divisional Councils considered vital for greater administrative and electoral efficiency.

The Conservatives consequently became a new force in Glasgow's

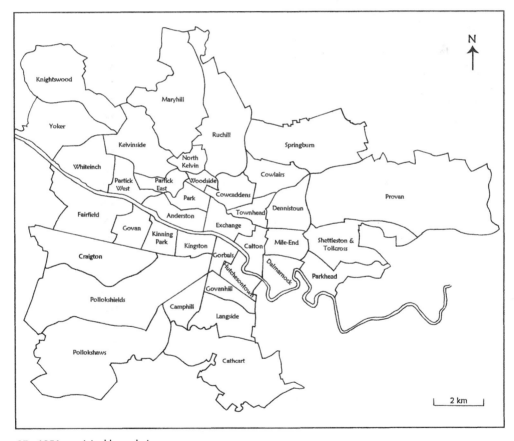

87. 1951 municipal boundaries.
Glasgow underwent unprecedented expansion during the inter-war period when the territory of the city more than doubled. New peripheral land was developed for council housing, and the creation of 'township' communities had a political impact as Labour supporters were dispersed throughout the city. The map shows the municipal boundaries in 1951, extending over thirty-seven electoral wards. (*The author.*)

88. Walter Elliot, circa 1950. Elliot round about the time he represented the Kelvingrove constituency for the Unionists in the 1950s. One of the longest-serving Glasgow MPs, Elliot was also an energetic Secretary of State for Scotland between 1936 and 1938. This drawing by W. O. Hutchison captures his distinctive, craggy looks. (*Scottish National Portrait Gallery. Copyright © the estate of W. O. Hutchison.*)

municipal politics; or rather, they gradually supplanted the Progressive Party, which since 1936 had solidly stood ground in the City Chambers. Using an assertively populist appeal, William Shearer became the first Conservative councillor to win a Corporation seat in 1967. Five years later the Progressives had disappeared, erstwhile councillors now rallying under the Conservative banner. At the time the coalescence of the right seemed to be an astute move, because the economic downswing was alienating public opinion from the policies of the Labour government. Distancing Conservatism from the politics associated with Scottish Unionism also had the advantage of identifying the party with more secular, post-colonial modernity. There had been a decidedly Orange tinge to several electoral successes in Glasgow, even during the 1950s, but the erosion of religious affiliation as a politically determining factor allowed the contentious issue of sectarianism to become muted.[31] Moreover, the Conservative hierarchy was anxious to go with the flow of popular opinion by projecting plans during the late 1960s in favour of Scottish devolution under a directly-elected Assembly. Strategy seemed to be vindicated by the unexpected Conservative victory in the 1970 general election, even though there was no advance on the two Glasgow constituencies.

The repackaging of Glasgow Unionism corresponded with a dramatic surge of support for the nationalist cause, as the SNP overcame years in the political doldrums to make major electoral inroads. There had been an augury of revival in the 1961 Bridgeton by-election, won by Labour but with a disconcertingly strong showing on the part of the nationalists. However, as the decade progressed, the SNP performance shifted gear from the steady to the spectacular. The sudden death of Pollok's Labour MP (Alex Garrow) precipitated a by-election in 1967, where the nationalist candidate polled over 10,000 votes and helped to ensure the return of a Conservative (Esmond Wright) until 1970. Then in 1968 the SNP 'roared like young lions rampant into the corridors of local government', according to the picturesque assessment of the *Glasgow Herald*.[32] The 'lions' triumphantly took thirteen Corporation seats, all but one from Labour. For the first time since 1952 municipal control passed out of Labour hands, with the nationalists holding the balance between the main parties. However, this early success was transient, as if voters were giving a cautionary warning to the Labour Party about taking its electoral base for granted. The SNP's breakneck momentum was abruptly halted in the 1970 general election, and the Corporation reverted to Labour control in 1971. Nevertheless, the issue of devolution came to dominate politics during the 1970s, the nationalist presence proving to be a profound irritant to Labour leaders in their attempts to safeguard parliamentary and municipal hegemony.

Significantly, the Glasgow Labour Party (like the Unionists) was suffering from an image problem which the youth and exuberance of SNP activists cast in a particularly unattractive light. As the total number of municipal votes plummeted from 121,248 in 1963 to 68,538 in 1968, the once formidable Labour 'machine' was exposed by the press to be in somewhat creaking order.[33] The City Labour Party was in dire financial straits, dependent on the inconsistent beneficence of trade unions. To compound the crisis, lurid 'graft' and corruption scandals unravelled within the Corporation towards the end of 1968, which were used by the Conservatives and others as evidence of previous Labour mismanagement. Less sensational, but just as damaging, was the perception of Labour as a bastion of elderly male worthies, still locked in the heroic pioneering days of the inter-war period and not prepared to make way for younger blood. John Rankin was aged eighty-three when he died, still MP for Govan, in 1973. The candidate selected for the by-election, Harry Selby, was aged sixty. Margo MacDonald was thus an astute choice to fight the seat for the SNP, as she eloquently represented the aspirations of the new generation. Jimmy Allison, then Glasgow Labour

Organiser, later commented that the party leadership doggedly refused to recognise the dangers of putting forward the unprepossessing (if dedicated) Selby.[34] In November 1973 MacDonald took the seat amidst a blaze of national media attention, to become the first nationalist and only the fourth woman to represent a Glasgow constituency at Westminster.

Govan was a stunning blow to Labour morale. Another warning had come from Glasgow's electorate, with the clear message that a Scottish Assembly had to be incorporated into official Labour strategy in order to stem further embarrassing loss of working-class constituencies. However, after the Labour Party (along with Harry Selby) was returned to government in 1974, it was the London leadership rather than Scottish politicians who proved keenest to emphasise their pro-devolution credentials. In Glasgow there was unease about the complex implications of legitimising the devolution option, with local activists determined to protect their own home base. When Corporation councillors debated the issue in June 1974, Labour group leader Dick Dynes argued forcefully that the call for devolution would not be addressed by an Assembly, but by transferring power to local government.[35] 'Municipal socialism' was still buried deep within the Labour consciousness as a practical solution to regenerating society, without the ambiguous trappings of emotional national identity. Conversely, Conservative councillors stated the familiar case against the dangers of too much state centralisation and the healthy boost to local democracy that would result from devolution. It was therefore ironic that political attitudes had reversed sharply once the Devolution Referendum took place in March 1979, with the Conservatives implacably opposed.

The 1970s was a decade of political flux in Glasgow, as the devolution drama unfolded and four general elections were fought in 1970, 1974 (twice) and 1979. The city's diminishing population was reflected in the realignment of parliamentary boundaries in 1974 and a drop in the number of constituencies from fifteen to thirteen. At the municipal level, major legislation implemented in 1975 had a drastic impact on the traditional notion of Glasgow as the unified 'city state'. As was explained in the previous chapter, local government became two-tier. Strathclyde Regional Council's remit stretched over a vast area from Argyllshire to Ayrshire, its responsibilities including social work, roads, education and water. The focus of Glasgow District Council was on such areas as town planning, housing, environmental services, leisure and recreation. Its area of jurisdiction extended over 20,250 hectares, including the old royal burgh of Rutherglen, where residents had not generally welcomed annexation to the neighbouring city in 1975.

The division of responsibility was meant to be cost-effective, although there were those who bitterly resented the break-up of the Corporation. Appearing latterly as a rather toothless old lion, devoid of functions from the glory days such as health, gas and electricity, it nevertheless retained majestic qualities and represented a focus for unity and civic pride in the city. In contrast, the dual entities of Strathclyde Region and Glasgow District created their own distinctive power bases, which could often clash. This was an internal party struggle, as Labour reaped the main electoral advantage out of local government reorganisation, provoking accusations that the regional boundaries had been deliberately carved out to create an electoral fiefdom. Not that Labour initially was secure, losing control of the District Council in 1977 when the SNP revived again briefly to hold the balance of power.

The inconclusive 1979 Devolution Referendum and the subsequent general election temporarily stemmed the tide of nationalism and shifted the orientation of Glasgow politics firmly towards the economic recession and growing unemployment crisis. However, the return of Margaret Thatcher's Conservative government had the paradoxical effect of intensifying that party's deteriorating fortunes in the city. In 1979 Teddy Taylor lost his Cathcart seat to Labour in a sensational result that probably robbed the ebullient Conservative of the Scottish Secretaryship and a Cabinet position. Taylor had worked his way through the Progressive ranks on the Corporation to parliamentary success in 1964. He subsequently attributed his party's decline in Glasgow to the centralising policies of the mid-1960s, which undermined long-standing Unionist grass-roots structures and resulted in perceptions of Conservatism as alien and English-dominated.[36] Thus, far from defining identity, Conservative reorganisation had confused it. Thatcher's brittle brand of English patriotism, especially apparent during the 1982 Falklands War, did nothing to mellow the image north of the Border. Of course, many urban areas in England repudiated Conservatism in the 1980s, and so general factors relating to deprivation and deindustrialisation also contributed towards the shift of electoral allegiance. As the recession deepened in Glasgow, the last remaining Conservative seat was lost in a famous 1982 by-election. Former Labour Home Secretary Roy Jenkins was the victor in Hillhead, now standing for the recently-created (and short-lived) Social Democratic Party.

By 1987 Labour returned all of Glasgow's MPs. However, further boundary reorganisation had reduced the representational base to only eleven constituencies, including Rutherglen, which formally ceased to be part of the city after another round of local government reorganisation in 1996. The appearance of Labour invincibility also belied serious tensions within the party. The far-left Militant phenomenon was exuberantly championed by Tommy Sheridan in his domain of Pollok, once Glasgow's Unionist stronghold. Sheridan's ardent approach to community activism safely secured a seat on the District Council, despite his widely-publicised expulsion from the Labour Party for factional tendencies. Then in 1988 Govan confirmed its reputation as territory of ill-omen for Labour when the SNP's Jim Sillars achieved victory in yet another parliamentary by-election. The Labour campaign was singularly inept, as if nothing had been learned over the past decades about projecting a positive image for the party at a time when the constitutional question was beginning to resurface forcefully in politics. Indeed, although Govan reverted to Labour in 1992, the general election was notable for the SNP's shift into second position in terms of overall party preference in the city.

The return of John Major's Conservative government entrenched existing political attitudes in Glasgow. Local government reforms, intended to dismantle the juggernaut of Strathclyde Region and restore the city to unitary control, resulted in near obliteration for the Conservatives in the 1995 elections for the new Glasgow City Council. Out of eighty-three seats, Labour took seventy-seven and the Conservatives three. The solitary SNP success revealed that despite solid support, the party still had a long way to go in terms of breakthrough. However, the onset of the new municipal regime from April 1996 immediately brought problems for Labour. Shorn of Strathclyde Region's financial support and with little prospect of Scottish Office assistance to meet public expenditure, councillors found themselves in a cash-flow crisis with serious implications for the preservation of jobs and services. Moreover, irreconcilable differences began to emerge in the amalgamated authority, resulting in a prolonged and deeply damaging power struggle. An attempt to expel Lord Provost Pat Lally and his deputy Alex Mosson over what the *Herald* called 'sleaze, factionalism and the breaking of party rules' backfired disastrously and exposed long-simmering tensions to the glare of publicity.[37] That unsavoury scandals had also emerged in Paisley and Airdrie prompted London's *Evening Standard* to comment scathingly in 1997 about the need to clear up Labour fiefdoms in Scotland's 'Wild West'.[38] However, Lally survived the controversy with his ebullient reputation as strong as ever, as did Mosson, who succeeded him as Lord Provost in 1999. The landslide victory of Tony Blair's revitalised Labour Party in the 1997 general election was seen as a further opportunity to redeem Glasgow's tarnished reputation. Frank McAveety, Labour group leader, acknowledged the contradictions of near monopoly control, which turned politics dangerously inwards and meant that ego could get in the way of 'honourable intentions'.[39]

Whatever the reality of Glasgow's Tammany Hall image during the mid-1990s, with the onset of the new century it seems likely that internal administrative structures will be fundamentally overhauled, to ensure that the blighting personality factor does not overwhelm professionalism and damage the city's carefully cultivated international prestige. As part of this strategy, moves towards proportional representation and a popularly-elected Lord Provost have been tentatively considered within government circles. Another new direction for Glasgow has been the historic implementation of a Scottish parliament, following overwhelming national endorsement in the 1997 Referendum. Nationally, Glaswegians recorded the

89. 1999 municipal boundaries.
Local government reorganisation in 1996 had the effect of contracting Glasgow's municipal boundaries for the first time, when Rutherglen and Cambuslang ceased to be part of the city. This map shows the seventy-nine municipal wards in 1999. (*The author.*)

second highest 'yes' vote, with 84 per cent in favour of the parliament. There were intriguing results when inaugural elections eventually took place in 1999. Voting arrangements combined the traditional first-past-the-post system with a quota of proportionally elected Scottish MPs (MSPs). While Labour took all ten Glasgow seats in the former category, the proportional vote allowed for the return of four SNP representatives, plus one apiece from the Conservatives, Liberal Democrats and Tommy Sheridan's Scottish Socialists. Out of the seventeen MSPs, eight were women. Significantly, at one level of government in Glasgow, constitutional change has given a more balanced electoral profile. It remains to be seen how the Scottish parliament will progress, and whether the loyalty of so many Glaswegians to Labour, manifested spectacularly in 1922 and retained (by and large) thereafter, will continue to be the characterising feature of city politics.

Notes

1. J. Cunnison and J. B. S. Gilfillan (eds), *The Third Statistical Account: Glasgow* (Collins: Glasgow, 1958), p. 439.
2. Michael Dyer, *Capable Citizens and Improvident Democrats: the Scottish Electoral System, 1884–1929* (Scottish Cultural Press: Aberdeen, 1996), pp. 113–14.
3. David Howell, *A Lost Left: Three Studies in Socialism and Nationalism* (Manchester University Press: Manchester, 1986), p. 192.
4. Alan McKinlay, '"Doubtful wisdom and uncertain promise": strategy, ideology and organisation, 1918–22', in Alan McKinlay and R. J. Morris (eds), *The ILP on Clydeside, 1893–1932: from Foundation to Disintegration* (Manchester University Press: Manchester, 1991), p. 138.
5. Quoted in Iain McLean, *The Legend of Red Clydeside* (John Donald: Edinburgh, 1983), p. 124.
6. Emanuel Shinwell, *Conflict Without Malice* (Odhams Press: London, 1955), p. 62.
7. *Glasgow Herald*, 1 February 1919.
8. Robert Blake, *The Unknown Prime Minister: the Life and Times of Andrew Bonar Law* (Eyre and Spottiswood: London, 1955), pp. 473–4.
9. Gilbert McAllister, *James Maxton: Portrait of a Rebel* (John Murray: London, 1935), pp. 119–31.
10. I. G. C. Hutchison, *A Political History of Scotland, 1832–1924: Parties, Elections and Issues* (John Donald: Edinburgh, 1986), p. 312.
11. I. G. C. Hutchison, 'Unionism between the two world wars', in. C. M. M. Macdonald (ed.), *Unionist Scotland, 1800–1997* (John Donald: Edinburgh, 1998), pp. 87–8.
12. Ian S. Wood, *John Wheatley* (Manchester University Press: Manchester, 1990), p. 155.
13. *Glasgow Herald*, 22 October 1921.
14. Ibid. 2 November 1921.
15. Ibid. 8 November 1933.
16. William Knox (ed.) *Scottish Labour Leaders, 1918–1939* (Mainstream: Edinburgh, 1984), p. 177.
17. Tom Gallagher, 'Protestant extremism in urban Scotland, 1930–1939: its growth and contraction', *Scottish Historical Review* 64 (1985), pp. 147–50.
18. *The Bailie*, 2 March 1935.
19. George Rawlinson, 'Mobilising the unemployed: the National Unemployed Workers' Movement in the west of Scotland', in Robert Duncan and Arthur McIvor (eds), *Labour and Class Conflict on the Clyde, 1900–1950* (John Donald: Edinburgh, 1992), pp. 186–93.
20. *Parliamentary Debates* (173), 9 May 1924, p. 794.
21. J. M. MacCormick, *The Flag in the Wind: the Story of the National Movement in Scotland* (Victor Gollancz: London, 1955), p. 14.
22. Richard J. Finlay, *Independent and Free: Scottish Politics and the Origins of the Scottish National Party, 1918–1945* (John Donald: Edinburgh, 1994), p. 72.
23. Quoted in Richard J. Finlay, 'Pressure group or political party? The nationalist impact on Scottish politics, 1928–1945', *Twentieth Century British History* 3 (1992), p. 283.
24. James Mitchell, *Conservatives and the Union: A Study of Conservative Party Attitudes to Scotland* (Edinburgh University Press: Edinburgh, 1990), p. 47.
25. *Glasgow Herald*, 4 November 1947.

26. Douglas Young, *Labour Record on Scotland, 1945–1949* (Scottish Secretariat of the Labour Party: Glasgow, 1949), p. 20.
27. MacCormick, *Flag in the Wind*, p. 134.
28. Ian Hamilton, *A Touch of Treason* (Lochar: Moffat, 1990), p. 52.
29. *Glasgow Herald*, 9 October 1959.
30. Quoted in Arnold Kemp, *The Hollow Drum: Scotland Since the War* (Mainstream: Edinburgh, 1993), p. 100.
31. James Kellas, 'The party in Scotland', in Anthony Seldon and Stuart Ball (eds), *Conservative Century: the Conservative Party since 1900* (Oxford University Press: Oxford, 1994), p. 678.
32. *Glasgow Herald*, 8 May 1968.
33. Ibid. 29 May 1968.
34. Jimmy Allison, *Guilty by Suspicion: A Life and Labour* (Argyll: Glendaruel, 1995), pp. 171–3.
35. *Glasgow Herald*, 28 June 1974.
36. Quoted in David Seawright, 'Scottish Unionism: an east-west divide?', *Scottish Affairs* 23 (1998), pp. 61–2.
37. *Herald*, 24 March 1998.
38. *Evening Standard*, 15 August 1997.
39. *Herald*, 23 February 1998.

CHAPTER ELEVEN

Social Change and Modernisation

The confidence that characterised Glasgow prior to 1914 was seriously eroded by the war, especially as the city's industrial base manifested such unsettling signs of weakness by the early 1920s. While problems of overcrowding and deprivation had a long pedigree, a negative image of the city began to overwhelm the popular consciousness during this time. The expansion of the media helped to perpetuate such notions. Investigative journalism and sensationalist fiction aimed to expose the city's nether side, and the legend of *No Mean City* was born during the 1930s. Yet inter-war Glasgow was far from the bleak cultural wasteland that some contemporary commentators suggested, and this chapter will show the vibrancy of social life, especially in leisure and recreation.

After the Second World War ambitious plans for reconstruction were progressed for Glasgow. The scale of the post-war housing project was massive, involving the relocation of a substantial percentage of the population, the wholesale clearance of inner-city communities and the development of new municipal housing estates. While the overall quality of life did improve, there was a social price to pay as communities fragmented and many of the new development areas failed to provide adequate amenity resources. By the 1970s the city planners recognised that their policies were creating disturbing new problems, and shifted priorities. This was the genesis of inner-city regeneration which, despite vicissitudes, proved to be instrumental in reversing the pervasive image of negativity, and made Glasgow culturally one of the United Kingdom's most dynamic cities during the last decades of the twentieth century.

Social Problems and the Coming of War

Prior to the First World War Glasgow's public relations profile was projected as a flourishing combination of culture and industry, overseen by benevolent civic government. As local historian George Eyre-Todd proudly put it in 1911: 'Glasgow has long been pointed out as perhaps the best-governed city in the world. With fleets upon every sea, and enterprises in every corner of the earth, it is the successor of the famous merchant cities of the past – Tyre, Carthage, and Venice'.[1] However, previous chapters have shown how the buoyancy reflected in these words seemed to deflate after 1918. Even though the Corporation remained a pivotal force for binding the community together, the invincibility of its great utilities was seen to falter, notably the tramways against the challenge of new technology. The political base also fundamentally altered, due to Liberal decline and Labour's sweeping general election successes of the early 1920s. Glasgow's leading Labour politicians shrewdly understood the power of the media and refined their propaganda skills in response to the social upheavals of war. The subsequent image of 'Red Clydeside' ran starkly counter to evocations of the prosperous pre-war community. One controversial exposé of city life was the book *Cancer of Empire*, written by journalist William Bolitho in 1924, which included much information supplied by 'the Clyde Reds themselves'. The threat of revolution was depicted as lurking menacingly because of the extent of social deprivation, with St Rollox MP and housing campaigner James Stewart describing the city as 'earth's nearest suburb to hell'.[2] In 1921 official figures revealed that over 66 per cent of Glasgow families lived in one or two-roomed dwellings, serving as a basis for Stewart's claims about the damaging impact of congestion on the quality of life.

The focus on Glasgow's social problems was double-edged. The Clydeside MPs were projecting the needs of their community in a direct appeal to the emotions. From a different political perspective the deteriorating urban fabric was used as a metaphor for Scotland's declining industrial prosperity. Assorted writers exploited the image of negativity to strengthen their case for remedial action. For instance, decrepitude featured forcefully in the writing of George Malcolm Thomson, who in 1927 claimed that: 'Half Scotland is slum-poisoned. The taint of the slum is in the nation's blood; its taint in their minds has given birth to a new race of barbarians'.[3] A journalist for the Scots-Canadian newspaper mogul, Lord Beaverbrook, Thomson's literary success reflected the growing influence of the popular press during the inter-war period. Beaverbrook had set up production in Glasgow when the *Scottish Daily Express* was founded in 1928. Together with the *Glasgow Herald*, the *Daily Record* and *The Bulletin*, plus three evening dailies, the city was well-served for newspapers. Editorially there was scant sympathy for Labour from the Glasgow dailies, although populist politics became more prominent with the arrival of the *Scottish Daily Express*. Indeed, a press war was fought between that organ and the *Daily Record*, then owned by Allied Newspapers, with both using the vexed question of Scottish regeneration as a major sales pitch.

The social problems of Glasgow loomed large in journalists' interpretations of contemporary events. Housing conditions were a perennial theme, as was evidence of anti-social behaviour emanating from those areas identified as the city's slum heartland. Bridgeton, Calton and Cowcaddens were among the most notorious, with *the* Gorbals (as it was invariably known among Glaswegians) becoming a by-word for urban corrosion in the United Kingdom. Unquestionably the district was deteriorating. In 1921 the municipal wards of Gorbals and Hutchesontown contained nearly 9 per cent of the city's population, and up to the 1960s the Gorbals ward was consistently among the most congested communities of Glasgow. Although density figures eased latterly, living conditions in some areas still had the power to shock. However, definitions of the Gorbals could be elastic. The district accommodated Laurieston and its elegant (if decaying) Georgian terraces as well as the teeming slum tenements of Crown Street in Hutchesontown. Known as 'the Harley Street of Glasgow', Laurieston's Abbotsford Place still served as a favoured address for the medical profession during the 1930s. One general practitioner operating from Abbotsford Place, Dr George Gladstone Robertson, took pains in his memoirs to qualify the lurid Gorbals reputation for violence.[4] While he was well aware of aggressive behaviour, he claimed that this was not so much the incidence of street-fighting among rival gangs as domestic violence against women, especially after public house closing.

By the 1920s gangs were identified even beyond the city as a malignant symptom of Glasgow's deterioration. The war was thought to have encouraged the phenomenon, due in part to the depleted manpower resources of the city's police force, although there had been vocal concern prior to 1914 about the 'hooligan' propensities of aimless youth in Glasgow and elsewhere in Britain.[5] During the 1900s the rapid commercialisation of association football and the intense rivalry that developed between Celtic and Rangers helped to fuel aggression. Brake clubs, which were called after the mode of transport that originally conveyed groups of supporters to matches, became identified with provocative sectarian partisanship. Sectarianism was an ingrained feature of inter-war gangs like the Billy Boys of Bridgeton, who flaunted their allegiance to Orangeism on and off the football terraces. According to Percy Sillitoe, who became Glasgow's controversial Chief Constable in 1931, there was a gang elite in the city, as represented by the Billy Boys and their arch-rivals, the Catholic Norman Conquerors (from Norman Street, Bridgeton).[6] The Billy Boys even charged subscriptions and issued membership cards, which pledged patriotic allegiance to crown and constitution. The funds were used for paying court fines, showing that gang activity in Glasgow could be rather more organised than the mindless, razor-wielding image of the newspapers.

The disturbing threat of organised crime had brought Sillitoe to the city, his appointment a statement by civic leaders of their commitment to tackle the issue. In his memoirs Sillitoe conveyed his impressions of a community urgently in need of strong leadership, which as an experienced police officer he felt he could provide. The new Chief Constable had served a tough policing apprenticeship in Rhodesia, which contributed to his missionary, pioneering approach. Sillitoe's self-assurance caused hackles to rise in Glasgow, especially when he claimed that policing standards previously had been allowed to slip. Despite the city's force being the largest in the United Kingdom outside London, he considered the police establishment to be woefully inadequate and in need of radical overhaul. Accordingly, Sillitoe extended the force and even appointed a corps of policewomen. He brought in state-of-the-art techniques, such as police telephone boxes, patrol cars and forensic science. In 1933 he visited the United States where he met J. Edgar Hoover, the high-profile head of the Federal Bureau of Investigation. This was at the height of a transatlantic moral panic over gangsters, and there was much in Glasgow's anti-crime campaign taken from FBI example. Sillitoe targeted individuals like Billy Fullerton, eponymous leader of the Billy Boys, whose jailing was depicted as a police triumph. He also used electronic surveillance to expose a 'graft ring' among councillors, who had been accepting bribes for procuring drinks' licences and other favours. An astute manipulator of the media, he formed a particularly warm relationship with Sir Robert Bruce, editor of the *Glasgow Herald*, who lauded Sillitoe's attempts to purge the city of crime.

The economic crisis sharply intensified the argument that a controlling influence was necessary in Glasgow, and by the early 1930s public opinion was accosted on all sides by the rhetoric of negativity and fear of social disintegration. Thus, from the left of the political spectrum, writer Lewis Grassic Gibbon penned a wry assessment in 1934 of the city's blighted identity, claiming that: 'The monster of Loch Ness is probably the lost soul of Glasgow, in scales and horns, disporting itself in the Highlands after evacuating finally and completely its mother-corpse'.[7] From a less picturesque perspective, the gangland novel *No Mean City* hit the bookstalls one year later, triggering a long-standing debate about the myth and reality of inter-war slum conditions. Councillors immediately banned the book from public libraries because of its 'unfair and inaccurate representation of working-class life', which had the inevitable effect of boosting sales publicity.[8] The authors of *No Mean City* were Alexander McArthur, an unemployed Gorbals baker, and H. Kingsley Long, an experienced English journalist brought in by the publishers to polish McArthur's prose and render the Glasgow dialogue more accessible. Their efforts were instrumental in disseminating the unsavoury image of the Gorbals, which was reinforced by successive reprints of the sensational tale of Johnny Stark, the doomed 'Razor King'. Significantly, Sillitoe had used the media to alert the public to the gang menace in Glasgow, and journalism underpinned this fictional representation of the problem.

Partly to counter the sombre stereotypes, regeneration was promoted ardently in Glasgow during the 1930s. As Chapter 9 explained, business confidence and civic consciousness were projected as the necessary economic restoratives, a strategy ironically given much press encouragement. Crucially important was the equation of progress with technical innovation. Percy Sillitoe made good use of this in his quest to combat crime, and councillors generally were concerned to espouse novelty, demonstrating that the Corporation was not behind the times. For instance, smoke and its debilitating health impact were all too evident in Glasgow's high incidence of respiratory diseases, but a cleaner solution was suggested by making wider use of the municipally-produced power source of electricity. From such modern and efficient alternatives the notion of the restructured city emerged. Probably more than any single event, the 1938 Empire Exhibition was intended to point the way forward. Economic revival was the rationale behind the Exhibition, first mooted by Sir James Lithgow in the forum of the Scottish National Development Council and encouraged by Walter Elliot as Secretary of State for Scotland. However, the Exhibition's remit extended much further than Glasgow, serving as a showcase for Scottish enterprise as well as a marketing device for Empire trade.

Using old symbols in a new context, the Exhibition's logo represented a lion rampant, which potently combined imperial and Scottish aspirations.

90. Empire Exhibition Lion, 1938.
The pugnacious lion rampant proved to be a hugely successful logo for the 1938 Empire Exhibition. This is a minimalist, monochrome version, but on the cover of the official Exhibition Guide the lion is set against a colourful background of patriotically entwined thistles, roses, leeks and shamrocks. (*Author's collection.*)

91. Empire Exhibition, 1938.
The sleek, Modernist architecture of the Empire Exhibition stands out against the skyline during this sunny day in 1938. In the centre, Tait's Tower points assertively upwards, while the ICI Pavilion and the *Glasgow Herald* Building feature in the foreground. (*By courtesy of the Mitchell Library, Glasgow City Libraries and Archives.*)

The soaring Tower of Empire was further testimony to the Exhibition's assertive profile, an edifice of over ninety metres placed prominently on the crest of Bellahouston Hill, at the heart of one of Glasgow's largest municipal parks. Scottish architect Thomas Tait's design for the Tower was sleek and Modernist, and the Exhibition generally was lauded as a tour de force of architectural innovation. The contrast with the monochrome landscape of Glasgow was deliberate, the parkland reflecting an alternative city of 'light, colour, spaciousness, spectacle and gaiety', according to the official guide.[9] Energy was a key theme, from the motive power displayed imposingly in the Palace of Engineering to assorted fitness and sports demonstrations aimed at promoting health. A different kind of energy outlet was supplied by Billy Butlin's Amusement Park and an impressive roster of entertainers, especially visiting dance bands.

When it finally closed in October 1938 the Exhibition had attracted just over 12.5 million visitors. This was much to the dismay of the organisers, who had predicted figures of twenty million. While the unusually wet weather (even for Glasgow) deterred the crowds, one uncomfortable reminder of old traditions may have helped to keep numbers down. For all its glamour, vibrancy and futuristic pretensions, the Exhibition was required to close on Sundays in deference to the still powerful Scottish Sabbatarian lobby. Destabilising international developments also detracted from the Exhibition's upbeat message to the citizens of Empire. European war was narrowly averted in September 1938 when Prime Minister Neville Chamberlain met Hitler at Munich to determine the fate of Czechoslovakia. Although peace among nations was a key objective of the Exhibition, the likely prospect of war had been evident in the Services Pavilion, which reassuringly displayed Britain's latest military hardware.

In the uneasy months after the Munich crisis there was intensification of civil defence arrangements to prepare for air attack. By the outbreak of war in September 1939 Glasgow's police, air-raid precautions and fire services were functioning as a combined unit, staffed by volunteers as well as professionals. The night-time black-out was implemented immediately, the *Glasgow Herald* reporting that an atmosphere of 'tense excitement and happy-go-lucky abandon' prevailed among crowds who had gathered on the first weekend of total darkness.[10] At the same time Lord Provost Dollan rallied the civic consciousness of Glaswegians, urging them determinedly to face up to war 'in the knowledge that your city will emerge from the combat a greater and friendlier community'. It seemed ironic that Dollan and his vivacious wife Agnes should have taken on this crucial leadership role, given their outspoken anti-war stance between 1914 and 1918. Yet the aims of the 'people's war' were qualitatively different from the previous conflict. The very achievement of a former conscientious objector as first citizen was depicted as an important symbol of unity and egalitarianism in a city undergoing profound social upheaval.

Housing, Reconstruction and Redevelopment

Towards the end of the First World War reconstruction plans had featured forcefully in government rhetoric, with electoral reform, education, health and housing forming part of a legislative package intended to boost living standards and promote equal opportunity. The Coalition government's seminal 1919 housing legislation sanctioned schemes for municipal homes helped by state subsidies. Consolidating its existing city improvement operations, Glasgow Corporation immediately created a Housing Department to co-ordinate building strategy. The target was 57,000 new houses, an objective that technically was achieved by 1939, with the completion of over 50,000 Corporation dwellings plus 10,000 jointly constructed by municipal and private enterprise.[11] Land was acquired for building, the territory of the city more than doubling from 7,763 hectares in 1912 to 16,076 in 1938. During the inter-war period the bulk of Glasgow's new housing was provided by the civic authority, with private speculative dwellings generally

92. Auxiliary Fire Service, circa 1940.
A corps of volunteer fire-fighters pose purposefully around 1940. The Auxiliary Fire Service was an integral component of Glasgow's civil defence arrangements after the outbreak of war in 1939. (*Author's collection, now in keeping of the Mitchell Library.*)

built beyond the city boundaries in middle-class residential areas like Bearsden and Newton Mearns. Here the bungalow was the favoured form of architecture, while in Glasgow early municipal developments such as Mosspark and Riddrie reflected the 'cottage' design promoted by John Wheatley prior to 1914. This showpiece quality accorded with long-standing Corporation determination to promote excellence and looked suitably attractive in publicity material. Less impressively, the tenants were drawn overwhelmingly from skilled, white-collar and professional backgrounds, as the category of citizen who could afford rents for these superior properties.

Historians have expressed conflicting opinions about the Corporation's vision for housing during the inter-war period. Assessments vary from criticism of the alien, 'Merrie England' conformity of cottage architecture to commendation of 'energy, imagination and innovation' in building design.[12] This dichotomy was reflected at the time. Labour's Jean Mann was one civic activist who abhorred Glasgow's tenement tradition and manifested missionary commitment in disseminating garden city principles. Serving as Housing Convener on the Corporation between 1933 and 1935, she vigorously pursued cottage construction to the extent that part of the new Pollok estate was modelled on Manchester's Wythenshawe Garden

City.[13] In accordance with the ideas of Ebenezer Howard, the English town planning pioneer, Mann was one of the main proponents of a satellite town for Glasgow, to help ease population congestion and offer a wholesome environment with modern amenities. Yet there were practical problems about building in the garden city style, not least costs and availability of sites. Moreover, between 1919 and 1939 some 18,000 houses, predominantly in the inner-city, were closed as unfit for habitation. Of these, 15,000 were demolished. There was consequently pressure to build low-rent tenement properties for relocated slum dwellers. One extensive example was the Blackhill housing scheme in the north-east of the city. Constructed in the 1930s, the bleak, barrack-like quality of Blackhill contrasted starkly with the cottages of neighbouring Riddrie, visibly demonstrating the contradictions of inter-war housing strategy.

Far more intensely than after the First World War, reconstruction policies from 1939 stressed the need for the fundamental re-planning of Scotland to provide a secure economic base and better homes. Glasgow accommodated over a million people, some 22 per cent of the national total, and so was understandably a prime focus of interest for planning reformers. One scheme for urban transformation was outlined in 1941 by Sir William

93. Damshot Road, Pollok, 1946.
Prestigious cottage-style housing in Damshot Road, Pollok. Located in the south-west of the city, the estate was developed by the Corporation from the late 1930s. Garden city influences were evident in some, but by no means all, of the inter-war municipal projects. (*By courtesy of the Mitchell Library, Glasgow City Libraries and Archives.*)

Whyte, who wrote with passion of the need to create 'utility, beauty, culture, healthfulness' in the substantially depopulated city.[14] A public servant rather than an elected representative, he nevertheless shared Jean Mann's idealistic quest for 'breathing space'. In pursuit of his vision Whyte was instrumental in bringing Patrick Abercrombie to Scotland, to co-ordinate a radical plan for the Clyde Valley region. Another luminary of the British town planning movement, Abercrombie had already taken on the daunting challenge of the Greater London Plan. He applied the same principles to the Clyde Valley project, advocating the relocation of urban population to new towns, industrial diversification and controlled regional development. Overcrowding was identified firmly as the scourge of Glasgow, with Abercrombie commenting that 'nowhere else in Great Britain are 700,000 people crowded into approximately 1,800 acres – an average *gross* residential density of nearly 400 persons per acre'.[15] The area referred to was located centrally and to the south of the river, representing 4.5 per cent of Glasgow's total territory.

The Clyde Valley Plan was initiated in 1943 at the behest of central government through the Scottish Office. Abercrombie submitted his proposals three years later. At the same time, Corporation councillors themselves commissioned an in-house scheme for the city's future, which proved to be radically different from Abercrombie. Robert Bruce, City Engineer, produced two reports in 1945 and 1946 aimed at transforming the physical appearance of Glasgow under wholesale redevelopment. In a fifty-year programme the old city would be obliterated to make way for a masterpiece of civic monumentalism, including a complex of imposing administrative buildings placed strategically on the north banks of the Clyde.[16] An intricate road and transport network, based partly on North American examples, would allow for ease of mobility. Bruce argued against relocation of population outside the boundaries and instead proposed a massive new housing development in garden suburbs on the city's periphery. He also vigorously defended tenement design, although his preference was for high-rise flats in the inner-city, reflecting modern architectural style. Underlying this grand strategy was civic determination to retain the city's population and taxation base. Recognising Corporation distrust of decentralisation, Abercrombie condemned the Bruce proposals as deriving from 'too short-sighted a view of Glasgow's place as the capital of the Region'.[17] The notion of the 'Greater Glasgow', which for decades had driven municipal policy, thus became the subject of heated debate as the war ended and reconstruction policies began to be implemented.

Whatever the precise plan for reshaping Glasgow, the war had seriously dislocated the slum clearance and rebuilding programme. Bomb damage also contributed to housing shortages, although Glasgow did not suffer to the same extent as neighbouring Clydebank where 35,000 people were left homeless after sustained attack over two nights in 1941. Immediately after

94. Bruce Plan, 1945–6.
A highly stylised representation of the Corporation's controversial Bruce Plan, taken from a contemporary children's guide to Glasgow. The reconstructed city has been compartmentalised into residential, industrial and administrative blocks, with multi-storey apartments looming over the landscape. While the helicopters give a futuristic transport touch, the old ways are glaringly apparent with the dominating masculine figures of authority. (*By courtesy of the Mitchell Library, Glasgow City Libraries and Archives.*)

" *The greatest changes will take place in the centre of the city* "

the war deteriorating tenements seemed omnipresent in Glasgow, and an eerie metaphor for structural corrosion was a particularly virulent plague of rats. In 1946 an organised squatting campaign caused embarrassment for the Labour-controlled Corporation, as homeless families occupied empty properties to demonstrate the severity of the crisis. Yet even as the post-war period progressed no meaningful dent could be made on the percentage of the population living in unacceptable conditions. The 1951 Census revealed the grim statistic that over 50 per cent of city households had no fixed bath and 37 per cent shared a water closet. That overcrowding was now defined according to more rigorous Scottish Office standards meant that over 44 per cent of Glasgow's dwellings fell into this category. During the early

1950s the Corporation's housing waiting list was approaching 100,000 families. The Corporation had already erected 2,550 temporary prefabricated houses, while building commenced in earnest in the vast peripheral 'townships' of Castlemilk, Drumchapel and Easterhouse. However, despite the exploitation of new materials and undeveloped sites there was an acute shortage of available land in the city, which meant that hopes to build 186,000 new homes were not a realistic option.

A combination of these and other factors helped to force a reappraisal of strategy, and in 1952 councillors reluctantly accepted the need for overspill to alleviate the chronic housing problem. New towns, as recommended by the Clyde Valley Plan, were to be substantial receiving areas. The first, in East Kilbride, had been designated in 1947, with ex-Lord Provost Dollan as

95. Lawmoor Street, Hutchesontown, 1947. The graffiti is a telling comment on living conditions in the immediate post-war period. (*By courtesy of the Mitchell Library, Glasgow City Libraries and Archives.*)

chairman. Notwithstanding this compliment to Glaswegian leadership qualities, the Corporation objected strenuously to the East Kilbride development, which was located only five kilometres from the city boundaries. It thus took considerable political horse-trading with the Scottish Office for sceptical councillors to support a second new town at Cumbernauld, finally designated in 1956. Some 40,000 Glaswegians were to be relocated to Cumbernauld, and to speed up the process the Corporation was authorised from 1957 to enter into overspill agreements with other Scottish housing authorities. This was a significant factor in reducing the number of inhabitants from 1.1 million in 1951 to 765,000 in 1981, thus meeting the aims of the Clyde Valley Plan to disperse 250,000 from the city. However, relocation was not confined to overspill agreements. From 1948 building was proceeding in the new peripheral estates at as high a density as standards would allow. The Corporation's annual statistics were impressive, with an unprecedented 6,460 council homes constructed in 1954 alone.[18] However, 6,150 of these were flats, by far the favoured form of architecture during the post-war period. Cottages, which for so long embodied Labour aspirations for the regenerated Glasgow, constituted a fraction of building output.

As for old, decaying Glasgow, slum clearance and rebuilding were co-ordinated by city planners in the largest comprehensive development programme in the United Kingdom. Eventually twenty-nine individual

96. Apartments, Drumchapel, 1955.
Standard Corporation apartment blocks in Drumchapel. Although there is a stark, pristine look to the dwellings constructed in this post-war estate, the presence of children shows that there is life in the new community. (*By courtesy of the Mitchell Library, Glasgow City Libraries and Archives.*)

97. Old housing and new, Castlemilk, 1990s.
Apartments remain a forceful feature of Castlemilk, another of Glasgow's massive post-war housing estates.
Yet, as this 1990s photograph shows, new building has had the effect of diversifying the landscape. (*Glasgow City Council Corporate Graphics.*)

plans were drafted, although not all got beyond the blueprint stage. Comprehensive development became a symbol of resurgent, modernising Glasgow, not least because an integral component was a motorway network which derived much inspiration from the Bruce prototype of the 1940s. A telling sign of the times was the dismantling of Glasgow's once renowned tramway system in 1962, although the demise had been coming since the early 1950s as traffic congestion intensified. 'Sadness and feeling of loss' was how one contemporary writer summed up the popular reaction, especially among older Glaswegians who still recalled the Dalrymple glory days.[19] Nor did nostalgia feature in the Corporation's ambitious plans for housing. The overall aim was to demolish 97,000 dwellings. Communities like Anderston, the Gorbals, Springburn and Townhead were altered indelibly after the bulldozers moved in. The magnitude of redevelopment was stressed, above all the preference for multi-storey apartment blocks as a quick and cost-effective housing solution. Such was the conversion of civic opinion to this mode of architecture that between 1961 and 1968 Glasgow had the most determined multi-storey drive of any British city, with high flats constituting almost 75 per cent of all completions.[20]

At the time there were some showpiece examples. In the Hutchesontown-Gorbals comprehensive development area, architect Basil Spence's lofty

Queen Elizabeth flats paid homage to the Clyde by echoing the design of ocean liners. Declaring that his mission was to 'civilise the tenement', Spence's words were later to have considerable irony, as his prize-winning, ship-inspired tower blocks were demolished in 1993 because of recurring vandalism and prohibitive maintenance costs.[21] Not surprisingly, given the focus of Corporation priorities during the 1960s, the thirty-one-storey Red Road flats at Balornock were built as the tallest in Europe and at first represented a considerable publicity coup. As one politician subsequently put

98. Queen Elizabeth flats, Hutchesontown, late 1950s. Sir Basil Spence's monumental flats are under construction. The scale of development is shown by the figure seated in the park. (*By courtesy of the Mitchell Library, Glasgow City Libraries and Archives.*)

99. High-rise hits Glasgow, 1950s. Multi-storeys as depicted in the *Daily Record* by cartoonist Bud Neill. During the 1940s and 1950s Neill provided a wry insight into the social life of the city that immediately touched a chord. Publication of his collected cartoons has ensured that Neill remains hugely popular both in Glasgow and beyond. (*Zipo Publishing Limited*.)

**"That's Bessie's on the top.
Wi' the edelweiss in the windae box . . ."**

it, with reference to the controversial role of Housing Convener David Gibson in leading the high-rise programme, 'He defied anybody, and he built as fast as he could'.[22] The single-minded Gibson was the antithesis of Jean Mann in his approach to housing, although there were intriguing continuities with Victorian precedents in his identification of Glasgow with structural monumentalism. A further contradiction in the Corporation's assertive modernising policy was lingering attachment to the pre-war notion of 'Greater Glasgow', which stressed that size and status mattered. However, in the search for building space, civic tentacles no longer stretched outwards but instead pointed resolutely upwards.

Despite the modernity of high-rise living, the environment proved to be isolating, insecure and alienating for many of the residents. As the Queen Elizabeth flats demonstrated, they were also expensive to maintain. In 1974, faced with accusations of creating costly 'new slums', the Corporation sanctioned its last multi-storey development. Labour leader Dick Dynes commented:

> . . . we will not be building any more after this. It is just not worth the candle. We have had a large number of complaints from both young and

old people. The planners should have told us about the difficulties before they were built – but they did not. We had to find out for ourselves.[23]

It was disingenuous of Dynes to blame Glasgow's planners, as politics had played a substantial part in directing the high-rise drive. However, the reaction against multi-storeys reflected the paradox of post-war redevelopment strategy. The ideal was often difficult to translate into reality, despite undoubted improvements in basic living standards. By 1971 the Corporation's post-war building record stood at over 100,000 houses and congestion had eased considerably. Yet this did not necessarily represent success, as slum clearance had the effect of fracturing community identity. Moreover, many Glaswegians were hastening the decrowding process by abandoning the city altogether. Planned overspill was not wholly responsible for the massive outflow, which had much to do with Glasgow's decaying industrial base and uncertain employment prospects. In 1974 the *West Central Scotland Plan* reported that some 25,000 people were leaving the city annually, a high percentage of them professional and skilled workers.[24] The GEAR project of 1976 was implemented in the hope of reversing this disturbing exodus. Significantly and symbolically, a planned new town for Stonehouse, Lanarkshire, was cancelled by the Labour government and the funds channelled to GEAR for inner-city regeneration.

Health and Education

Along with housing, health was an integral component of the First World War reconstruction programme. In 1918 the Coalition Government created a centralised Ministry of Health to co-ordinate provision. From 1919 the Scottish Board of Health was delegated to negotiate levels of grant from the Treasury, and the funds were then passed to the relevant authorities, including Glasgow Corporation. Despite hopes to integrate health care administration, responsibility for treatment was divided among assorted voluntary and public bodies up to the inauguration of the National Health Service (NHS) in 1948. Accordingly, public health remained a municipal preoccupation, especially the control of infectious diseases. Smallpox, diphtheria, measles, whooping cough and enteric fever were among the range of serious ailments treated in the six municipal 'fever' hospitals operational by 1919. Within this category, pulmonary tuberculosis (also known as consumption or phthisis) was recognised as particularly pervasive in Glasgow, despite steadily falling death rates from the disease. The prevalence of tuberculosis and other respiratory diseases was exacerbated by the high levels of overcrowding. Pollution was another major contributory factor. Smoke created the dense fogs that periodically engulfed the city up to the 1960s and the 'asphyxiating effect' inevitably undermined the well-being of Glaswegians.[25]

100. Tower block, Roystonhill, 1992 (before demolition). At twenty-four storeys it was a monumental symbol of the problems arising from the 1960s high-rise boom. (*Glasgow City Council Corporate Graphics.*)

During and immediately after the First World War, the need for better health care was made all the more glaring by the return of ex-combatants who had been physically or psychologically damaged by the conflict. The influenza pandemic of 1918–19 was a further uneasy reminder of post-war dislocation, resulting in approximately 4,000 deaths in Glasgow. Schools closed temporarily to prevent the contagion from spreading among youngsters, who at the same time became vulnerable to a particularly virulent outbreak of pneumonia. As the campaigns of the Clydeside MPs illustrated, of all the health issues affecting the city during the inter-war period, child

101. Tower block, Roystonhill, 1992 (after demolition). Seagulls scatter as the Roystonhill tower block is obliterated. (*Glasgow City Council Corporate Graphics.*)

welfare was the most emotive. Evidence from the statistics reinforced the belief that not enough was being done to improve the quality of life. Between 1911 and 1931 infant mortality levels had decreased from 139 to 105 per 1,000 live births, yet this gave scant cause for comfort as by the later date Glasgow was lagging behind other British cities. In Liverpool, for example, the figures were ninety-three per 1,000 live births, while Edinburgh's had fallen to sixty-nine per 1,000, after exceeding Glasgow's at the turn of the century. Understandably, maternal and child welfare provision featured prominently in concerted Corporation efforts to counter the disturbing levels of infant mortality. Health education aimed to disseminate the need for 'high standards of mothercraft associated with improved housing conditions'.[26] A corps of female health visitors formed part of this strategy; a movement inaugurated in the city as far back as 1908, but which was extended and professionalised during the inter-war period.

Plans for a comprehensive health service were promoted in earnest during the Second World War, following the publication of Sir William Beveridge's historic 1942 report on social security provision. As with housing, there were detailed investigations of the state of the nation to plan for reconstruction. One of the most revealing for Glasgow was the 1943 report issued by Sir John Boyd Orr's Committee on Infant Mortality in Scotland.[27] The toll of Scottish infant deaths was identified as among the highest in western Europe, with the west central region (including Glasgow) condemned as Scotland's blackspot. Environmental conditions were largely to blame, although it was ironic that such concern was manifested at a time when the war effort had the effect of relaxing smoke controls and shrouding the city in a permanent dusky haze. When it finally arrived in 1948, the NHS was important for integrating the administration of Glasgow's general practitioner and hospital services. Although the Corporation relinquished control of its fever hospitals to the new Western Regional Hospital Board, it retained provision of environmental health and social services, including child welfare. The scale of overall health improvements in Glasgow was revealed by the sharp drop in infant mortality levels from seventy-seven per 1,000 live births in 1947 to thirty-six per 1,000 in 1955. Yet Glasgow still compared unfavourably with other British cities, showing how much inadequate housing was inhibiting the full benefits of the post-war 'welfare state'.

By the 1950s the main cause of death for Glaswegians was coronary disease, followed by cancer. To the alarm of the health authorities, war conditions had increased the incidence of pulmonary tuberculosis and death rates from the disease were well ahead of other urban communities. In response, Glasgow's mass X-Ray campaign of 1957 was a pioneering health initiative, co-ordinated by the Corporation and NHS to identify tuberculosis carriers. Some 715,000 people were screened in mobile radiography units across the city and almost 2,000 active cases were discovered among Glasgow residents. The exercise was considered to be a milestone in efforts to raise the public consciousness about better health, although it failed to wholly eradicate tuberculosis from the city. Indeed, the high hopes for a healthier Glasgow were soon shown to have been misplaced. By the 1970s the new housing estates were displaying some disconcerting parallels with the old slum districts, especially in the recurrence of infectious diseases like tuberculosis. NHS reform in 1974, together with local government reorganisation the following year, was also criticised for failing to come to grips with the problems of the deprived areas. Public health (although not environmental health) had been removed from municipal control, and it was felt by some commentators that its status declined drastically thereafter.[28]

102. X-Ray Centre, George Square, 1957.
George Square, taken from a vantage point in the City Chambers, showing queues at the tuberculosis X-Ray centre in 1957. This major drive in health awareness proved to be remarkably successful in identifying cases and carriers of the disease. (*By courtesy of the Mitchell Library, Glasgow City Libraries and Archives.*)

Significantly, the functions of Glasgow's Medical Officer of Health, previously a formidable civic figurehead for the city, were dispersed among a series of designated Community Physicians. Despite some excellent and innovative medical services, the overall health record continued to compare badly with other cities. Coronary disease, chronic bronchitis and lung cancer were latterly among the major killers, associated notoriously with high-risk lifestyles (notably smoking and alcohol) and deprivation. Growing levels of drug abuse became a further chilling symbol of social dislocation.

Closely connected with health considerations, at least for younger Glaswegians, was the provision of schooling. The 1918 Education (Scotland) Act had replaced the Glasgow School Board with an elected local education authority, which was itself absorbed by the Corporation in 1930. As was seen in Chapter 10, a key feature of the legislation was the agreed transfer of denominational schools to the management of the new authority, with safeguards for their religious character. As 25 per cent of Glasgow's school population was estimated to be Roman Catholic, this process had considerable bearing on staffing and resources. By 1930 the Corporation was catering for 190,000 scholars in 194 primary and secondary day establishments. The massive scale of operations was magnified by the precarious economic climate, which focused attention on the vexed question of child welfare. The impact of the depression was revealed strikingly by Education Department figures, which between 1930 and 1933 showed a rise in recipients of free boots and clothing from 28,000 to 49,000.[29] There was no significant increase in school numbers, indicating that more than a quarter of state-educated children in the city had become 'necessitous' cases. As for educational standards, efforts towards improvement had been made with the reduction of the maximum primary class size from sixty to fifty scholars. Additional teachers were recruited, boosting numbers to 5,254 by 1930, almost three-quarters of them women.

At the outbreak of war in 1939 Glasgow's schools had closed and elaborate plans were implemented by the civil defence authorities for the removal of young people to safe areas. Evacuation was a voluntary process with just over 105,000 school-age children formally registered, the largest figure outside London. The receiving areas were predominantly rural and in the early days the health benefits were emphasised to encourage registration. However, for many Glasgow children the experience was far from idyllic.

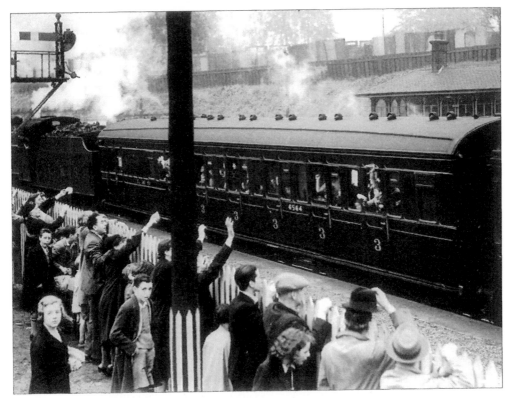

103. Evacuees, 1939.
Young evacuees depart the city in September 1939. Glasgow's wartime evacuation programme was the largest in the United Kingdom after London. (*By courtesy of the* Herald *and* Evening Times.)

The culture shock of their new environment was compounded by the class divisions exposed in the reactions of some host communities. The Earl of Mansfield represented worried Perthshire residents when he spoke about 'the filthy and verminous condition in which the majority of the children arrived'.[30] One letter to the *Glasgow Herald* stigmatised evacuees as 'pollution' and 'the odour of the slums', eliciting the curt response from Lord Provost Dollan that, 'These children may not have reached aristocratic standards of hygiene, but are more deserving of sympathy than censure'.[31] Although there were successes, the social experiment of evacuation proved to be impractical, with large numbers of homesick children returning by the end of 1939. The city's schools, now protected against air raids, had already re-opened. More positively, the evacuation controversy strengthened the case for meaningful reconstruction policies, as it brought evidence of urban deprivation directly into the homes of many Scots who had not appreciated the extent of the problem.

The post-1945 clearance and rehousing programmes inevitably reorientated the city's educational needs, although school building initially was slow in the new peripheral 'townships'. Such was the scale of the problem that by 1955 nearly 17,000 children were transported distances of up to eleven kilometres by the Corporation to schools in the old city.[32] An acute shortage of qualified teachers further stretched resources, the enforcement of improved standards (such as reduced class sizes) contributing to the deficit. The balance began to be rectified during the educational growth era of the 1960s. The exodus of Glaswegians beyond the city boundaries further eased the pressure, as did a general decrease in the school population due to falling birth-rates. By the 1990s there were just over 100,000 state scholars in Glasgow, plus 9,000 attending private schools. In a direct reversal of 1950s priorities, school closures and the amalgamation of existing institutions began to be implemented by Strathclyde Regional Council, which had taken over as the education authority in 1975. The Region's successor, Glasgow City Council, continued this controversial streamlining process. Conversely, there was sustained expansion in higher education, tangibly demonstrated by the creation of Strathclyde University in 1964 and Glasgow Caledonian University in 1993. Strathclyde was the former Royal College of Science and Technology and opted to remain in a central location, despite being offered the opportunity to move to a greenfield site in East Kilbride.

Leisure and Recreation

Emphasis on fresh air and physical well-being during the inter-war years derived considerable impetus from the nineteenth-century public health debate in Glasgow. A practical example was the schools' holiday camp scheme, which despatched thousands of necessitous children annually to 'hill and glen and seaside' for an invigorating break from the city.[33]

However, the benefits of escaping from Glasgow's smoke-tainted atmosphere were just as relevant to adults. In 1937 English journalist Cicely Hamilton cautioned prospective visitors that the city had 'no particular appeal' and 'beauty must be sought beyond its borders'.[34] The close proximity of the Firth of Clyde, the 'Burns Country' and the Trossachs boosted Glasgow's profile as a gateway for tourists and featured prominently in Corporation-sponsored publicity material during the Empire Exhibition. The growing popularity of motor transport opened out travel opportunities further and helped to stimulate a passion for rambling and hill-walking. Such energetic pastimes were by no means confined to tourists and better-off Glaswegians. Many of the unemployed made use of enforced leisure to discover the landscape outside the city. The peaks of Ben Lomond and other mountains beckoned the more intrepid, who joined working-class climbing clubs like the Lomonds, the Ptarmigan and Craig Dhu. As one devotee subsequently explained: 'I did at that time fear the city. You could have your imagination stunted if you lived all your life in a city surrounded by buildings. And the antidote to this situation was to get away at weekends as we did'.[35]

Of course, Glasgow's parks represented long-standing municipal efforts to maintain healthy public space within the city. From the 1900s demand increased for recreational facilities, and by the 1930s Corporation provision included eight golf courses, twenty-two putting greens, twenty-five swimming pools, sixty-nine bowling greens, 131 tennis courts, nine cricket grounds, seventeen hockey pitches and 109 football pitches. A diverse assortment of private clubs extended scope for sporting participation, although lack of available space in the city restricted opportunities for the construction of new recreation grounds, especially in the post-1945 'townships'. Spectator pastimes also thrived, notwithstanding the vagaries of the inter-war economy, and wholly new activities made a deep impression on the popular consciousness. For instance, in 1926 greyhound racing was introduced to Britain from the United States, and Glasgow soon acquired four well-patronised dog tracks. Boxing was another pursuit with an enormous following. For young working-class males it potently displayed qualities of skill, dexterity and tenacity, and could be the means of making a reasonable living for the most talented. Above all others, Benny Lynch secured legendary, if tragic status. In 1935 he was the first Scot to achieve triple success as world, European and British flyweight champion, titles he held for the next three years. Born in Hutchesontown, the meteoric rise of 'Wee Benny' was a boost to Gorbals pride and more generally reflected the spirit of Clydeside indomitability after the worst of the depression. That Lynch died an alcoholic, aged thirty-three, revealed the pressures of success in the ruthlessly competitive world of professional boxing.

Association football continued to stir powerful emotions, especially among die-hard followers of Rangers and Celtic. In George Blake's 1935 novel, *The Shipbuilders*, Old Firm players were identified lyrically as 'peer-less and fearless warriors, saints of the Blue and Green', offering spectators vicarious release from the profound insecurities of industrial depression.[36] In terms of performance Rangers dominated the Scottish Football League during the inter-war period, winning the First Division championship fourteen times. Celtic's heroic years came much later, under the inspired direction of Jock Stein, who in 1965 took over as manager. In 1967 Celtic triumphed against the illustrious Inter Milan to become the first British club to win the European Cup. Fundamental changes in the organisation of Scottish professional football during the 1970s considerably raised the commercial stakes for Glasgow's two premier clubs. In order to compete in the prestigious international sporting arena the unsavoury sectarian element was forced to recede. Rangers much-publicised signing of Catholic player Maurice Johnston in 1989 was described as 'revolutionary' by one historian, because the club previously had refused to countenance such a gesture.[37] However, football in Glasgow has always represented far more than the Old Firm, with two other senior teams, Partick Thistle and Queen's Park, still based in the city. The Thistle, especially, has served as a refuge for aficionados who eschew Old Firm domination and the lingering trappings of sectarianism.

Passion was by no means monopolised by football in inter-war Glasgow. By 1930 the city accommodated 127 cinemas, their frequently exotic archi-tectural style standing out against the urban landscape. George Green continued to invest in this highly lucrative business, opening Green's Playhouse in 1927 as a combined super-cinema and leisure centre. With facilities for over 4,000 film-goers and with a ballroom that reputedly could accommodate up to 6,000 dancers, the Playhouse reflected the dual pre-occupations of young men and women at the time.[38] The need to seek glamorous horizons beyond the confines of crowded tenements was often put forward as a prime reason for the allure of the cinema and dancing. Pursuing this theory, a series of *Glasgow Herald* articles in 1955 pointed out that there were more dance halls in the city per head of population than in London.[39] Choices ranged from elaborate 'palais' ballrooms such as the Albert and the Plaza to a plethora of smaller municipal and church halls, providing food, soft drinks and romance. The pastime had surged in pop-ularity during the 1920s, and it is revealing that the novel *No Mean City* depicted professional dancing as an important outlet for young people wishing to escape from the slums. The scale of enthusiasm was shown in 1932 by the vogue for the Afro-Cuban rumba, when over 1,000 dancers took lessons at Green's Playhouse during the course of two weeks.[40] Momentum was maintained up to the era of rock and roll jiving in the 1950s, when new musical trends accelerated the decline of strict tempo dancing. By the 1970s Glasgow's ballroom hey-day had passed, although traditional dancing, Scottish and Irish, continued to hold their own.

As the rise of the cinema illustrated, technology helped to diversify popular culture, and in Glasgow old enthusiasms often co-existed with the new. Thus, while the cinema dented the popularity of live performance to some extent, it was quite usual for inter-war picture shows to be interspersed with variety entertainments. The luxurious, American-owned Paramount cinema, opened in 1934, boasted a full orchestra and a troupe of high-stepping Tiller Girls.[41] Variety had a long pedigree in Glasgow and combined an eclectic array of influences, from transatlantic culture to the ethnic, penny-theatre traditions of the nineteenth century. Tommy Lorne, Tommy Morgan and Dave Willis were highly visual 'Scotch comedians' who sustained Glasgow's earthy and enduring pantomime style. The city's performing venues had multiplied from 1900, accommodating sixteen custom-built theatres by the outbreak of war in 1914. Drama made particular headway when the Glasgow Repertory Company was formed in 1909. Although it did not survive beyond 1914, playwright James Bridie was profoundly influenced by the locally-based stock company. He made it his mission to further professional drama in Glasgow, becoming the driving-force behind the Citizens' Theatre, established in 1943 and based in the Gorbals.

The new medium of radio was an alternative outlet for drama. The BBC first broadcast from Glasgow in 1923, and the swashbuckling melodrama

104. Jivers, 1950s. Glasgow style in the 1950s, when rock and roll added raw dynamism to the city's dance floors. Bud Neill's ability to uniquely capture the mores of the time are reflected in such detail as the Teddy boy's crepe soles and the pencil skirt and pony-tail of his jiving partner. (*Zipo Publishing Limited.*)

**"I'm no jivin' this wan, Mac.
I've jist new regained ma poise . . ."**

Rob Roy proved to be an enormous success later that year.[42] Glasgow and Aberdeen were the two main relay stations in Scotland, and both became noted for the quality of their output, especially music, drama and children's programmes. As technology progressed, the appeal of radio broadened. By the 1940s a humorous Glasgow soap-opera, *The McFlannels*, was commanding huge audiences, the family's experience of the black-out, rationing and assorted romantic encounters touching a chord throughout wartime Scotland. Significantly, the founding General Manager of the BBC, John Reith, had spent his formative years in Glasgow. He imbued the organisation with a paternalistic controlling influence that suggested much about his upbringing as the son of a Free Church minister. The Reith concept of public service broadcasting lingered long after his departure from the BBC in 1938 and inevitably influenced television, which arrived in Glasgow (under BBC auspices) in 1952. However, unlike radio until the 1970s, the government allowed for commercial competition in television from 1954. One year later the Canadian newspaper magnate, Roy Thomson, launched Scottish Television (STV) from its first headquarters at Glasgow's Theatre Royal. Thereafter the BBC and STV retained a strong base in the city, augmented by the highly successful commercial enterprise of Radio Clyde, which commenced broadcasting in 1973.

The Reinvention of Glasgow

A recurring feature of Glasgow's history, at least from the eighteenth century, was the projection of an image both cosmopolitan and progressive, yet with a strand of conservatism underpinning its identity. During the twentieth century the ambiguous response to immigrant communities illustrated the tensions arising from this dualistic focus. At times of uncertainty prominent Glaswegians did not hesitate to attribute social problems to alien influences, as was shown by the overt anti-Irish flavouring to certain political pronouncements after 1918. In a direct riposte to such defensive attitudes, Lewis Grassic Gibbon paid tribute to multi-ethnic Gorbals in the 1930s, which he described as 'lovably and abominably and delightfully and hideously un-Scottish'.[43] As well as the long-standing Scoto-Irish presence, the district had become the main centre for Glasgow's 35,000 Jewish community, overwhelmingly Eastern European in origin. As Gibbon conveyed, the Gorbals Jews added a dynamically different quality to the city's cultural life. A distinguished example from the 1930s was the Jewish Institute Players, founded by tailor Avrom Greenbaum and one of the most innovative contributors to Scottish community drama. Italians formed another important component of Glasgow's population at this time, their domain the ice-cream parlours and fish-supper shops that provided an indispensable catering outlet throughout the city.

It is salutary to note that anti-Italian riots erupted in certain areas of the city after Mussolini declared war on the allies in June 1940. Anti-Catholic sectarianism has been suggested as one reason for the particularly violent attacks on Italian properties in Glasgow.[44] The war and its aftermath generally had a marked impact on altering the city's ethnic profile, not least by dispersing the Gorbals Jews as the district was radically redeveloped. Yet if there was change to the old communities there were also new groups of immigrants who came to live permanently in Glasgow. The Chinese, overwhelmingly from Hong Kong, carved out a niche by providing specialist cuisine in a city not then known for the variety or quality of its restaurants. The Indo-Pakistani community was larger, with around 3,000 in the city by 1960. It was a long-established if not settled community, until wives and children were brought to Scotland during the 1950s to establish family units.[45] The distinctively Glaswegian love affair with chilli-fired curries derived from this ethnic presence and dated from at least 1938, when the Taj Mahal restaurant was advertised at the Empire Exhibition as 'a breath of the East'. Of course, the contribution of the Indo-Pakistani and other groups to Glasgow became increasingly wide-ranging and influential. The Jewish community produced a Lord Provost in the person of Sir Myer Galpern in

105. Chinese dragon, 1990s.
The dragon, Chinese symbol of good luck and leadership qualities, shows its mettle in a New Year parade during the 1990s. Although Glasgow has long been a multi-ethnic city, cultural diversity became more pronounced during the second half of the twentieth century when groups like the Hong Kong Chinese came to settle. (*Glasgow City Council Corporate Graphics.*)

1958, and he went on to represent the Shettleston constituency in parliament. Although the twentieth century did not produce a Lord Provost from an Asian background, Mohammed Sarwar was elected MP for Govan in 1997. Like Galpern, he stood in the Labour interest.

Notwithstanding anti-Italian sentiments, the experience of the Second World War suggested that more outgoing attitudes were developing among Glaswegians. War weariness had served as a focus for discontent during the previous conflict, which meant that maintaining morale remained a government priority after 1939. Glasgow's theatres and cinemas consequently were encouraged to provide entertainment, despite initial anxieties about the safety of public buildings. Dance hall attendance boomed and added piquancy was provided by visiting personnel from the armed forces. Agnes McLean, who was as passionate about dancing as trade unionism, retained fond memories of one American GI and his flamboyant footwork.[46] Moreover, although hours were restricted and whisky was in short supply, public houses remained resolutely open. Compared with the First World War, official attitudes were far more mellow about drinking, which in turn brought about a small but significant social change. From 1902 temperance movement pressure had prohibited women from serving in Glasgow's bars, but a dearth of barmen by 1940 repealed the notorious by-law.

In the wake of the war more of the moral strictures that directed the lives of Glaswegians began to be challenged. Sabbatarianism steadily lost its grip, and Glasgow's municipal parks opened their gates to Sunday sport in 1955. As for drinking, in 1954 the *Glasgow Herald* reported on glaring inconsistencies in the housing schemes, where there was vigorous enforcement of prohibition on Corporation-owned property.[47] The policy dated from 1890 and was again a temperance movement initiative, which had the effect of turning Pollok (post-war population 40,000) into a dry area. Whatever the worthy intentions behind the original measure, the scant amenities of Pollok and other newly-developed areas were seen by the *Herald* as creating a sense of social alienation that temperance attitudes only reinforced. There were ultimately a number of factors that combined to shift opinion decisively in favour of licensing law liberalisation. Declining membership of the Church of Scotland, especially among the younger generation, undermined the influence of one of the most outspoken guardians of temperance. Material considerations also were crucial, given the loss of potential revenue to the economy at a time when Scotland was being promoted assertively as a tourist destination. In terms of health and welfare, the proliferation of shebeens in Glasgow's housing schemes substantiated the argument that restrictions encouraged illegal drinking and perpetuated alcohol abuse.

A government review of Scottish liquor licensing, under Dr Christopher Clayson, reported in 1973 and unreservedly recommended a relaxation of the laws. The Licensing (Scotland) Act of 1976 subsequently extended opening hours, including Sundays. The hard-drinking stereotype of Glasgow began to break down, a process accelerated by British membership of the European Community in 1973. The reduction of duties on imported wines meant that tastes became more eclectic and sophisticated, and continental-style bistros, brasseries and wine-bars opened as a fashionable alternative to the public house. The reorientation of drinking habits eventually had a major impact on Glasgow's regenerated image, as *Sunday Times* journalist Ian Jack reported in 1984:

> . . . the new laws have made drunkenness less obvious . . . Now increasing numbers of Glasgow men and women get argumentative and sentimental over wine and cocktails in palatial saloons with names – Nico's, Lautrec's, Zhivago's – which suggest their owners were on nodding terms with Gertrude Stein.[48]

The literary doyenne of bohemian Paris, Gertrude Stein, was scarcely a name to be coupled with grey and industry-scarred Glasgow. Yet part of the striking success of the 'Miles Better' campaign was the ironic interplay of old stereotypes with Glasgow's phoenix-like resurgence, in order to contrast more sharply the metamorphosis into post-industrial city. Glasgow's gritty reputation was used to advantage by ostentatiously defying the lingering and deep-rooted image of depression. Significantly, the *Sunday Times* investigation included an interview with Harry Diamond, journalist and Gorbalonian, who was described as a 'reformed character' after taking on his high-profile role as the District Council's public relations manager in 1975. Sensationalism and negativity, the stock-in-trade of countless newspaper assessments of Glasgow since the 1920s, were replaced by self-assured rhetoric about Glasgow as a city of world importance. It was initially a daunting task to convince outsiders, as a 1982 survey of London-based civil servants revealed that Glasgow still evoked grim impressions of the Gorbals, tenement slums, violence and industrial corrosion.[49] Edinburgh, by comparison, represented culture, tourism, Scottish heritage and shopping, qualities that the reshapers of Glasgow not only strived to emulate, but audaciously attempted to improve upon. As has been seen, competition with Edinburgh or any other city was no new experience for Glasgow, and was a proven device for arousing an assertive brand of local patriotism.

The shift in strategy towards inner city restructuring had been stimulated by the need to create more congenial surroundings to boost Glasgow's flagging economic base. The proposed renewal of 1,600 hectares in the East End under GEAR was a pioneering initiative within the United Kingdom because it directed substantial resources back to the centre. Recognition that the old communities still mattered also represented a new awareness of the city's architectural heritage, above all the unique legacy of the nineteenth century. Shifting generational attitudes were important for rehabilitating the past, as many older Glaswegians had mixed feelings about the tenement city and its associations with deprivation and overcrowding. However, by the 1970s memories of the single-end were receding, and what remained of the old city appeared less threatening. A telling symbol of changing times was official concern to protect the fabric of buildings, blackened by industrial pollution. The Clean Air Act of 1956 was crucial for creating the environmental conditions conducive for stone-cleaning, which began systematically in Glasgow during the early 1970s. There were impressive results in the terraces and tenements of the West End, which shed their sooty patina to reveal the original red and honey-coloured sandstone. Conservation policies were extended and became a growing commitment of central and local government, with whole areas of the city designated architecturally important.

At the same time, the rediscovery of Charles Rennie Mackintosh as a pioneer of art nouveau conferred stylistic prestige on Glasgow that had not been assumed for decades. Mackintosh's international cult status accelerated the conservation process, as it alerted the authorities to the need for greater sensitivity in redevelopment strategy. The extent of changing environmental priorities was demonstrated by the protection of prestigious Mackintosh buildings like the Martyrs' Public School, which at one point had been threatened with demolition to make way for a motorway. The revived spirit of Mackintosh did much to exorcise the pervasive ghost of the 1940s Bruce plan, which although never formally implemented, had directed much of the post-war vision for Glasgow. Mackintosh was a prime attraction for the growing number of visitors during the 1980s, and the lesson of using heritage was not lost on the city's planners. The conserved central area was named the 'Merchant City' in tribute to the men who shaped Glasgow's commercial destiny during the eighteenth and nineteenth centuries. It was a manufactured title that suggested more about the spirit of 1980s enterprise culture than historic Glasgow, yet it was also iconoclastic, as it was intended quite deliberately to dissolve the depressed stereotype. The SDA, in partnership with local government, was the guiding force in this ambitious residential, leisure and commercial initiative. A major aim was to convert derelict warehouses into up-market housing, reflecting contemporary concern to encourage the private property market and bring people back to the urban heartland. On the other hand, part of the success of the Merchant City was that the District Council still owned much of the area, and so was in a key position to stimulate and control development.[50]

Inevitably, there was criticism of Glasgow's 1980s make over. Deindustrialisation and its devastating effects on employment seemed to sit incongruously with a glittering inner-city of wine-bars, art galleries and designer clothes shops. 'Red Clydeside' had apparently yielded to Thatcherite market economics, in a city with an entrenched Labour power-base. High-profile initiatives, intended to bolster civic pride, were regarded suspiciously as public relations ploys to gull the people and render them politically quiescent. One example was the 1988 Garden Festival, which recreated the flamboyant style of the Empire Exhibition fifty years previously. Sited on former docklands space on the south banks of the Clyde, the blighted industrial landscape was depicted as blooming again. Poet Liz Lochhead was not convinced:

> Well, jolly japes
> Like cutting hedges inty fancy shapes
> And trying to make some kinna Eighth Wonder
> Oot o' plantin' oot the coat o' arms in floribunda
> Are making Scotland just a theme park,
> A dream park,
> A Disneyland where work disnae exist.[51]

The designation of Glasgow as European City of Culture for 1990 provoked even more furore, the *Glasgow Herald* devoting extensive column inches to a vitriolic and highly personal debate about the precise meaning of culture in the city. That Glasgow followed on directly from Berlin and Paris in the European Community's roster of cultural excellence seemed to critics like winning a surreal beauty contest, where appearances had been wholly deceptive. 'Glasgow's problem', suggested one writer, 'is that it is a workers' city whose rulers resolutely pretend that it is something else'.[52]

Barbs of gentrification, elitism and betrayal could not stop the momentum of the regeneration programme, at least in relation to Glasgow's hard-won status as a city of international standing. As one *Scotsman* journalist suggested, this created conflicting images: 'So which is the new Glasgow? . . . Sales of designer clothing unmatched anywhere outside London. Private housing rising from the ashes of the Gorbals. And unemployment and violent crime statistics that are worse than any other Scottish city'.[53] Yet if there was disconcerting familiarity about Glasgow as a media curiosity, the reporting was far from despairing. Journalists and broadcasters focused relentlessly on the booming culture phenomenon and the much-vaunted Glasgow style. Passion was expended on such questions as whether the municipal Gallery of Modern Art, opened in 1996, was aesthetically a folly or a triumph. Controversy also demonstrated that considerable creative energy was being released over cultural aspirations. As Moira Burgess points out in her detailed and entertaining study of Glasgow fiction from the eighteenth century, writing in the city took off precipitately during the 1980s and continued to thrive in the 1990s.[54] There was much irony in the award of the prestigious Booker Prize for fiction to Glasgow writer James Kelman in 1994, because he had been a leading City of Culture sceptic. Yet his raw, uncompromising prose became another component of Glasgow's eclectic image, showing that the spirit of place had taken on many voices.

During 1999 an ambitious programme of events was launched to celebrate

Glasgow's year-long status as United Kingdom City of Architecture and Design. Arts Council judges had been impressed by the bid made five years previously, considering the populist edge to projected plans as imaginative and daring in comparison with the more conventional offering from Edinburgh. Such an accolade would have been unthinkable in the 1960s, and showed how far confidence in the landscape had been restored by the reinvention process. In unconscious acknowledgement of nineteenth-century pretensions to be the 'Venice of the North', Glasgow was dubbed the 'New York of the North' by the London-based *Guardian* newspaper. [55] The city's cosmopolitan ambience was summed up as flash, brash and bustling, 'a complex mongrel' of Scottish, Irish and other roots. That Glaswegians

106. Crown Street Regeneration Project, 1990s.
New building in Hutchesontown, once the corrosive community of *No Mean City* notoriety. The Crown Street Regeneration Project was first promoted by the Glasgow Development Agency in 1989, and the 'New Gorbals' has steadily emerged under public and private sector initiative. (*Glasgow City Council Corporate Graphics.*)

107. Gallery of Modern Art, 1996.
The Cunninghame mansion took on another identity in 1996 when the Gallery of Modern Art was opened.
Despite controversy about the artistic merits of some exhibits, the gallery proved to be popular. In front of the
Corinthian pillars is an equestrian statue of the Duke of Wellington, making a suitably post-modern statement
with a traffic-cone. (*Glasgow City Council Corporate Graphics.*)

seemed to be more at ease with cultural diversity reflected generational
changes. For all the pervasive North American influences, awareness of
Glasgow's place among European urban communities was broadening
horizons. Younger residents had grown up with the post-industrial image
that emerged in the 1970s and were not so hidebound by definitions of the
'authentic' city. While the historic legacy was respected, there were fewer
cultural constraints and greater scope to accommodate multiple identities.

At the opening of the twenty-first century economic prospects are uncertain, as is the role of the city's government in the unpredictable era of constitutional change, but Glasgow style continues to be celebrated with panache.

Notes

1. George Eyre-Todd, *The Story of Glasgow: From the Earliest Times to the Present Day* (Blackie: Glasgow, 1911), pp. 7–8.
2. William Bolitho, *Cancer of Empire* (G. Putnam: London, 1924), p. 17.
3. George Malcolm Thomson, *Caledonia, Or, The Future of the Scots* (Kegan Paul, Trench, Truber: London, 1927), p. 21.
4. George Gladstone Robertson, *Gorbals Doctor* (Jarrolds: London, 1970), pp. 128–37.
5. Bill Murray, *The Old Firm: Sectarianism, Sport and Society in Scotland* (John Donald: Edinburgh, 1984), pp. 147–8.
6. Sir Percy Sillitoe, *Cloak Without Dagger* (Pan Books: London, 1955), p. 145.
7. Lewis Grassic Gibbon, 'Glasgow', an essay in his collection *A Scots Hairst* (Hutchinson: London, 1967), p. 82. First published in 1934.
8. Quoted in Seán Damer, 'No mean writer? The curious case of Alexander McArthur', in Kevin McCarra and Hamish Whyte (eds), *A Glasgow Collection: Essays in Honour of Joe Fisher* (Glasgow City Libraries: Glasgow, 1990), p. 32. The speaker was Patrick Dollan.
9. Empire Exhibition (publisher), *Official Guide* (Glasgow: 1938), p. 109.
10. *Glasgow Herald*, 4 September 1939.
11. A. G. Jury, *Housing Centenary: A Review of Municipal Housing in Glasgow from 1866 to 1966* (Glasgow Corporation: Glasgow, 1966), p. 31.
12. For these contrasting approaches, see the criticisms in Charles McKean, 'Between the wars', in Peter Reed (ed.), *Glasgow: The Forming of the City* (Edinburgh: 1993), pp. 130–45, and more positively, Nicholas J. Morgan, '"£8 cottages for Glasgow citizens": innovations in municipal house-building in Glasgow in the inter-war years', in Richard Rodger (ed.), *Scottish Housing in the Twentieth Century* (Leicester University Press: Leicester, 1989), pp. 125–34.
13. Miles Horsey, *Tenements and Towers: Glasgow Working-Class Housing, 1890–1990* (HMSO: Edinburgh, 1990), p. 22.
14. Sir William E. Whyte, 'Planning for post-war Glasgow', in *Proceedings of the Royal Philosophical Society of Glasgow* 66 (1941–42), p. 28.
15. Sir Patrick Abercrombie and Robert H. Matthew, *The Clyde Valley Regional Plan 1946* (HMSO: Edinburgh, 1949), p. 174.
16. Robert Bruce, *First Planning Report* (Glasgow Corporation: Glasgow, 1945), pp. 52–3.
17. Abercrombie and Matthew, *Clyde Valley Regional Plan*, p. 15.
18. Jury, *Housing Centenary*, p. 45.
19. C. A. Oakley, *The Last Tram* (Glasgow Corporation: Glasgow, 1962), p. 118.
20. Horsey, *Tenements and Towers*, p. 49.
21. Brian Edwards, *Basil Spence, 1907–1976* (Rutland Press: Edinburgh, 1995), pp. 82–5.
22. J. Dickson Mabon, 'Rebuilding Scotland: the role of government', in Miles Glendinning (ed.), *Rebuilding Scotland: The Post-War Vision* (Tuckwell Press: East Linton, 1997), p. 57.
23. Quoted in Charles Gillies, 'High rise living reaches low ebb', *Glasgow Herald*,

19 November 1974.

24. Michael Keating, *The City that Refused to Die: Glasgow, the Politics of Urban Regeneration* (Aberdeen University Press: Aberdeen, 1988), pp. 27–8.

25. A. K. Chalmers, *The Health of Glasgow, 1818–1925: An Outline* (Glasgow Corporation: Glasgow, 1930), p. 447.

26. David Stenhouse, *Glasgow: Its Municipal Undertakings and Enterprises* (Glasgow Corporation: Glasgow, 1933), p. 76.

27. J. Cunnison and J. B. S. Gilfillan (eds), *Glasgow: the Third Statistical Account of Scotland* (Collins: Glasgow, 1958), p. 479.

28. David Hamilton, 'Health and health-care in west central Scotland', in H. M. Drucker and M. G. Clarke (eds), *The Scottish Government Yearbook, 1978* (Paul Harris: Edinburgh, 1978), p. 84.

29. Compare the 1931 edition of Stenhouse, *Glasgow: Its Municipal Undertakings and Enterprises*, p. 106, with the revised 1933 edition, p. 114.

30. *Glasgow Herald*, 16 September 1939.

31. Ibid. 13 and 14 September 1939.

32. Cunnison and Gilfillan (eds), *Glasgow: the Third Statistical Account*, p. 521.

33. Sir Charles Cleland, 'Public education in Glasgow', in J. Graham Kerr, *Glasgow: Sketches by Various Authors* (Robert Maclehose: Glasgow, 1928), pp. 168–9.

34. Cicely Hamilton, *Modern Scotland: As Seen by an Englishwoman* (J. M. Dent: London, 1937), pp. 12–13.

35. Ishbel Maclean, 'Mountain men: the discovery of the hills by Glasgow workers during the Depression', in Billy Kay (ed.), *Odyssey: Voices from Scotland's Recent Past* (Polygon: Edinburgh, 1980), p. 87. The speaker was Jock Nimlin.

36. George Blake, *The Shipbuilders* (B. & W. Publishers: Edinburgh, 1993 edition), p. 69. First published in 1935.

37. Graham Walker, '"There's not a team like the Glasgow Rangers": football and religious identity in Scotland', in Graham Walker and Tom Gallagher (eds), *Sermons and Battle Hymns: Protestant Popular Culture in Modern Scotland* (Edinburgh University Press: Edinburgh, 1990), pp. 137–8.

38. Bruce Peter, *100 Years of Glasgow's Amazing Cinemas* (Polygon: Edinburgh, 1996), p. 40.

39. *Glasgow Herald*, 25 January 1955.

40. Elizabeth Casciani, *Oh, How We Danced! The History of Ballroom Dancing in Scotland* (Mercat Press: Edinburgh, 1994), p. 68.

41. Peter, *100 Years of Glasgow's Amazing Cinemas*, p. 48.

42. Adrienne Scullion, 'BBC Radio in Scotland, 1923–1939: devolution, regionalism and centralisation', *Northern Scotland* 15 (1995), p. 69.

43. Gibbon, 'Glasgow', p. 90.

44. Terri Colpi, *The Italian Factor: The Italian Community in Great Britain* (Mainstream: Edinburgh, 1991), pp. 105–8.

45. Bashir Maan, *The New Scots: The Story of Asians in Scotland* (John Donald: Edinburgh, 1992), p. 160.

46. Neil Rafeek, 'Agnes McLean, 1918–1994', *Journal of the Scottish Labour History Society* 30 (1995), p. 128.

47. *Glasgow Herald*, 26 January 1954.

48. Ian Jack, 'The repackaging of Glasgow', reprinted in his collection, *Before the Oil Ran Out: Britain in the Brutal Years* (Vintage: London, 1997), p. 207.

49. Michael Pacione, *Glasgow: the Socio-Spatial Development of the City* (Wiley: Chichester, 1995), pp. 237–8.

50. *Architects' Journal*, 21 November 1984.

51. Liz Lochhead's poem, 'The Garden Festival, Glasgow 1988' in her collection

Bagpipe Muzak (Penguin Books: Harmondsworth, 1991), pp. 18–19.

52. Seán Damer, *Glasgow: Going for a Song* (Lawrence and Wishart: London, 1990), p. 210.

53. Brian Pendreigh, 'The wild west', *The Scotsman*, 27 February 1995.

54. Moira Burgess, *Imagine a City: Glasgow in Fiction* (Argyll: Glendaruel, 1998), p. 300.

55. Jonathan Glancey, 'New York of the north', *The Guardian*, 18 January 1999.

Further Reading

What follows is a selective list of further reading, divided chronologically. In order to make the list manageable, the focus is on publications coming after Charles Oakley's classic 'urban biography', *The Second City*, which first appeared in 1946. For a useful account of earlier Glasgow histories, see Joe Fisher's *Glasgow Encyclopedia* (1994), pp. 172–4. The subject matter of several books and articles extends beyond the precise cut-off dates, but have been cited once only, to avoid repetition.

General Historical Studies

Berry, Simon and Whyte, Hamish (eds) (1987), *Glasgow Observed*, John Donald: Edinburgh.

Burgess, Moira (1998), *Imagine a City: Glasgow in Fiction*, Argyll: Glendaruel.

Cunnison, J and Gilfillan, J. B. S. (eds) (1958), *Glasgow: the Third Statistical Account for Scotland*, Collins: Glasgow.

Daiches, David (1982), *Glasgow*, Grafton: London.

Damer, Seán (1990), *Glasgow, Going for a Song*, Lawrence and Wishart: London.

Fisher, Joe (1994), *The Glasgow Encyclopedia*, Mainstream: Edinburgh.

Gibb, Andrew (1983), *Glasgow: The Making of a City*, Croom Helm: Beckenham.

Gomme, Andor and Walker, David (1987), *Architecture of Glasgow*, Lund Humphries: London.

King, Elspeth (1993), *The Hidden History of Glasgow's Women: The Thenew Factor*, Mainstream: Edinburgh.

McKean, Charles, Walker, David and Walker, Frank (1989), *Central Glasgow: An Illustrated Architectural Guide*, Mainstream: Edinburgh.

Oakley, C. A. (1946), *The Second City*, Blackie: Glasgow.

Pacione, Michael (1995), *Glasgow: The Socio-Spatial Development of the City*, Wiley: Chichester.

Reed, Peter (ed.) (1993), *Glasgow: The Forming of the City*, Edinburgh University Press: Edinburgh.

Smart, Aileen (1988 and 1996), *Villages of Glasgow*, two volumes, John Donald: Edinburgh.

Whyte, Hamish (ed.) (1993), *Mungo's Tongues: Glasgow Poems, 1630–1990*, Mainstream: Edinburgh.

Williamson, Elizabeth, Riches, Anne and Higgs, Malcolm (1990), *Glasgow*, Penguin: London.

Wordsall, Frank (1979), *The Tenement, A Way of Life: A Social, Historical and Architectural Study of Housing in Glasgow*, Chambers: Edinburgh.

The Pre-Industrial City

Devine, T. M. (1978), 'An eighteenth-century business elite: Glasgow-West India merchants, c.1750–1815', *Scottish Historical Review*, 57, pp. 40–67.

Devine, T. M. (1990), *The Tobacco Lords: A Study of the Tobacco Merchants of*

Glasgow and Their Trading Activities, c. 1740–90, Edinburgh University Press: Edinburgh.

Devine, T. M. and Jackson, Gordon (eds) (1995), *Glasgow, Volume I: Beginnings to 1830*, Manchester University Press: Manchester.

Driscoll, Stephen (1998), 'Church archaeology in Glasgow and the Kingdom of Strathclyde', *Innes Review*, 49, pp. 95–114.

Durkan, John (1998), 'Cadder and environs, and the development of the church in Glasgow in the twelfth century', *Innes Review*, 49, pp. 127–42.

Edward, Mary (1993), *Who Belongs to Glasgow? 200 Years of Migration*, Glasgow City Libraries: Glasgow.

Fraser, W. Hamish (1988), *Conflict and Class: Scottish Workers, 1700–1838*, John Donald: Edinburgh.

Hamilton, H. (1954), 'The founding of the Glasgow Chamber of Commerce, 1783', *Scottish Journal of Political Economy*, 1, pp. 33–48.

Hook, Andrew and Sher, Richard (eds) (1995), *The Glasgow Enlightenment*, Tuckwell Press: East Linton.

King, Elspeth (1987), *The Strike of the Glasgow Weavers, 1787*, Glasgow Museums: Glasgow.

Macfarlane, Leslie J. (1992), 'The elevation of the diocese of Glasgow into an archbishopric in 1492', *Innes Review*, 43, pp. 99–118.

Macinnes, Allan I. (1991), 'Covenanting, revolution and municipal enterprise', in Jenny Wormald (ed.), *Scotland Revisited*, Collins and Brown: London, pp. 97–106.

MacKenzie, John M. (1999), '"The Second City of the Empire": Glasgow – Imperial Municipality', in Felix Driver and David Gilbert (eds), *Imperial Cities*, Manchester University Press: Manchester, pp. 215–37.

Macquarrie, Alan (1997), 'St Kentigern of Glasgow', in Macquarrie, *The Saints of Scotland: Essays in Scottish Church History, AD 450–1093*, John Donald: Edinburgh, pp. 117–44.

McQueen, John (1992), 'The dear green place: St Mungo and Glasgow, 600–1966', *Innes Review*, 43, pp. 87–98.

Markus, Thomas A. (ed.) (1982), *Order in Space and Society: Architectural Form and its Context in the Scottish Enlightenment*, Mainstream: Edinburgh.

Riddell, John F. (1979), *Clyde Navigation: A History of the Development and Deepening of the River Clyde*, John Donald: Edinburgh.

Smout, T. C. (1960), 'The development and enterprise of Glasgow, 1556–1707', *Scottish Journal of Political Economy*, 7, pp. 194–212.

Smout, T. C. (1968), 'The Glasgow merchant community in the seventeenth century', *Scottish Historical Review*, 47, pp. 53–71.

Withers, Charles W. J. (1998), *Urban Highlanders: Highland-Lowland Migration and Urban Gaelic Culture, 1700–1900*, Tuckwell Press: East Linton.

Industrial Transformation, 1800–1860

Allan, C. M. (1965), 'The genesis of British urban redevelopment with special reference to Glasgow', *Economic History Review*, 18, pp. 588–613.

Aspinwall, Bernard (1984), *Portable Utopia; Glasgow and the United States, 1820–1920*, Aberdeen University Press: Aberdeen.

Brown, Callum (1996), '"To be aglow with civic ardours": the "Godly Commonwealth" in Glasgow, 1843–1914', *Records of the Scottish Church History Society*, 26, pp. 169–95.

Brown, Stewart J. (1982), *Thomas Chalmers and the Godly Commonwealth in Scotland*, Oxford University Press: Oxford.

Cage, R. A. (ed.) (1987), *The Working Class in Glasgow, 1750–1914*, Croom Helm: Beckenham.

Checkland, Olive (1980), *Philanthropy in Victorian Scotland: Social Welfare and the Voluntary Principle*, John Donald: Edinburgh.

Checkland, S. G. (1964), 'The British industrial city as history: the Glasgow case', *Urban Studies*, 1, pp. 34–54.

Collins, Kenneth (1990), *Second City Jewry: Jews in Glasgow in the Age of Expansion, 1790–1919*, Scottish Jewish Archives Centre: Glasgow.

Devine, T. M. (ed.) (1991), *Irish Immigrants and Scottish Society in the Nineteenth and Twentieth Centuries*, John Donald: Edinburgh.

Donnelly, F. K. (1976), 'The Scottish rising of 1820: a reinterpretation', *Scottish Tradition*, 6, pp. 27–37.

Fraser, W. Hamish (1976), 'The Glasgow cotton spinners, 1837', in John Butt and J. T. Ward (eds), *Scottish Themes*, Scottish Academic Press: Edinburgh, pp. 80–97.

Fraser, W. Hamish (1996), *Alexander Campbell and the Search for Socialism*, Holyoake: Manchester.

Fraser, W. Hamish (1996), 'Owenite socialism in Scotland', *Scottish Economic and Social History*, 16, pp. 60–91.

Fraser, W. Hamish and Maver, Irene (eds) (1996), *Glasgow, Volume II: 1830 to 1912*, Manchester University Press: Manchester.

Gordon, George (ed.) (1985), *Perspectives of the Scottish City*, Aberdeen University Press: Aberdeen.

Gordon, George and Dicks, Brian (eds) (1983), *Scottish Urban History*, Aberdeen University Press: Aberdeen.

Handley, James E. (1964), *The Irish in Scotland*, John S. Burns: Glasgow.

Hartman, Mary S. (1973), 'Murder for respectability: the case of Madeleine Smith', *Victorian Studies*, 16, pp. 381–400.

Kellett, J. R. (1964), 'Glasgow's railways, 1830–80: a study in "natural growth"', *Economic History Review*, 17, pp. 354–68.

Kellett, J. R. (1979), *Railways and Victorian Cities*, Routledge and Kegan Paul: London.

King, Elspeth (1979), *Scotland Sober and Free: The Temperance Movement, 1829–1979*, Glasgow Museums: Glasgow.

McCaffrey, John F. (1981), 'Thomas Chalmers and social change', *Scottish Historical Review*, 60, pp. 32–60.

McCarra, Kevin and Whyte, Hamish (eds) (1990), *A Glasgow Collection: Essays in Honour of Joe Fisher*, Glasgow City Libraries.

McFarland, Elaine (1990), *Protestants First: Orangeism in Nineteenth Century Scotland*, Edinburgh University Press: Edinburgh.

Mahood, Linda (1990), *The Magdalenes: Prostitution in the Nineteenth Century*, Routledge: London.

Maver, Irene (1994), 'Politics and power in the Scottish city: Glasgow Town Council in the nineteenth century', in T. M. Devine (ed.), *Scottish Elites*, John Donald: Edinburgh, pp. 98–131.

Maver, Irene (1997), 'Children and the quest for purity in the nineteenth-century Scottish city', *Paedagogica Historica (International Journal of the History of Education)*, 33, pp. 801–24.

Michie, Michael (1997), *An Enlightenment Tory in Victorian Scotland: The Career of Sir Archibald Alison*, Tuckwell Press: East Linton.

Mitchell, Martin J. (1998), *The Irish in the West of Scotland, 1797–1848: Trade Unions, Strikes and Political Movements*, John Donald: Edinburgh.

Montgomery, Fiona A. (1979), 'Glasgow and the movement for Corn Law repeal', *History*, 64, pp. 363–79.

Montgomery, Fiona A. (1980), 'The unstamped press: the contribution of Glasgow, 1831–1836', *Scottish Historical Review*, 59, pp. 154–70.

Montgomery, Fiona A. (1982), 'Glasgow and the struggle for parliamentary reform,

1830–32', Scottish Historical Review, 61, pp. 130–45.

Murray, Norman (1978), The Scottish Handloom Weavers, 1790–1850: A Social History, John Donald: Edinburgh.

Phillips, Alastair (1982), Glasgow's Herald: Two Hundred Years of a Newspaper, 1783–1983, Richard Drew: Glasgow.

Roach, W. M. (1972), 'Alexander Richmond and the radical reform movements in Glasgow in 1816–17', Scottish Historical Review, 51, pp. 1–19.

Saunders, Laurance James (1950), Scottish Democracy, 1815–1840, Oliver and Boyd: Edinburgh.

Simpson, Michael (1972), 'Urban transport and the development of Glasgow's West End, 1830–1914', Journal of Transport History, 1, pp. 146–60.

Simpson, Michael (1977), 'The West End of Glasgow, 1830–1914', in M. A. Simpson and T. H. Lloyd (eds), Middle–Class Housing in Britain, David and Charles: Newton Abbott, pp. 44–85.

Slaven, Anthony (1975), The Development of the West of Scotland, 1750–1960, Routledge and Kegan Paul: London.

Slaven, Anthony and Aldcroft, Derek (eds) (1982), Business, Banking and Urban History, John Donald: Edinburgh.

Sloan, William (1994), 'Employment opportunities and migrant group assimilation: the Highlanders and Irish in Glasgow, 1840–1860', in T. M. Devine (ed.), Industry, Business and Society in Scotland since 1700, John Donald: Edinburgh, pp. 184–97.

Wilson, Alexander (1959), 'Chartism in Glasgow', in Asa Briggs (ed.), Chartist Studies, Macmillan: London, pp. 249–87.

Wilson, Alexander (1970), The Chartist Movement in Scotland, Manchester University Press: Manchester.

Second City of the Empire, 1860–1918

Aspinwall, Bernard (1977), 'Glasgow trams and American politics, 1894–1914', Scottish Historical Review, 56, pp. 64–84.

Atherton, Cynthia (1991), 'The development of the middle-class suburb: the West End of Glasgow', Scottish Economic and Social History, 11, pp. 19–35.

Brotherstone, Terry (1969), 'The suppression of the Forward', Journal of the Scottish Labour History Society, 1, pp. 5–23.

Burkhauser, Jude (1990), Glasgow Girls: Women in Art and Design, 1880–1920, Canongate: Edinburgh.

Butt, John (1971), 'Working-class housing in Glasgow, 1851–1914', in S. D. Chapman, The History of Working-Class Housing, David and Charles: Newton Abbot, pp. 57–92.

Checkland, Olive and Lamb, Margaret (eds) (1982), Health Care as Social History: the Glasgow Case, Aberdeen University Press: Aberdeen

Checkland, S. G. (1981), The Upas Tree: Glasgow, 1875–1980, Glasgow University Press: Glasgow.

Damer, Seán (1980), 'State, class and housing: Glasgow, 1885–1919', in Joseph Melling (ed.), State, Class and Housing: Glasgow, 1885–1919, Croom Helm: Beckenham, pp. 73–112.

Donnachie, Ian, Harvie, Christopher and Wood, Ian S. (eds) (1989), Forward! Labour Politics in Scotland, 1888–1988, Polygon: Edinburgh.

Duncan, Robert and McIvor, Arthur (eds) (1992), Labour and Class Conflict on the Clyde, 1900–1950, John Donald: Edinburgh.

Foster, John (1992), 'Red Clyde, Red Scotland', in Ian Donnachie and Christopher Whatley (eds), The Manufacture of Scottish History, Polygon: Edinburgh, pp. 106–24.

Fraser, W. Hamish (1990), 'From civic gospel to municipal socialism', in Derek Fraser (ed.), *Cities, Class and Communications: Essays in Honour of Asa Briggs*, Harvester Wheatsheaf: Hemel Hempstead, pp. 58–80.

Fraser, W. Hamish (1993), 'From municipal socialism to social policy', in R. J. Morris and Richard Rodger (eds), *The Victorian City: A Reader in British Urban History*, Longman: London, pp. 258–80.

Gomme, Andor (1992), 'The city of Glasgow', in Boris Ford (ed.), *The Cambridge Cultural History of Britain: Volume 7, Victorian Britain*, Cambridge University Press: Cambridge, pp. 209–21.

Gordon, Eleanor (1991), *Women and the Labour Movement in Scotland, 1850–1914*, Oxford University Press: Oxford.

Hillis, Peter (1987), 'Education and evangelisation, Presbyterian missions in mid-nineteenth century Glasgow', *Scottish Historical Review*, 66, pp. 46–62.

Hume, John R. and Moss, Michael S. (1975), *Clyde Shipbuilding*, Batsford: London.

Hume, John R. and Moss, Michael S. (1979), *Beardmore: The History of a Scottish Industrial Giant*, Heinemann: London.

Kaplan, Wendy (1996) (ed.), *Charles Rennie Mackintosh*, Glasgow Museums: Glasgow.

Kenefick, William and McIvor, Arthur (eds) (1996), *Roots of Red Clydeside, 1910–1914: Labour Unrest and Industrial Relations in West Scotland*, John Donald: Edinburgh.

Kinchin, Perilla (1991), *Tea and Taste: the Glasgow Tea Rooms, 1875–1975*, White Cockade: Wendlebury.

Kinchen, Perilla and Kinchin, Juliet (1988), *Glasgow's Great Exhibitions*, White Cockade: Wendlebury.

King, Elspeth (1992), 'The Scottish women's suffrage movement', in Esther Brietenbach and Eleanor Gordon (eds), *Out of Bounds: Women in Scottish Society, 1800–1945*, Edinburgh University Press: Edinburgh, pp. 121–50.

Knox, William (1989), 'The Red Clydesiders and the Scottish political tradition', in Terry Brotherstone (ed), *Covenant, Charter and Party: Traditions of Revolt in Modern Scottish History*, Aberdeen University Press: Aberdeen, pp. 92–104.

Leneman, Leah (1991), *A Guid Cause: The Women's Suffrage Movement in Scotland*, Aberdeen University Press: Aberdeen.

McCaffrey, John F. (1971), 'The origins of Liberal Unionism in the west of Scotland', *Scottish Historical Review*, 50, pp. 47–71.

Macdougall, Ian (ed.) (1978), *Essays in Scottish Labour History*, John Donald: Edinburgh.

McFadzean, Ronald (1979), *The Life and Work of Alexander Thomson*, Routledge: London.

Mackay, James (1998), *The Man Who Invented Himself: A Life of Sir Thomas Lipton*, Mainstream: Edinburgh.

McLean, Iain (1983), *The Legend of Red Clydeside*, John Donald: Edinburgh.

McKinlay, Alan and Morris, R. J. (eds) (1991), *The ILP on Clydeside, 1893–1932: from Foundation to Disintegration*, Manchester University Press: Manchester.

Maitles, Henry (1995), 'Attitudes to Jewish immigration in the west of Scotland to 1905', *Scottish Economic and Social History*, 15, pp. 44–65.

Maver, Irene (1998), 'Glasgow's public parks and the community, 1850–1914: a case-study in Scottish civic interventionism', *Urban History*, 25, pp. 323–47.

Melling, Joseph (1983), *Rent Strikes: People's Struggle for Housing in the West of Scotland, 1890–1916*, Polygon: Edinburgh.

Moss, Michael S. and Hume, John R. (1977), *Workshop of the British Empire: Engineering and Shipbuilding in the West of Scotland*, Heinemann: London.

Nicholson, Murdoch and O'Neill, Mark (1987), *Glasgow: Locomotive Builder to the World*, Polygon: Edinburgh.

Robertson, Edna (1998), *Glasgow's Doctor: James Burn Russell*, Tuckwell Press: East Linton.

Roxburgh, James M. (1971), *The School Board of Glasgow, 1873–1919*, University of London Press: London.

Slaven, Anthony and Checkland, Sidney (eds) (1986 and 1990), *Dictionary of Scottish Business Biography, 1860–1960*, two volumes, Aberdeen University Press: Aberdeen.

Smith, Joan (1986), 'Class, skill and sectarianism in Glasgow and Liverpool, 1880–1914', in R. J. Morris (ed.), *Class, Power and Social Structure in British Nineteenth Century Towns*, Leicester University Press: Leicester, pp. 157–215.

Stamp, Gavin and McKinstry, Sam (eds) (1994), *'Greek' Thomson*, Edinburgh University Press: Edinburgh.

Sweeney, Irene (1992), 'Local party politics and the temperance crusade: Glasgow, 1890–1902', *Journal of the Scottish Labour History Society*, 27, pp. 44–63.

Tarn, J. N. (1968), 'Housing in Liverpool and Glasgow: the growth of civic responsibility', *Town Planning Review*, 39, pp. 319–34.

Treble, James H. (1986), 'The characteristics of the female unskilled labour market and the formation of the female casual labour market in Glasgow, 1891–1914', *Scottish Economic and Social History*, 6, pp. 33–46.

Walker, Graham (1988), *Thomas Johnston*, Manchester University Press: Manchester.

Wannop, Urlan (1986), 'Glasgow/Clydeside: a century of metropolitan evolution', in Gordon, George (ed.), *Regional Cities in the United Kingdom, 1890–1980*, Harper and Row: London, pp. 83–98.

Wood, Ian S. (1990), *John Wheatley*, Manchester University Press: Manchester.

Wilson, R. Guerriero (1998), *Disillusionment or New Opportunities? The Changing Nature of Work in Offices, Glasgow, 1880–1914*, Ashgate: Aldershot.

Glasgow Since 1918

Booth, Peter and Boyle, Robin (1993), 'See Glasgow, see culture', in Franco Bianchini and Michael Parkinson (eds), *Cultural Policy and Urban Regeneration: the West European Experience*, Manchester University Press: Manchester, pp. 21–47.

Boyle, Raymond and Lynch, Peter (eds) (1998), *Out of the Ghetto? The Catholic Community in Modern Scotland*, John Donald: Edinburgh.

Brown, Gordon (1986), *Maxton*, Mainstream: Edinburgh.

Cage, R. A. (1994), 'Infant mortality and housing: twentieth-century Glasgow', *Scottish Economic and Social History*, 14, pp. 77–92.

Crampsey, Bob (1988), *The Empire Exhibition of 1938*, Mainstream: Edinburgh.

Damer, Seán (1989), *From Moorepark to 'Wine Alley': The Rise and Fall of a Glasgow Housing Scheme*, Edinburgh University Press: Edinburgh.

Donnison, David and Middleton, Alan (eds) (1987), *Regenerating the Inner City: Glasgow's Experience*, Routledge and Kegan Paul: London.

Englander, David (1981), 'Landlord and tenant in urban Scotland: the background to the Clyde rent strikes, 1915', *Journal of the Scottish Labour History Society*, 15, pp. 4–14.

Foster, John and Woolfson, Charles (1986), *The Politics of the UCS Work-In: Class Alliances and the Right to Work*, Lawrence and Wishart: London.

Gallagher, Tom (1985), 'Protestant extremism in urban Scotland, 1930–39: its growth and contraction', *Scottish Historical Review*, 64, pp. 143–67.

Gallagher, Tom (1985), 'Red Clydeside's double anniversary', *Journal of the Scottish Labour History Society*, 20, pp. 4–14.

Gallagher, Tom (1987), *Glasgow – the Uneasy Peace: Religious Tension in Modern Scotland*, Manchester University Press: Manchester.

Glendinning, Miles and Muthesius, Stephan (1994), *Tower Block: Modern Public Housing in England, Scotland, Wales and Northern Ireland*, Yale University Press: New Haven & London.

Horsey, Miles (1990), *Tenements and Towers: Glasgow Working-Class Housing, 1890–1990*, HMSO: Edinburgh.

Howell, David (1986), *A Lost Left: Three Studies in Socialism and Nationalism*, Manchester University Press: Manchester.

Jack, Ian (1997), 'The repackaging of Glasgow', in Jack, *Before the Oil Ran Out: Britain in the Brutal Years*, Vintage: London, pp. 200–20.

Johnstone, Charlie (1993), 'Early post-war housing struggles in Glasgow', *Journal of the Scottish Labour History Society*, 28, pp. 7–29.

Keating, Michael (1988), *The City that Refused to Die: Glasgow, the Politics of Urban Regeneration*, Aberdeen University Press: Aberdeen.

Knox, William (ed.) (1984), *Scottish Labour Leaders: A Biographical Dictionary*, Mainstream: Edinburgh.

Knox, William (1987), *James Maxton*, Manchester University Press: Manchester.

McArthur, Colin (1986), 'The dialectic of national identity: the Glasgow Empire Exhibition of 1938', in T. Bennett, C. Meyer and J. Woolacott (eds), *Popular Culture and Social Relations*, Open University Press: Milton Keynes, pp. 117–34.

McGoldrick, Jim (1982), 'Crisis and the division of labour: Clydeside shipbuilding in the inter-war period', in Tony Dickson (ed.), *Capital and Class in Scotland*, John Donald: Edinburgh, pp. 143–85.

Macinnes, John (1995), 'The deindustrialisation of Glasgow', *Scottish Affairs*, 11, pp. 73–95.

McKean, Charles (1987), *The Scottish Thirties: An Architectural Introduction*, Scottish Academic Press: Edinburgh.

McShane, Harry and Smith, Joan (1978), *No Mean Fighter*, Pluto Press: London.

Marks, Richard (1983), *Burrell: Portrait of a Collector*, Richard Drew: Glasgow.

Miller, Ronald and Tivy, Joy (eds) (1958), *The Glasgow Region*, British Association: Glasgow.

Murray, Bill (1984), *The Old Firm: Sectarianism, Sport and Society in Scotland*, John Donald: Edinburgh.

Peter, Bruce (1996), *100 Years of Glasgow's Amazing Cinemas*, Polygon: Edinburgh.

Rodger, Johnny (1999), *Contemporary Glasgow: The Architecture of the 1990s*, Rutland Press: Edinburgh.

Rodger, Richard (ed.) (1989), *Scottish Housing in the Twentieth Century*, Leicester University Press: Leicester.

Spring, Ian (1990), *Phantom Village: the Myth of the New Glasgow*, Polygon: Edinburgh.

Wishart, Ruth (1991), 'Fashioning the future: Glasgow', in Mark Fisher and Ursula Owen (eds), *Whose Cities?*, Penguin: London, pp. 43–52.

Walker, Graham and Gallagher, Tom (eds) (1990), *Sermons and Battle Hymns: Protestant Popular Culture in Modern Scotland*, Edinburgh University Press: Edinburgh.

Index